# Yin-Yang

# Yin-Yang

## American Perspectives on Living in China

Edited by
Alice Renouf and Mary Beth Ryan-Maher

ROWMAN & LITTLEFIELD PUBLISHERS, INC.
*Lanham • Boulder • New York • Toronto • Plymouth, UK*

Published by Rowman & Littlefield Publishers, Inc.
A wholly owned subsidiary of The Rowman & Littlefield Publishing Group, Inc.
4501 Forbes Boulevard, Suite 200, Lanham, Maryland 20706
http://www.rowmanlittlefield.com

Estover Road, Plymouth PL6 7PY, United Kingdom

British Library Cataloguing in Publication Information Available

**Library of Congress Cataloging-in-Publication Data**

Yin-yang : American perspectives on living in China / edited by Alice Renouf and
Mary Beth Ryan-Maher.
    p. cm.
    Summary: "China has become one of the largest study and teach-abroad,
travel, and business destinations in the world. Yet few books offer a diversity
of perspectives and locales for Westerners considering the leap. This unique
collection of letters offers a rarely seen, intimate, and refreshingly honest view
of living and working in China. Here, ordinary people—recent college graduates,
teachers, professors, engineers, lawyers, computer whizzes, and parents—recount
their experiences in venues ranging from classrooms to marketplaces to holy
mountains. The writers are genuine participants in the daily life of their adopted
country, and woven throughout their correspondence is the compelling theme of
outsiders coping in a culture that is vastly foreign to them and the underlying
love-hate struggle it engenders. Written in a down-to-earth, personal, often
humorous, always authentic style, these tales of trials, successes, and failures
offer invaluable insight into a country that remains endlessly fascinating to
Westerners"— Provided by publisher.
    Includes bibliographical references and index.
    ISBN 978-1-4422-1269-5 (hardback : alk. paper) — ISBN 978-1-4422-1270-1 (paper :
alk. paper) — ISBN 978-1-4422-1271-8 (electronic)
    1. China—Social life and customs. 2. China—Travel and description. 3.
Americans—China—Correspondence. I. Renouf, Alice, 1946– II. Ryan-Maher, Mary
Beth, 1967–
    DS779.23.Y56 2012
    951.061'1—dc23

                                                                    2011034074

Printed in the United States of America

To our families
Jon, Cassidy, and Whitney Rush
Robert, Anna, and Nora Maher

We all live under the same sky,
but we don't see the same light.

—*Chinese Fortune Cookie*
Courtesy of Jen Powers
Colorado China Council teacher
Kunming, Yunnan, China

# Contents

*Contents*

# Foreword

Short of actually going to live and work in China, this book is the next best thing. And if in fact you are planning to spend time in China, *Yin-Yang: American Perspectives on Living in China* will serve as an invaluable guide.

Here we have a selection of vignettes from letters, e-mails, and blogs written by foreigners (mostly Americans) who are teaching English in China for a year or longer. Their stories present the unvarnished, firsthand experiences of discovering and adjusting to day-to-day life in a world that sometimes seems like a parallel universe. Hard-won nuggets of truth are derived from their immersion in Chinese classrooms and culture, without the safety net of a tour guide. The results can be surprising, revealing, touching, or amusing.

Focused mostly on the past decade, this edited volume reflects a China that is increasingly confident, cosmopolitan, and comfortable with outsiders in its midst. The first installment, published in 1998 (*Dear Alice: Letters Home from American Teachers Learning to Live in China*), showed a higher degree of mutual uncertainty and mistrust between Chinese and Americans.

Alice Renouf, executive director of the Colorado China Council in Boulder, is the "Alice" behind these messages. During the past twenty years, she has recruited some seven hundred people to teach at Chinese universities, sending them to a variety of cities, mostly off the well-trodden expatriate path—places like Chengdu, Fuzhou, Hangzhou, Lijiang, Qingdao, and Tianjin.

While a number of US programs send English teachers to China, the Colorado China Council is distinctive in providing opportunities not only for recent college graduates, but for men and women of all ages, some of them with families. They head off for China with a variety of motives and backgrounds, and usually are encountering Asia for the first time.

I first met Alice in 1977, when she was a graduate student at the University of Colorado. She directed the newly established Colorado China Council, and I had just joined the staff of the national China Council under the auspices of the Asia Society in New York City. Led by Robert Oxnam, with funding by the National Endowment for the Humanities and several private foundations, the council was a nonpartisan response to growing American interest in China at a time when access for foreigners was still limited and there were few sources of reliable information. It was an exciting time— Deng Xiaoping was launching reforms to modernize China in the wake of the disastrous Cultural Revolution, and Americans were debating the terms for diplomatic recognition of the People's Republic of China.

The Colorado China Council, based in Boulder, was one of eleven regional affiliates in cities and states across the United States, and my job was to help coordinate them. Alice, with her boundless energy and infectious enthusiasm, organized an array of activities ranging from art exhibitions and lecture series to media briefings and conferences. She has a gift for organization and for bringing people together. So as China became more open, it was a natural step for her to start the China Teachers Program.

Alice Renouf goes beyond the mechanics of hiring and training teachers, arranging visas and travel, and negotiating placements with universities in China. She provides the electricity that brings the program to life and the spirit that keeps it humming. We do not find her responses to her teachers in this book, but reading between the lines one easily can see that she is there, offering steady support and encouragement, reassuring her charges to "think Chinese, be Chinese."

As you would expect, their experiences and reactions run the gamut. They include food ("I also love the dumplings. They are served in round steaming bamboo boxes, and you dip them in vinegar with a chili garlic sauce."); health issues ("I now know how to say cough, syrup, medicine, and green mucus in Chinese."); language ("My Chinese still gets me into more trouble than it gets me out of."); and travel ("Going to buy a train ticket is a little like answering the riddle of the Sphinx: if you don't know exactly what you're going to say, and if it isn't exactly right, you will be eaten.")

Teaching—"a seriously exhausting endeavor!"—is a major topic, of course. There are different approaches to schoolwork: "The students here have spent so much of their time up to now either at school or at home studying that there is practically no time for any social life." And in the end there are gratifying outcomes: "I now know about one hundred Chinese students who will bring tears to my eyes whenever I think of them." Another writes, "My teaching has been the most rewarding thing I have done in my whole career. I love it very much."

Alice's emissaries discover the contradictions of a society that is both cosmopolitan and authoritarian, a country where modern technology coexists with age-old customs, a culture with a seemingly endless capacity to charm as well as aggravate. Observations range from the prosaic to the profound: "I guess I am living the cliché foreign experience here: intense periods of frustration followed by the occasional event that puts a smile back on my face. I've quit trying to figure it out."

The Colorado China Council is part of a thriving web of intercultural and international exchanges that play a vital role in informing and explaining Americans and Chinese to one another. So while the primary audience for this collage of impressions is in the United States, readers in China would also find it useful to learn what Americans find surprising, interesting, demanding, and delightful about their country. As one author ruefully notes, "Unfortunately, what most often gets shipped out of America is the top level of trash in the form of our pop culture."

*Yin-Yang* sends an important message that gets beyond stereotypical thinking; it is told through the lives of outsiders (*waiguoren*) who ponder China with insight and humor. These tangible, human "snapshots" provide much needed perspective on China and on ourselves. As one teacher puts it, "I am sometimes literally breathless when I consider the scope of my adventures in China that have covered the full breadth of the country and the full range of emotions."

Terry Lautz, former vice president
Henry Luce Foundation

# Preface

Ever wonder if moving to a foreign country like China with radically differ-ent socioeconomic, political, and historical roots would be a good idea for you personally? If you have ever asked this question, then this book will open up an intercultural window into China's vast, complex, and fascinating culture. *Yin-Yang: American Perspectives on Living in China* offers a rare, often hilarious, and totally genuine reflection on life as a foreigner in China with all its wonder and warts, pathos and levity as the voices of recent college graduates, teachers, professors, engineers, lawyers, computer techies, and parents are strung together like the irregular freshwater pearls ubiquitous in Chinese tourist markets. Far outside their comfort zones amidst the cacoph-ony that is cultural immersion, the message that most often bounces back from these writers is, "I love it, and I hate it." The book compiles Western-ers' perceptions of China from the classroom to the marketplace to China's holy mountains and everyplace in between. It is organized to reflect the phases of adjustment to such a major relocation. Initial highs shift to general discomfort, then to full-blown culture shock and slowly regaining a sense of balance, identity, and normalcy, and finally, to coming home, or not.

The Colorado China Council (CCC), a not-for-profit, educational outreach organization founded in Boulder, Colorado, in 1977 has sent nearly seven hundred teachers[1] to universities throughout China since 1991. The first book, *Dear Alice: Letters Home from Americans Learning to Live in China*, pub-lished in 1998 and edited by Phyllis L. Thompson, was composed of letters sent by CCC teachers to me, Alice Renouf, the council's director. By the late 1990s, email access was slowly filtering into China, and an email sequel to the first book began to take shape.

Much like the letters, the emails have a real sense of immediacy, humor, joie de vivre, and occasionally, deep angst and frustration. People emailed about what they were experiencing as they learned to live, teach, travel, and come to terms with a life that did not fit into any familiar paradigms. These emails tell us a lot about China during one of the fastest growth periods any nation in history has ever experienced, but they tell us even more about the human condition, and especially about how Americans adapt to radical change.

I contacted Mary Beth Ryan-Maher, former CCC teacher and codirector of CCC's Shanghai Summer TESL Institute. As a teacher, writer, and editor, I wanted to see if she would be willing to work on this project, and of course, she was. She and her husband, Robert, taught in Kunming for a year (1999–2000), and then ran the Summer Institute in Shanghai for four summers. Just prior to the start of the institute in 2000, Mary Beth and Robert spent time looking up words like "pregnancy test" in Chinese, went to the pharmacy and learned they were going to be parents. Their made-in-China baby, Anna, traveled to China three times by the time she was three years old. Younger sister Nora joined the family for the 2004 Summer Institute at seven months of age. The stories of a half dozen families are unique to this book.

Reading through over a decade of emails, blogs, and some letters and then selecting, editing, reformatting, and weaving them into a narrative was a Herculean task. The writers include people of all ages, from their early twenties to early sixties; they are primarily natives of the United States, but include a handful of other Westerners who spent much of their adult lives in the United States: Barbara Gambini from Italy, Mary Barton from Canada, and Hélène North from France. These writers lived in fourteen different cities throughout China and worked in twenty different universities from the mid-1990s to the present.

Compared to their counterparts in the 1980s and early 1990s, this "email generation" of CCC participants usually enjoyed better housing, access to high-speed Internet, and a vastly improved infrastructure for travel, as well as a university bureaucracy that was more malleable and open to Westerners. There are still stories about problems related to water, electricity, and housing, but for the most part, the complaints are fewer and farther between.

By the late 1990s, many of the Foreign Affairs officials (*waibans*) at the universities had studied in the West and were more understanding and sympathetic to American teachers; Chinese students' English had also dramatically improved. Many of the same frustrations and emotional roller-coaster relationships with China, however, carry over from the letter-writing generation to the email generation. These emails are a vibrant reflection on the unavoidable cultural confusion that Westerners experience when living in China. The fascination and frustration of trying to understand Chinese rhythms and routines from how the traffic flows to how to buy bus tickets intensify to questions about how to politely refuse a gift, how to return a favor, and when might the group's performance be more important than the individual's.

When traveling or living in another country, we all occasionally live under the illusion that the people, their lives, and much of what they think, say, and do is similar to our ways. In fact, this is not the case at all. The differences on both the superficial and subterranean levels are in fact dramatic. Some obvious differences these writers encounter are that brides traditionally wear red; white is the appropriate color to wear to a funeral; standard paper is legal-sized paper; and stamps are glued on to the back side of packages and letters. In China, the geographic axis is east–west, not north–south. For example, in the United States, you would say your friend lives in the northeast part of the city; in China, your friend lives in the east-north side of town. The Chinese have always looked at history from a cyclical perspective, while Westerners have a more linear vision. The more time you spend in China, the more the differences multiply. These anomalies tend to keep the level of edginess rather high, but as you will see, with a sense of humor, patience, perseverance, and cultural flexibility, most of the teachers come to terms with the vast cultural differences.

Having taken about thirty-five long and short trips to China since 1970 (when I lived in Taiwan for a year), I have witnessed from the ground up and the top down the vast changes in China's infrastructure, living standards, urbanization, explosion in architectural style, and elegance and opening of the marketplace at an unprecedented level in human history. Occasionally, I miss the "old" China of blue and gray Mao suits, stores with empty shelves, shop clerks asleep on their counters, donkey-drawn carts, bicycles everywhere, and motorcycles with families of four hanging on for dear life, perhaps even with a pig, headed to market on the back of a scooter. Cars were relatively rare. When China opened its doors to Americans in 1979, it presented a very dark, foreboding picture due to years of isolation, grueling poverty, government-sponsored chaos, and a naiveté about dealing with Westerners that was disarming, as well as priceless.

When I traveled to Shanghai in 1979 with the International Society of Burn Surgeons our breakfast was a glass of warm beer and a variant on lemon meringue pie! We thought it bizarre, but we loved it. It was exciting to be in a country where everything seemed unpredictable by our standards. To be fair, when the first Chinese delegations began to arrive in the United States, we were also very naive as to how to host them properly. And truly, the Chinese can still out-host anybody, anywhere, anytime!

We flew in an old Russian Ilyushin plane from city to city in 1979 and landed about every half hour. I finally asked the flight attendant why, and she said, "So the pilot can use the bathroom, and we want to show you the new airport and gift store." We would all be asked to disembark and walk through the gift store while the pilot and some passengers used the facilities. Have times ever changed!

Today in Shanghai a good hotel breakfast is usually a buffet as good as any in the world. Airports in China are arguably some of the finest anywhere and certainly the biggest. The new trains can reach speeds of four hundred kilometers an hour, and one can take a train from Beijing to Shanghai in five hours, less than half the time it used to take. It has been fascinating to watch this society cut loose from its Maoist moorings to reach for the moon, the stars, and everything in between. For me personally, it has been gratifying and enriching to watch Americans weave themselves into this burgeoning society that is trying to simultaneously modernize and yet preserve its Confucian and Communist roots.

On my trips to visit teachers over the last five or six years, there has been hardly a ripple of discontent. The modernization in infrastructure, housing, and general amenities in its major cities has made China a much more comfortable and inviting place to live. And from my vantage point, one qualitative measure illustrates the impact of this change. In 1992, CCC sent thirty-three young Americans, mostly recent college graduates, to teach at Chinese universities. They wrote deeply personal letters about their hardships and triumphs and how much they loved their experience, but every teacher came home after one year. Today, however, about a quarter to one-third of our teachers stays on for another year or more, and a couple have never permanently returned to the States.

Post-China, many former teachers go to work for the State Department, Foreign Service, and Peace Corps. Others attend graduate school in Chinese or international studies or business. Many return to their old jobs. The time spent in China for most of our teachers was enormously enriching because it provided a stage in which they could explore their own Western heritage within a radically different cultural context and learn the skills, adaptability, and understanding needed to find their own China rhythms.

Writing in 1999 before his stay in Chengdu, Josh Leslie answered the questions the Colorado China Council asks of all applicants: *What do you hope to personally accomplish, and what challenges do you think you will encounter living and teaching in China? Why do you think you will make a good teacher?* He graciously agreed to let us reprint it here:

My goals for spending a year in China fall into two general categories: the material and the spiritual. Materially, I hope, and I believe I will accomplish several things: gain a basic level of fluency in Mandarin, travel throughout China, make new friends, and learn to be a teacher, hopefully a good one. The spiritual goals are less easily attainable. I hope, in some sense, to learn about myself. I hope to test the limits of my patience, and then establish a new limit. I hope to gain a profound understanding of China, how it is different and what I can learn from it. I hope to rise to all challenges and meet them head on, but not at the risk of anyone losing face. Most importantly, I hope to make lasting connections with my students.

As for challenges, I am sure there will be many. The water will be bad, I will get sick (more than once), I will miss my family, I will yearn for good old American cooking (although I never do now), I will become frustrated by bureaucracy, I will become tired of teaching, I will be cold, I will be hot, I will feel moral indignation and institutional skepticism. However, these are superficial challenges. My real challenge will be to accept others as they are, to accept events as they come to pass and to accept beliefs without passing moral judgment. My challenges, in a nutshell, will be patience and acceptance, two concepts that have intellectual appeal, but little practical application in my life pre-China.

I believe that I will be a good teacher because I was a bad student. The fundamental understanding I gained was every student learns differently and has individual needs. Teaching is about finding the key to each student and unlocking his or her potential. It is about making your passion for a subject contagious. The courses in college that I learned anything in were those that I was excited about. A good professor could make me excited about anything—like China. Who would have known?!

The writers in this book have discovered a passion for China. We hope to pass along their enthusiasm and insights.

Alice Renouf

# Acknowledgments

This book exists because of the teachers who were willing and enthusiastic about sharing their heartfelt, spontaneous roller-coaster China experiences: the good, the bad, the ugly, and the magical. The other catalyst was Mary Beth Ryan-Maher's willingness to take these threads and weave them into a vibrant tapestry. As a former CCC teacher, she understood the essence of the experience and its value as a legacy to pass on to other prospective sojourners. Without Mary Beth's editorial mastery, as well as her understanding of the program and commitment to make this happen, this book would have always remained just another interesting idea.

The Colorado China Council's (CCC) Advisory Board, many of whom have been on the board since its inception in 1977, has always been generous with insights, advice, and support. Especially in the early days, the advisory board formed the network that helped with program development and Chinese university access. Joe and Toni Stepanek, now deceased, were among the original local sponsors who, along with their son Jim, helped move CCC forward.

Terry Lautz, a founder of the China Council of the Asia Society of New York City, was instrumental in the establishment of the eleven original regional China Councils throughout the United States in the late 1970s. From Terry's foresight in planting those seeds so much has blossomed.

We owe Howard Goldblatt special thanks for steering us to Rowman & Littlefield and acquisitions editor Susan McEachern. She saw the book's merit, encouraged us every step of the way, and tracked countless details. We are so grateful for Susan's support, as well as that of Carrie Broadwell-Tkach at Rowman.

Harrison (Xinshi) Tu, a highly acclaimed calligrapher, has been incredibly generous for allowing us to use his powerful, yet delicate, calligraphy. The characters on each chapter opening page represent the chapter title. The stunning photos generously provided by Ken Driese, John McGee, and Tim Lewis, who went to China with their spouses and children, greatly enrich our perspective and appreciation for living in a land so different from our own.

Jeanne Phillips, Phyllis Thompson, and Betsy Armstrong made invaluable editorial suggestions and never flagged in their enthusiasm for the project. Julie Segraves, along with Henry Strauss, have always being willing to listen and encourage in all aspects of program development. Ellen Axtmann put in endless amounts of administrative time and effort to help me keep the program going when it became overwhelming.

CCC, especially since it transitioned around 1991 from an outreach program into a program for Americans to teach in China, has flourished because of the support of my family. Our son, Cassidy Rush, worked on the seemingly intractable issues of collecting, organizing, and formatting the hundreds of emails, letters, and blogs from teachers from over a decade so that Mary Beth and I could begin work on the book. He also designed and maintains the website while living overseas himself. Our daughter, Whitney, participated in the program and opened my eyes on a deeply personal level to the day-to-day joys and hardships of living and teaching in China. She is also a good recruiter.

Lastly, but most importantly, my husband, Jon Rush, who was also in China studies, has been the backbone and patron saint of CCC. For three decades, he has listened patiently to me anguish over every little detail of the program and all the issues and problems of an ever changing, endlessly challenging conundrum of trying to put a square peg in a round hole! He also set up the computer, technical, and accounting systems to keep the program running smoothly. He provided the support rhythms that have kept this program alive decades longer than anyone could ever have imagined. I am eternally grateful to Jon, Cassidy, and Whitney and all the teachers, friends, and colleagues who helped bring this book to life.

Alice Renouf
Boulder, Colorado

☯

This book would not be possible without the vision and stamina of Alice Renouf. Working with Alice is a sheer pleasure. Her sense of life as a celebration at home and abroad kept this work afloat for three years, until it found a home at Rowman & Littlefield with Susan McEachern. Thank you, Susan and Carrie Broadwell-Tkach, for your tireless efforts!

I'm also extremely grateful to the teachers who were willing to share their emails and blogs with us for publication and whose words I've delighted in reading and rereading for the images, memories, and truths they evoke. The photographs by Ken Driese, Timothy Lewis, and John McGee and the calligraphy by Harrison Tu are marvelous and magical gifts to this book.

I am greatly indebted to Phyllis Thompson whose *Dear Alice* has been the beacon, benchmark, and catalyst for this book! Thank you, Melissa Wavelet and Jack and Yvette Connell, for reading various drafts and chapters of this book and for your insights and support along the way.

I never would have gone to China without my husband, Robert. He and his colleague Steve O'Connor plotted and planned the trip during the days when we were all teaching high school in the Bronx. Robert has truly been a patient partner in this endeavor. She Yi, our Chinese tutor, and her family were our lifeline during our year in Kunming and continue to be treasured friends. My mother Joan Ryan, my aunt Bonnie Agan, and uncles Richard Agan and Michael Whalen deserve special thanks for traveling to China to visit us and to Shanghai to babysit while Rob and I led the Summer Institute. Finally, thanks to my darling daughters, who are great travelers, linguists, and wordsmiths.

Mary Beth Ryan-Maher
New York, New York

# Contributors

*Note:* Contributing writers granted permission to use excerpts from their emails and blogs and indicated how they wished to be identified throughout the manuscript. Some writers chose only their first name or initials.

Christopher Angell
Ann
Lauren Anneberg
Ellen Axtmann
Mary Barton
Stopher Beck
Ian Bledsoe
Jim Boyd
Tom Brennan
Mat Brown
Bryna
Heather Bugni
Jennifer Bulmash
Susan Burnett
Seth Cagle
S. Lauren Carpenter
Rodney Chin
Ian Clark
Dana
Daniel
Larry Davis
Ken Driese

Jack Early
E. H.
Eric Fish
Barbara Gambini
Kevin A. Gee
Tim Gerber
Clio Goldsmith
Dana Hagengruber
Michael Hsu
JB
Lisa A. Johnson
Julie
Elene Johnston Kapp
Kim
Barbara Kramarz
Tim Lehmann
Josh Leslie
Brian E. Lewis
Sue Lewis
Timothy Lewis
Bev McGee
John McGee

Jake McTigue
Adrian Neibauer
Ellen Neibauer
Ryan Noll
Hélène North
Elizabeth Phelps
Jeanne S. Phillips
Steven J. Platz
Jessica Davis Pluess
Karen Raines
Jennie Richey
Peggy Rosen
Whitney Rush
Mary Beth Ryan-Maher

Cilla Bosnak Shindell
Carl Siegel
Bill Snyder
Collin Starkweather
Catt Stearns
Jennifer Szeto
Eva Tam
Patrick Tartar
Shana Tarter
Kimberly Te Winkle
Theresa
Brian T. Vick
Alex Weymann

# Cities and Provinces Where Teachers Lived and Taught

Beijing
Chengdu, Sichuan
Fuzhou, Fujian
Guangzhou, Guangdong
Hangzhou, Zhejiang
Jiaxing, Zhejiang
Kunming, Yunnan
Lijiang, Yunnan
Nanjing, Jiangsu
Putian, Fujian
Qingdao, Shandong
Shanghai
Tianjin
Wanzhou, Chongqing Municipality

*Cities and Provinces Where Teachers Lived and Taught*

# Travel Destinations

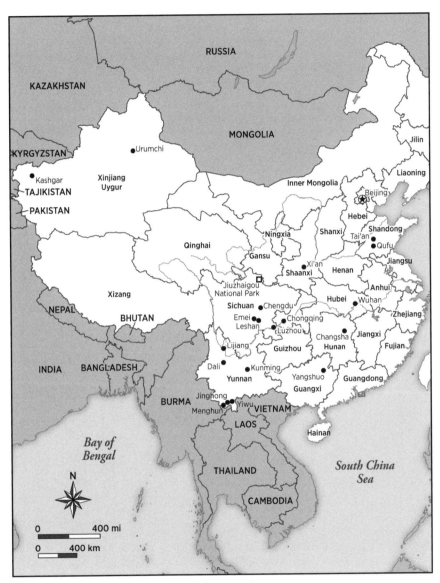

*Travel Destinations*

# 1

# China Arrival

*Settling In Can Be So Unsettling*

So many bizarre things occur all the time, and everyone acts like it's just normal.

—Ian Bledsoe, Hangzhou

*Bizarre, incredible, amazing, unbelievable. These words color the emails sent to Alice from her teachers shortly after they arrive in China. The intensity is palpable as the teachers wade into a new culture. The first few writers in this chapter are writing from the Council's Summer Institute, which is held in Shanghai every August. The Summer Institute is an intensive two- or three-week preparation for the rigors of teaching, complete with a teaching practicum. The summer program includes a Chinese language learning component and many conversations about cultural differences. It is the launching pad for this diverse group of individuals as they embark on a year of teaching English as a Foreign Language in cities throughout China. The time in Shanghai also affords some enjoyable sightseeing and time to be a tourist before taking up residency in their respective Chinese cities.*

**Jennie Richey**, Seattle to Shanghai to Nanjing
August 2001

We are now heading into our third week in Shanghai, population 10.8 million. We will stay here until Thursday at which time we will board a train for a three-hour ride to Nanjing where we will be greeted by my program hosts and escorted to our new home. Thus far, we have definitely been on a "China High." Everything is new and exciting, and each moment is full of learning experiences. Shanghai ranges from poverty-stricken areas to areas of extreme wealth. We have walked down trash-ridden, rotten-smelling, grimy streets where small children run around nearly naked, and we have also walked down streets flashier than Vegas where people stroll around in fancy outfits talking on their cell phones.

The markets here are absolutely unbelievable. They are crawling with live delicacies such as crickets, frogs, snakes, pigeons, spiny sea creatures, and more. "Shopkeepers" (if you could call them that) have mastered this squatting position, and they hover on top of the tables over their goods. Some of the food is wonderful, and some of it is odd and frankly disgusting (i.e., sucking the eyeball out of a fish head is a delicacy). We have both been stricken with massive and miserable diarrhea attacks which come at the most inopportune times. It may be the food or a combination of other factors (i.e., climate, water, etc.), but hopefully our bodies will adjust to the changes soon.

As white Americans we are definitely a sight to be seen around here. I am not used to the staring and snickering and sometimes feel like an alien when glassy eyes unabashedly stare at me. Since we arrived, we've seen the Shanghai Acrobats (the most talented group of gymnasts and jugglers

I have seen in my life), a Confucian Temple, a traditional Chinese garden, and walked streets and streets lined with shops selling traditional Chinese clothes, Mao paraphernalia (we bought a Little Red Book[1]), and much more. It has been a whirlwind of events and experiences intermingled with three hours a day of classes and two hours of teaching.

We have also been caught outside during monsoon-like rains that sweep through the city accompanied by *loud* thunder and bright lightning. We now take our umbrellas everywhere as the rains sneak up on a sunny day entirely unexpected.

Fortunately, through the training, we have had a chance to learn a lot about Chinese culture and customs. It is very interesting to move from a strong individualistic, efficiency-oriented society to one of collectivism, communism, and numerous formalities. Functioning within a society so completely different from what I am used to definitely inspires me to question my own beliefs and the influence my culture has had on shaping who I am.

**Karen Raines**, Sacramento to Shanghai
August 2007

It is my first week living in China, and I am in a state of constant awe. The awe is not always because I see something amazing, rather it is often because I see something, well, unbelievable. For instance, the first time I felt like I had truly gone through the figurative looking glass was on day three when I saw a lady selling frogs on the street. At first, I actually smiled at the jumping and squirming frogs confined underneath a wire tent. My interest increased as I saw a local woman in a mismatched pair of checkered pajamas (which, by the way, people wear pajamas all day long here), amble over to purchase a frog. Though I knew the frog would be the woman's dinner, I curiously watched as she poked the frogs to determine who would be the lucky (unlucky?) purchase. Finally, she chose one that met her specific, yet unknown, requirements. My amazement turned to horror, however, when I saw the seller grab the frog and proceed to dismember it with a pair of bright red kitchen scissors. China! I have a feeling that the frogs are only the beginning.

**Lauren Anneberg**, Denver to Shanghai to Hangzhou
August 2006

Yesterday's trip to Tong Li (a water town) was memorable mostly due to the scintillating sex museum. How unexpected! The canals were charming, and the shaded boat ride a welcome respite from the sun. I think we might have sweat off about a half a stone.

Last night a few of us ate at the Punjabi Indian restaurant near Nanchang Lu. We enjoyed a huge buffet and many laughs. Tonight we are going to a local hot pot place.[2] Days seem to revolve around the next meal, full of things I can honestly say I have never seen or eaten, but we're all well and enjoying each other's company (minus the ubiquitous "digestive trouble").

I have loved walking through the park in the early morning, visiting the fabric market, eating steaming soup-filled dumplings, and being ever-impressed with the students at the high school (where the Summer Institute practicum with volunteer Chinese students takes place). I would say that Shanghai is far more sprawling and glamorous than I expected. I ventured into the Shanghai Centre and wandered past every haute couture label I could never afford in my lifetime. It seemed out of place and yet strangely established. I was envisioning the neighborhood around the campus to be more of the standard, and perhaps it is. I haven't done enough exploring on my own to get a fair sense of the place. This afternoon I'm heading to the Shanghai Museum, so I better get going if I hope to make it back by dinner!

**Brian E. Lewis**, Denver to Shanghai to Tianjin
August 2002

Don't get the impression that I'm tired or frustrated or displeased in any way with China. By "intense," I merely meant that it is a big change. But really, it's been far easier than I had imagined. The only problem is the food; we all have found that learning the names of dishes that we like is a slow and time-consuming process, which none of us has really mastered. We've all settled on a handful of dishes we know and pretty much eat these constantly.

I'm actually ready to get on to Tianjin and start with the business I came here for. Shanghai was just preparation and a safe haven from which to settle into China. In Tianjin, I'll be on my own resources for the first time. I'm ready.

*After the brief sojourn in Shanghai, the new teachers depart for their respective universities and new residences. Ready or not, they will have to rely mostly on their own resources to navigate the next ten months. Aside from Alice's long-distance support, their one formal source of support in China is the* waiban, *a member of the university's Foreign Affairs Office. Since the majority of arrivals know minimal Chinese, basic communication outside of the university is generally an adventure, as is travel by bus, bike, or taxi and shopping for food, books, or computer equipment. While there are many surprises, there are also numerous amenities and conveniences. Susan Burnett writes from Shanghai in 2007, "The school has been very expedient in getting all of our paperwork with the government completed. They*

*are even opening bank accounts for us for direct deposit of our paychecks! They're going to be deposited at the Bank of Shanghai, which is right across the street from the guest house."* This is quite a difference from Rob's and my payday experience in 1999, which involved stopping by the Foreign Affairs Office to pick up an envelope stuffed with small bills, and then returning home to deposit it in the university-issued safe, which was conveniently installed in the bathroom of our apartment (and was too heavy to move.) The conveniences of the "New China" speed the ease of adjustment on some levels, but this is usually tempered with plenty of surprises.*

*Let's start with some stories from teachers in Hangzhou, the capital city of Zhejiang Province in eastern China only about one hundred miles from Shanghai. Hangzhou has a population exceeding four million and is known for its natural beauty, particularly West Lake and the temples and pagodas that surround it.*

**Ian Bledsoe**, Hangzhou
October 2003

So far everything's great here. My apartment is very nice and in a relatively quiet area, whereas most of the city is being built and torn down at all hours of the day and night! My apartment is on a small street, Xixi Lu, that winds its way between two more major streets and is lined with little stores, fruit stands, noodle shops, and old men playing cards at all hours of the day. I'm also only about a ten or fifteen minute walk from West Lake and right next to a path that goes up into the hills above the lake. I can't complain!

You're right! China's beyond fascinating. I can hardly peel my eyes away every night. So many bizarre things occur all the time, and everyone acts like it's just normal—though I guess such things happening all the time does make them normal by default. For example, the other night the other teachers and I were eating in a restaurant and a cat fell out of a hole in the ceiling right next to our table. Of course, we were the only ones present who found this interesting! Needless to say, I've had my fair share of terrifying taxi rides and other Chinese specialties.

**Kim**, Hangzhou
August 2005

Our living arrangements are wonderful. We have fully furnished two room apartments with a large bathroom and kitchen. We have a refrigerator, microwave, rice-cooker, a hot pad for a frying pan, and an excellent clothes washer. The apartments also have air conditioners in both the main rooms. We are living on the fifth floor of the campus hotel.

We have received our meal cards so if we use the cafeteria our meals are free. Today we went to the bank and started savings accounts so the school can directly deposit our monthly salaries. Our residence permits have not been finalized yet, but the *waiban* is working on them, and she had us open bank accounts today because it will take a while for the processing of the residence permits, and she wanted the accounts ready before the first payment on the eighth of September. We are still very much in the dark as to what classes we will be teaching. I am not too worried as I know they will have to give us that information or we will not be able to teach.

**Lauren Anneberg**, Hangzhou
August 2006

The *waiban* is a legend and has been helpful in every way. He's shown me around town, taken me shopping, taken me to lunch with his wife, and arranged for one of his students, Blue, to show me around West Lake. I think he's a wonderfully understanding and trustworthy man, and his best quality is his dry wit! The second-year teachers have been equally incredible. I've seen them every day for a random meal or a walk around town. This morning they took me up Baoshi Hill, around some temples, to the hot shopping spots, and to one of about a dozen Starbucks. Tomorrow night, I'm having them over for dinner (after I explore the Carrefour, a French department store), and then onto ladies' night at the Irish pub. I think Hangzhou's wonderful! We just had a huge cracking storm, got drenched running home through it, made a cup of tea to watch it come down wall-length windows.

I have a draft teaching schedule: Writing, Spoken English, and Foreign Movie Appreciation (yes!). I teach Mondays through Thursdays from 3:55 until 8:05 p.m. Looks like I have mornings free for now. I will be meeting with the other foreign teachers and the Vice-Dean this Friday. I have also "volunteered" to edit the poetry magazine. And I might answer an ad to join a women's soccer team in the area. Never too late in life to take up a new sport!

*A few teachers settle in Beijing, China's capital city with a population of more than fourteen and half million. Beijing is home to numerous cultural and historical sites from the Forbidden City to the Summer Palace and to nearby sections of the Great Wall.*

**Daniel**, Beijing
September 2007

The university gave all the foreign teachers a plant for "Teacher's Day," which was Monday here in China. The university is having a banquet on Friday for all of the foreign teachers. Dress is formal so I guess this is an official picture-taking event. I'm looking forward to it. The *waiban* asked me to speak on behalf of the new teachers so I guess I'll have to think of a few nice things to say.

As for Beijing, the nightlife seems to be good, although I have not done too much of it. Maybe I'll go enjoy a beer and some western music tonight come to think of it. No class tomorrow. My students are great. I have two master classes that are a joy. They are small with twenty-one and twenty-four students in those classes. Who says Chinese classrooms are enormous? Multi-media in the classroom is decent, especially in the newer buildings on campus.

As for my housing, yes, I do live in one of those typical six-floor walkups. I'm on the fifth floor so I get a little Stairmaster workout every day. My neighbors are other foreign teachers and the Chinese. It's nice to be mixed in with the locals. I like that.

*Seventy-two miles to the southeast of Beijing is Tianjin, Beijing's port city, now only twenty minutes away by high-speed train. Tianjin is one of China's largest cities with a population of nearly twelve million. Attractions include the Boxer Rebellion Museum, the Antique Market, and numerous temples.*

**Brian T. Vick**, Tianjin
December 1996

It is fascinating to see how technology is changing and shaping the country. Tianjin is one of China's several Economic Development Areas, and it exemplifies the contrast of old and new China. It is an amazing blend of tradition and technology. BMWs and donkey-drawn carts share the same street. Large families dwell in tiny single-room homes but have state-of-the-art TVs, VCRs, and stereos. Everyone has pagers and most have cell phones. Public messages are sent out via the paging system (stock exchange reports and weather forecasts and more). What is even more amazing is that most pagers have visible message capability which means Chinese characters scroll across the LCD screen. Modern props in a very rustic and rough setting.

**Lisa A. Johnson**, Tianjin
September 2000

Tianjin is awesome! Life here seems more relaxed, less crazy and definitely smaller than Shanghai! My classes begin on the thirteenth so I've had time to ride my bicycle around and prepare for my lessons. I'm in the post-graduate foreign languages department but am also doing some teaching for a small group of students in the pharmacy school. There are only four foreign teachers on this huge campus, so as you can imagine we are constantly getting phone calls and requests to teach various classes for various groups. I think that if a person wanted to they could teach twenty-four hours a day! Not me. I'm enjoying life and academia.

**Brian E. Lewis**, Tianjin
August 2002

### Split Pants and Road Rules

*Laowai* (pronounced laow-why) is the colloquial term for a foreigner. Tianjin does not receive many foreign visitors, so every time I go outside, it's a traveling circus. I've gotten *laowai* shouted at me so many times, I think it's my name.

Sunday I went to Heping Lu, a major pedestrian street downtown. I turned off of Heping Lu a few blocks, into a more quiet section. I didn't attract much attention on Heping Lu, but Chinese swarmed me like flies in this residential street. I was walking and smiling at all the friendly gawkers. An older man was with his grandchild, whose back was to me and who also happened to be in the middle of taking a big baby dump onto a tree. (Something you may not know, I didn't, is that the vast majority of Chinese children do not wear diapers. Instead, their pants have a slit or larger opening through which mostly digested matter may pass, usually onto the sidewalk or in this case, a tree.) The old man got very excited, pointed to me saying "*laowai!*," picked the kid up mid-defecation and turned him around so he could see me. Red letter day: baby's first *laowai*. He seemed very proud, and I was honored to be part of such a momentous occasion.

Tianjin itself is very quiet and laid-back as far as cities go. Tianjin has a climate quite like Denver's: very dry, dusty, hot in summer and cold in winter with little rain or snow. They burn coal for heat here in the winter, so most everyone here wears surgical masks to screen out the dust. At the same time, Tianjin is a very green city. The campus is actually quite beautiful. It is dominated by a vast lotus pond, ringed by large, leafy willows. The Hejin River rings the campus, channeled into sculpted canals. It's very peaceful. People lounge around in parks, reading books or fishing.

Even the traffic is less intense here. Road rules are more or less observed, and the bike lanes are more ardently marked and enforced.

However, a cab I was in this morning did make a U-turn on a six-lane highway, go the wrong way down a one-way street, block said street for five minutes getting directions, drive down a pedestrian only street, and almost run over four bikes in an intersection while running a red light. This was all in the same cab, same ride. The nearby Chinese protested only with an emphatic ringing of bike bells or car horns. The man would have been shot dead in Denver. I actually found myself hoping that some large truck would bring Mr. Toad's Wild Ride to an end so that I could switch to a less extreme cab. It was rather hilarious to be stalled out perpendicular to the flow of traffic in a six-lane highway with a huge truck bearing down on me and showing no sign of braking. I think in China, people have come to some sort of understanding with death.

August 2002

**The Road Warrior**

Monday I bought a bicycle, for 160 *kuai*,[3] which I had bargained down from the original price and got the guy to throw in a lock. I am now the Terror of Tianjin. If you think foreigners attract attention here, try riding a bike. The sight of a *laowai* on a bicycle blows the mind of many a native. Particularly one who, like me, feels completely at home weaving in and out of traffic, swerving inches from pedestrians, and jumping over potholes. On my bike, I'm more Chinese than the Chinese. Now, I must admit, that my first foray into the angry sea of chains and rust was a little anxiety ridden. But I've spent the vast majority of the day on the road, in the seething dust and grinding heat, battling for position, swooping down on unsuspecting intersections, holding my breath while I clip through a split-second opening between two taxis. I have arrived. I even beat a motorcycle for a few blocks through some adept maneuvering and high-speed pedaling. It's really not fair, though. Most Chinese ride very slowly. They have a kind of two-wheeled passive aggression. I'm assertive. I think "car," I ride "car." I am a car, except when there's a real car ahead of me. Still, I'm quickly developing a sense for the way Chinese drivers make decisions, and that's allowing me to adjust to the situation on the streets more rapidly than I had thought possible. I'm also getting a good feel for the layout. I rode around without my map today and made it everywhere I wanted to go just fine. Sure, sometimes I overshot, or had to loop around a little, but I always found my way. I'm completely stoked.

*Chengdu, located in Sichuan Province in southwestern China, is a financial and transportation hub, and sometimes called the Gateway to Tibet. Chengdu's population tops four and a half million.*

**Adrian Neibauer**, Chengdu
August 2003

Well, Ellen and I are finally here in the wonderful city of Chengdu. I'm glad we acclimated to the climate and time difference while in Shanghai, because there is no time for rest. We got in yesterday and were introduced to our lovely apartment. It is twice as big as the one in Boulder, but it comes with some special bonuses. Ready? Our bathroom and shower are in the same room, as in the shower is right above the toilet on the other wall. There is a smelly drain in the bathroom so the water goes down while taking a shower. I just have to be careful not to slip and hit the toilet while I am singing in the shower. The kitchen looks like something from the Bates Motel in *Psycho*. We have a lovely view of the alley, along with which comes a nice sewer/alley smell. Basically, our entire apartment is consumed with the smell, and it will take a lot of air fresheners to get used to it.

Next come the bugs. On our first night, we found a huge spider under our bed (about the size of a small frog). Using my shoe, I stepped on it, but it was so big I felt as if I were trying to kill a mouse or something. The fleas and mosquitoes are huge and everywhere. We may have to look for some sort of bug net to sleep under so we don't get eaten alive.

Chengdu is wonderful. We talked to someone who has been here for about three weeks who gave us a head start on where to find various things. We spent 600 *renminbi* last night buying everything from cleaning supplies to linens; that's only about US $60. Right now, we have to go to the train station in order to get our mailed suitcase and then spend some more time shopping for stuff to make our place feel like home.

August 2003

The cleaning lady came on Saturday afternoon, and she did a great job, but alas, the smell in the kitchen/bathroom is still there. We have decided that it is coming from the alley the kitchen window faces, and there is not much that can be done. Ellen's mother is sending us some baking soda from the States, and we think that it will help with the smell. We wanted to let you know that it is probably not a good idea to talk to the *waiban* about the smell. He has already replaced our broken bed, gotten us a water cooler, sent people to fix a leak in our kitchen, and will soon send someone out to fix the horrible connection on our phone. I think that we have bugged him enough. The smell, although unpleasant at times, is not unbearable. Thank you for your concern; we will keep you posted. This is turning into a wild and fun adventure, and we want to thank you for getting us here. Oh, and the weather has been cool and wet; it has rained every night in the last four days. It is much more comfortable than Shanghai.

**Bill Snyder**, Chengdu
February 2004

Here are some of our experiences in no particular order:

- In Southwest China, it is definitely "B.Y.O.T.P." (Bring Your Own Toilet Paper).
- It was fifty-three degrees the first night in our apartment (and that was the "warm" room). It was about thirty-eight in the bathroom. (When it is less than forty degrees in the bathroom, you really "have to go" badly to get out of bed at night.) We have since reached the high sixties with the addition of a heater, electric blanket, and more layers!
- Of course, the cold weather is beneficial for some of our neighbors. Like most people in Asia, we dry our clothes by hanging them on a line put up outside our window. Our neighbors across the courtyard took down their laundry and put up various pork products to keep chilled. Not entirely sure, but I believe there were some pig feet, pig intestines, and a slab of bacon.
- We tripped the circuit breaker three times in the first couple of days in our apartment, so we are now having the following conversations daily, "I need to use the microwave, can you turn off the heater?" and "I want to dry my hair, could you turn off the TV?" You must respect your power grid!
- There is a guy on a bicycle that wanders through our neighborhood almost every morning chanting something in a deliberate, but rather melodic and loud tone. We thought maybe he was spouting some Chairman Mao dogma to the masses each day, such as, "Remember the great Proletariat Revolution," or "Long live the Communist Party," or maybe the standard, "Power to the People." However, someone recently told us he is just asking for cardboard to recycle.
- There is both incredible wealth and incredible poverty here in Chengdu. We live on campus and across the road there is a brand-new multimillion dollar classroom and research building. Across the street from this building is what we assume are peasant workers living in "tarp housing" digging up the foundations of recently demolished buildings just to salvage the bricks. It is backbreaking work as all that they have are picks, shovels, and hammers.
- There is a US Consulate less than a mile from the university campus here. It is only about a hundred yards across the front of the building, but there were sixteen Chinese guards out in front of the building fence the other day and seven of them were carrying Uzi machine guns.

We are clearly in reverse sticker shock in terms of the costs of things after living in Tokyo. In Chengdu, three of us went to dinner at a dumpling place on campus, and for forty dumplings, hot vegetable soup, and drinks, it was seventy-five cents. Not per person, total! Also, we were debating whether we should hire a person to clean our apartment until we were told the cost was about a dollar an hour. We decided to have the cleaning lady come twice a week!

March 2004

Well, it took a little over three weeks, but we finally signed our contracts today. There was a lot of negotiating (or should we call it "gamesmanship"), but in the end we mostly got what we wanted due to a couple of things. First, the few key points you helped us get in writing before we left home were invaluable. It's funny how most of that information did not get passed to the people still here, but we had it all in writing when we really needed it.

Secondly, and not to be underestimated, they clearly have a lot of respect for you and that really helped. When they finally agreed to the key positions we had taken, it was clear they took into consideration "our good friend Alice" (their words, not mine). So, we certainly feel good about our decision to work with you as your experience and reputation here is obviously very high.

I will save you all the details, but we simply had to take a solid stand on the number of hours we would teach (they wanted a lot more), the types of courses we would teach (we agreed to subject courses only, but they at one point wanted Beatrix to teach six subject courses and then ten English classes on top of that), and where we would teach (we quickly vetoed anything off campus).

In the end, I am teaching thirteen hours of subject courses, and Beatrix is teaching six hours of subjects and two hours of English, which puts us right around the twenty hours we agreed to. The airfare worked out better than we imagined as they are paying our international fare here and domestic both ways. They are good negotiators, but we had a strong position with your help.

*Kunming, population two and half million, is the capital city of Yunnan Province in southwest China. Yunnan Province is home to at least twenty-five of China's ethnic minorities. Kunming highlights include Green Lake Park and the Garden of the World Horticultural Exposition.*

**Mary Beth Ryan-Maher**, Kunming
September 1999

So here I sit on this quiet Monday morning at the computer/Internet/copy shop down the lane listening to the news in Chinese and to the tinkering of a woman sitting on the roof of the building across the way pounding blocks of coal (?) into small pieces and loading them into her large bamboo basket. There is also the occasional buzz of a motorcycle and the constant hammering of the nearby construction sites. Kunming is under construction in a big way. To the east of our apartment the university is completing construction on a hotel. It will be a training ground for students studying tourism. To the south of us, a massive building is being built, and it is nowhere near being finished. The pounding goes on and on late into the night, and sometimes after dark from our window we see the sparks flying from the welding illuminating the workers. This is the noise in the background.

The hustle and bustle of the day are during three specific times. Between seven and eight in the morning everyone is going to school and work. Parents and children flood our lane on the way to the school that is at the other end creating an amazing flow of motorbikes, bicycles, pedestrians, and the occasional car or mini-van. The elementary school students wear sweat suits as their uniforms. These youngsters flow out of school again, along with the university students, high school students and parents at noon. School does not resume until two thirty, and school ends at five thirty, when again the street overflows with activity and street vendors. It is these younger students who always look curiously at us on the street, giggle, and occasionally throw out a "Hello" in a somewhat British accent. When you return their "Hello" and ask, "How are you?" their eyes widen, they cover their mouths, whisper to their friends, and practically run away. This scene is repeated over and over. We can only smile; they are quite adorable.

**Collin Starkweather**, Kunming
August 2006

I've been settling in this week as well. I'd been told I'd begin teaching last Monday (yes, two days after I arrived), but when I got here, they said classes wouldn't start for a week. Whew! In retrospect, I needed a week to acclimatize.

My apartment is really nice, a corner unit on the top floor of a "hotel." The school seems to rent some rooms out, and the maids come in regularly to randomly move my things about. My bedroom has two beds, so anyone who wants to make the trip to Kunming has a place to lay their head, but I should warn all travelers that the beds are even harder than those in Shanghai.

The weather in Kunming is gorgeous: temperatures in the sixties and seventies with regular evening showers. It's certainly a city, though it lacks the hustle and bustle of Shanghai. My initial impression is that it is also a bit more old school in Chinese terms. On the short half-mile walk from the apartment to the university administrative building, I pass maybe a half dozen police officers (definitely not mall cops, mind you), then pass by two more permanently stationed at the entrance to the building.

Kunming is also not as affluent as Shanghai. I visited the Economics Department and schmoozed with one of the few professors who spoke English. I believe he was the chair of the department and his computer was an ancient HP that wouldn't have surprised me if it had a 5.25" floppy drive and was running Windows 98. He was very friendly.

One funny incident happened while we were chatting. One of his colleagues came up and began asking me something in Chinese at a mile a minute. At that moment, I decided that my standard response to any flood of Chinese will be to smile and deadpan, slowly and carefully, "*Hen hao. Ni hao ma?*" (I'm very well. How are you?)

I've had many interesting experiences with *hanyu* (Chinese language) since I got here. My hot water device did not work, so I spent a good half hour with the dictionary writing up the nature of the problem. Maintenance guys came and gave me a stream of unintelligible Chinese. Fortunately, I had memorized the phrase "*Ni xiu li jin tian ma?*" (I think it means, "You repair today?"), and after the tenth or twelfth query, they said, "*Mingtian*" (tomorrow).

My Internet also didn't work, and I finally found someone who knows a graduate student whose English is primarily composed of computer terms and knows what a switch is (a networking device which is the central hub for Internet connections in a building). I got him to find out where the switch was in the building, then waved my hands and gesticulated wildly until they understood that the port to my room was dead and let me switch the connection to a working port. I also figured out that *yin te wang* is "Internet" and *yin te wang lian jie, huai le* means, "The Internet connection, it's not working."

When the guys came *mingtian* to give me a new hot water tank, they somehow locked the door to my bedroom in the course of the repair. A bit of a problem since my wallet and all my clothes were in the bedroom. Fortunately, my dictionary was with me, and a mere eight hours later, we established that they had lost the key. They sent a train of other maintenance guys up until someone finally got the bright idea to hack the doorknob off.

And finally, my iPod decided to reboot in a continuous cycle. #*!@&. After a long afternoon, I can now provide tech support in case anyone needs to flash their firmware and power cycle their iPod.

I hope it doesn't sound like my week has been trials and tribulations. I've had a blast learning new Chinese (*yaoshi* = key, *yushi* = bathroom, and *woshi* = bedroom) and figuring out how to have a conversation with six words or less.

September 2006

I spent the day negotiating the purchase of a new ink cartridge for my printer. While this may seem a relatively simple task, in China it is anything but. The transaction proceeds as follows:

1. Look up the word printer in the dictionary.
2. Look up the word ink in the dictionary.
3. Look up the word cartridge in the dictionary.

4. Ask a friend who speaks some Chinese whether the words "printer ink cartridge" together mean anything in Chinese.

   One cannot simply assume that putting the words "printer," "ink," and "cartridge" together will elicit even a glimmer of recognition. It could be that the Chinese for "printer ink cartridge" might be literally translated as "electric paper machine dark water container" or something even more obscure. Fortunately, "printer ink cartridge" translates.

5. Research prices online. One must negotiate for everything in China. Prices are not posted and you cannot simply assume that the business is going to have a reasonable markup. In fact, because you are a Westerner, they are going to try to stick it to you. (To give you an indication of scale, a friend here in Kunming recently told me she negotiated a vendor down from 5,000 *yuan* to 100 when trying to buy a pair of jeans.) One must simply accept that and do the relevant research to be sure you are not being taken advantage of.

6. Print out a picture of the ink cartridge and the prices so that I can show them a picture in case my Chinese elicits more confusion than clarification, and I can use the prices as a negotiating point. (Fortunately, my printer is not totally out of ink, so I am able to make said printouts.)

7. Go to a store that sells printers. Ask where to find ink cartridges. Of course, the store that sells printers wouldn't think of selling ink cartridges. They're a printer store. Silly American.

8. Tease out of the employees the location of the store that sells ink cartridges.

9. Ask how much it is to buy a cartridge.

10. Express shock and dismay at the price. (The gripping of one's heart translates well in any culture.) Try to tell them that your mother needs an important operation which you cannot afford if you pay the price that they're asking.

11. Tell them again there's no way you can possibly afford the cartridge.

12. Ask about refill kits.

13. No, not those refill kits. Refill kits made by Chinese companies that ignore WTO intellectual property regulations, but do make extremely inexpensive products.

14. Haggle some more over price.

15. Come to an arrangement and close the deal. Mother gets her operation after all.

Bear in mind that the step labeled "look up the word in the dictionary" is no simple matter. Looking up a word in Chinese can be a trying experience. You'll have to trust me on this.

All told, it was probably a four-hour operation from start to finish, even though the printer store is located about ten minutes away. The price started at 300 *yuan* (about US $35) and ended at 35 (about US $4.37). Not too bad, but I think I could have haggled them down another fifty cents or so.

*Many teachers also land in Nanjing, population five million. Nanjing, the capital of Jiangsu Province, is located along the Yangtze River approximately 175 miles west of Shanghai. Sites to see include the Ming Palace ruins, Fuzi Temple, Xuanwu Lake, the Chaotian Palace, and Zijin (Purple) Mountain where you can visit the mausoleum of Sun Yat-sen (1866–1925), the father of modern China.*

**Jennifer Szeto**, Nanjing
September 2000

I arrived in Nanjing safely. I met the *waiban* at the train station. You were right; she is wonderful and speaks very good English. So far things have been pretty good despite a few (big) bugs, broken sinks, and toilets. I can't complain too much. I must say though, Shanghai was almost a tease. The teachers there have it very good.

Well, I started teaching yesterday. I think it went well. The training was very helpful.

Also, I wanted to inform you that I needed to get a blood test for hepatitis. I didn't want to cause a scene so I just complied. The needles were safe.

September 2000

Nanjing is a nice city, and quieter than Shanghai, of course. The campus is lined with trees and gardens. I have a bicycle because you need one to get anywhere in less than ten minutes. My apartment is a bit old, but livable. There are only five foreign teachers here including me. Though they're all nice, I don't know how close we'll get. Two are rather religious in that they came to China because "God told them to." Then there's a girl from Ohio and a fellow from England; all of us are new teachers. I teach fourteen hours, and I've agreed to give a few "lectures," and I'm privately tutoring an older teacher here who wants to go to Canada. I have a Chinese tutor and plenty of enthusiastic students. I'm still looking for a person to teach me calligraphy.

**Jennie Richey**, Nanjing
September 2001

Sunday night at about seven, our power went out. After a lot of shuffling around trying to find our tiny little alarm clock flashlight and locating the apartment storekeeper, we found out we had run out of power. The concept of buying power before you use it was entirely foreign to me. The school never mentioned that we needed to purchase our own power. The least I would have expected is a phone number of who to call and instructions on where and how to read the power meter. I was irate. I had lessons to plan; I didn't have candles or a flashlight. The inconvenience was totally unnecessary.

**Mary Barton**, Nanjing
September 2003

Well, I have been here in Nanjing for two weeks now, and I have finished my first week of teaching!

It is still very hot and humid, and it's not pleasant being outside. Since everything in China takes five times longer than usual, I am outside more than I have wanted. The weather should break in a few weeks, and I understand that the fall is the best and most beautiful time in Nanjing. I am looking forward to being able to do the tourist things in this historic city.

We are celebrating "National Day" on October first. It is similar to the Fourth of July in the United States and First of July in Canada. I think the students and teachers will have the week off.

There are five foreign teachers here at the university: one from Britain, one from Australia, and three of us from the United States (i.e., Baltimore, San Diego, and me, from Denver/Canada). We have quite a melting pot. We all live in the same apartment building, two to an apartment.

I had a skirt made. Naturally, I couldn't speak Mandarin and the tailor couldn't speak English. I was afraid to pick up my order not knowing what the heck I was going to get. It turned out so well that I had another skirt and a pair of pants made. She is really quite good. I ventured out to a fabric store and purchased some fabric; one for a traditional Chinese-style long skirt. Oh, yes, I bargained for the fabric. You dicker for just about everything here; it is like a game, and I sure have fun bantering with the Chinese. They are really wonderful and very helpful.

I have been watching movies during any free time (very little) that I have; DVDs are very, very cheap here, but you get what you pay for. A lot of them are knockoffs and very bad copies. I was watching one movie and the laugh track was for another movie, and the subtitles were also for another movie! During this particular one, I saw a person get up in front of the screen and leave. Ah-ha! This movie was filmed in a theater and sold! Still, the good ones outweigh the bad ones.

**Cilla Bosnak Shindell**, Nanjing
February 2003

Greetings from the People's Republic of China! I arrived safely here about one week ago after an exhausting twenty-four-hour trip from Dayton to

Shanghai. I share an apartment on campus with a graduate of Smith College, who is delightful. She has studied Mandarin and speaks quite a bit, so we have been able to make a few trips to the grocery and post office. Our Chinese coordinator for foreign teachers, the *waiban*, has been simply wonderful and responsive to our questions and needs. He seems to understand that we need time to adapt physically, time to set up our home, and yesterday, he just introduced us to our teaching schedule. Although classes start today for most of the school, our classes won't start until next week, which gives us a full week to prepare. That's quite a blessing. Most of the people with whom we have interacted so far have some command of English, so we communicate basics generally well. The *waiban*'s English is excellent, and he has recruited several students to take us downtown to the main shopping area where there are huge, shiny bright department stores filled with beautiful, modern clothing, jewelry, shoes, and conveniences. Once we get outside the university, communicating becomes more challenging, but with my roommate's command of Mandarin, a phrase book, and a few handwritten notes from the *waiban* (with our home address on them), we've taken buses and taxis to get around.

❧

**Christopher Angell**, Nanjing
June 2007

As my mother calmly predicted, my bags failed to arrive with me, so at the moment, the apartment is a little barren but very clean and pleasant. It has all the amenities, including air conditioning (Nanjing is reputed to be one of the "Three Furnaces of China"), refrigerator, washing machine and outdoor clothesline for drying, and microwave. I also have an Internet connection in the apartment. The building itself is not much to look at. I would describe the architecture as "early Soviet-bloc" style, but it is conveniently located near two dining halls and a beautiful park on school grounds, complete with overhanging willow trees, lake with fountain, and a Chinese-style three-arch bridge.

June 2007

Despite the fact that I don't speak Chinese, life is becoming a little easier here because the Chinese people have been so kind. For instance, when I go into the local market, the clerks and I start laughing almost immediately because we know that my pantomiming is going to be fun and a little bit of a game. The cashier at the cafeteria now knows me and always helps me order what I want by walking around with me while I point at what other people are having. At the local roadside snack stand, I play with the little son of the shop owners and ask him to take the money for my ice cream, much

*Stone bridge in Xitang, Zhejiang. Photo by Tim Lewis.*

to everyone's delight. And I now know some of the bus routes that will take me to the sights I want to see.

June 2007

My trip into downtown Nanjing turned out to be quite an endeavor! My mission was to find and buy a pair of computer speakers, a city map showing where my school is located, and a Chinese-English dictionary with the words in Chinese written in the Roman alphabet (i.e., *pinyin*). I had a few obstacles to overcome: I didn't know which way to go, I didn't know how or how much to pay, and I didn't know where to get off. Fortunately, I did know that the Yangtze River is on the far side of the city. So if I crossed that, I could be sure I was on my way to Tibet!

First, I went to the bus stop that I thought would take me in the right direction, but just to be sure, I gestured for the crowd in both directions, asking with my best Chinese accent, "Nanjing? Nanjing?" After an odd look or two, the direction was pointed out to me, which was a good thing because I was ready to get on a bus headed the wrong way. After crossing the street and getting on the No. 5 headed the right way, I watched to see how much everyone else was putting in the coin slot and followed suit. I then edged my way toward the back of the bus, looked down, and saw bare pavement below me. I could also see the transmission, one axle, and the gear linkage through a rather large hole in the wooden floor. Next to the hole was a bucket of water that I think was used to cool down the engine when necessary, but who knows? (This was one of the older buses in the fleet; the one I came back on was much newer.)

Have you ever noticed that in some cities on public transportation, no one talks? Or if they do, it is in a hushed voice? Well, no such doings on this bus! People were chatting amiably away as loud as they cared to, either with one another or on cell phones, with not a hint of self-consciousness. It was refreshing to hear this and not surprising. With so many people, my guess is that personal privacy is a luxury that few are able to afford.

In any case, my attention rapidly focused on where I was going to get off the bus, so I kept a close eye on landmarks outside, including the huge and beautiful remnants of the Ming city walls, an imperial garden, and grand city canals. And I was amazed at the amount of construction! It seemed that nearly every city block had cranes and workers of some sort scurrying around, and my impression is that these jobs are going on twenty-four hours a day. Finally, a traffic circle with a statue of Sun Yat-sen[4] (also under construction) appeared, and I decided that this was the place to leave my bus family. Waving good-bye and promising to keep in touch, I descended to the pavement, looked up, and saw a huge sign for a university bookstore! Hah! "Living in China without speaking or reading the language is going to be a snap," said I to myself. What a foolish thought!

When I got inside, I discovered that there was not a single word in English to be seen on either a sign or bookshelf. I went up to the first employee I could find and asked, "English books?" I pantomimed opening and reading a book.

"No," came the reply. Then in a courteous gesture, the man motioned me outside the store, pointed me down the street and said, "English bookstore." And off I went.

Unfortunately, this next store had only a few books in English, but it *did* have a street map of Nanjing in both Chinese and English. After purchasing it, I now knew where I was, and I had a reasonable expectation of confining myself to the Nanjing city limits.

So I set off to meet with Sun Yat-sen again, and picking a street heading north from the traffic circle because it looked important, I began my search for computer speakers and a dictionary. I had no idea of how difficult it would be to find them!

In the first place, I did not see any stores for the two hours that I walked that had any computer equipment in them at all, except for the ubiquitous PlayStation2 stores. Further, the shopping malls where one might expect to find a computer shop were almost all clothing stores. Those few that had electronics were dominated by cell phones and appliances. So I knew I'd have to go "off the beaten path" if I were to be successful in my search, which meant heading down some streets that are best described as outdoor malls and are absolutely jammed with people. In addition, the streets tend to blend together to the uninitiated eye, and there are outdoor advertising shows going on everywhere, with stages and dancing set up in some locations and in others, employees with signs marching single file through the crowds in an attempt to attract attention. All these distractions make it even tougher to navigate.

After another hour of wandering, I thought I had stumbled across the Grail. I saw a huge, three-story building with a sign that appeared to have something to do with electronics. After entering and letting my eyes get adjusted to the new light, I looked around and saw a whole floor devoted to nothing but cell phones! Oh well, I thought, it might be worth trying the second floor, so I half-heartedly went up the escalator and found approximately four computers for sale and a set of speakers hooked up to one of them!

My next task was explaining that I wanted the speakers *without* the computer. (By the way, after my experience here, you definitely want me on your Charades team!) The salesperson could not have been more patient and helpful, and after a few trips to the manager's office, he was able to sell me the speakers separately (they cost a little less than ten US dollars). I never knew that a simple purchase could bring such a feeling of elation!

Deciding it was now time to try to find my way back to the bus stop, I left the store but immediately noticed a little bookstore that was located across the street from the electronics building. Sure enough, it had the Chinese-English dictionary I was looking for.

Now emerging from the bookstore as Caesar, Lord of All He Surveys, I triumphantly swaggered back toward the bus stop, booty in hand, and suddenly realized that having been turned around while in the outdoor mall, I had no idea which way the bus stop was, let alone the university. In the space of one block, I went from nobility to foreign idiot once again, and after plotting what seemed like as good a direction to take as any, I began my march. Fearing that this one might rival the Long March[5] for length and lack of direction, I was only too happy to accidentally run into, after a few blocks, my old friend Dr. Sun Yat-sen. Weary but content, he showed me the way to the bus, and from there it was a simpler matter to figure out how to get home.


June 2007

I realize I know next to nothing about what is going on here beneath the surface. However, my brief contacts with students and colleagues have led me to the following observations about China:

1. There are several different Chinas in existence here simultaneously; the most recognizable "societies" are the urban and rural. Most of the alarming stories one hears about China (abortion of female fetuses, factory working conditions, etc.) are directly linked to the problems in the

countryside, where traditional values, overpopulation, and a lack of jobs has led to drastic measures to limit the number of mouths to feed and to massive migrations to the city in a hunt for work. China has no social security system of which I am aware, so planning for retirement in rural areas means "smart" family planning and ensuring that there will be steady income streams being earned by the next generation.

2. My students are part of the urban society and think of themselves as modern, and in most respects they are. The boys' dress and behavior are almost indistinguishable from their American counterparts. While some girls still make some concessions to traditional modesty, super-tight jeans are the rage for them. But with a handful of exceptions, tops are modest and the girls will often avert their gaze and act shy when I speak to them.

3. Cell phones are everywhere and in constant use. I don't have one yet, and I feel naked!

4. Chinese kids don't want to be American. They want to be modern and as well-off as the average American, but they want to be modern as Chinese people and not modern as pseudo-Americans.

5. Co-existing with the younger kids, but seemingly living in a different reality, are the older folks who dress more traditionally, are more reserved, and look askance at the displays of "making-out" sometimes seen in public. Things are moving a little fast for them.

6. There is building going on *everywhere*! I am not exaggerating when I say that one cannot walk more than a few blocks in any direction in Nanjing without bumping into a major construction project. It is so common that there seems to be a layer of building dust that permeates the city. Here at the university, there are at least three huge buildings undergoing major renovations, and the city is in the midst of building a new subway line to supplement the one line it already has, with plans for more on the board.

7. If you want to find Americans in China, find the nearest McDonald's, KFC, or Pizza Hut.

8. On the other hand, if you want to meet some interesting foreigners, go to the Bureau of Public Security, where workers' permits are issued.

9. Not all Chinese food tastes good.

August 2007

## Language Impressions

Hello *Dajia*,

I'm using an extra Chinese word in my greeting because it demonstrates an interesting point that has been slowly crystallizing in my mind. *"Ni hao"* means "hello" (no mystery there), and the easiest translation of *dajia* is "everybody." If you look no further, there is little to be learned. But "dajia" is actually a combination of two words: *da* meaning "big," and *jia* meaning "house" or "family." So the literal translation of my greeting is "hello big family (or extended family)."

The Chinese way of saying "everybody" highlights a key difference between Chinese and American cultures. I would argue that the word "everybody" in Western culture has an impersonal tone to it. It merely signifies a certain group without mentioning the speaker's connection, if any, with that group. The Chinese word, however, tells listeners that the speaker feels he or she has at least a communal connection with everyone within earshot, whether he or she actually knows them or not. For me, this highlights an important difference between Western and Chinese culture. While Western culture focuses on the individual and often generates feelings of community through "artificial" means, such as loyalty to sports teams, colleges, political parties, and clubs to which we belong, a Chinese sense that the whole is greater than the sum of its parts seems to be innate. This is extremely appealing to me and is readily apparent. When I wanted to distribute information files to my students via computer, since the network here is unreliable, a few kids would invariably volunteer to copy them and take responsibility for seeing that they were distributed to everyone in the class. I worried about the reliability of this system, but I never heard any student complain about not getting what they needed. And I think the feeling of belonging to a whole also explains, to a certain extent, my warm reception by nearly all the people with whom I have had contact. I have a feeling that as a foreigner, I am not only a guest of my employer, but also of the greater Chinese community and that most Chinese believe I should be treated as such.

As my continuing attempts to learn the Chinese language lead me to new insights, they also continue to lead to a few new mishaps. The other day, while in the health club, I tried to tell a walking advertisement for weight training that I was an American citizen and managed instead to tell him I was his little sister. I have also implied to my hair stylist that he is the son of a horse. Best of all, though, I decided to learn my first Chinese pick-up line, "You are very beautiful." After practicing in front of a mirror for quite a long time, my pronunciation had not improved but I felt much better about myself. I ventured out on the street looking for a victim and ran across an adorable little girl with her parents. I proceeded to tell her she was very frightening, which irritated the parents and didn't make the girl happy either. After lots of smiles and gesturing, we figured it out.

## New China

I think most Americans still think that because China is Communist that it still bears many of the attributes it had in the 1970s, and that it resembles, in many ways, the old Soviet-style society. Nothing could be further from the truth.

There is no doubt that the single-party system here carries with it some practices that are onerous to democratic ideals. I cannot access, for instance, the Frontline website with the film about Tiananmen Square because of government censorship that simply snuffs out my Internet connection when I try. When the government decides it must remove people from their homes in order to gain access to their land, the people have no recourse except physical protest. Public criticism of the government that either advocates changing the whole system or is pointed at sensitive areas is not tolerated.

On the other hand, criticism of the government, short of calling for the overthrow of the Communist Party, is widely accepted here. My Chinese friends talk openly of policies that have failed and why, of public corruption and bribery, and of the directions they believe China should move in. They refer to their country now as "the new China," meaning a more open China in which the government acts as a facilitator for rapid development and growth. As long as it does so, Chinese people seem willing to tolerate authoritarian tendencies because there is a long history of this type of rule here and because they emphasize harmony over fractiousness. Most important, however, is that Chinese society is suddenly providing many opportunities for people to make money and raise their standard of living, which is perhaps the single most-often-repeated goal that I hear from the Chinese. As long as those opportunities keep appearing, major dissatisfaction with the government is unlikely to develop.

On a practical level, it is impossible to tell who is a Party member and who is not just by looking at people. Membership is not worn on the sleeve and there seem to be few symbols of Communist rule on the streets (remember, I don't read Chinese!). Were it not for TV and my Internet experiences, I would have no idea I was living in a communist state because it looks and feels just like a capitalist society. It turns out that the director of my teaching department is a Party member. She is one of the nicest people here. She spent at least six years in the States and has gone out of her way to make me feel at home. When I showed interest in an electronic mosquito-killer that looks like a tennis racquet she had in her office (sorry, the little kid in me may never die), a new one was delivered to me by a student with her compliments the next day.

In addition, my sense is that after a long period of terror, upheaval, and instability, many Chinese are burnt out on politics in the sense of wanting to try to change the system. Things are not perfect by any means, but they are obviously moving forward here, and the Chinese are very proud of that, as they should be. China is taking its place among the most important nations in the world, and as long as that trend continues and opportunities to climb the ladder remain available, most Chinese, especially the younger ones, are content to leave the governing system as is. If this trend ever stops, however, I would not want to be an official in Beijing!

**Ryan Noll**, Nanjing
September 2009

Pukou (a suburb of Nanjing) has its up and downs. So far the administration has done a good job. The head of the English department on my campus does a lot of talking at me, such as "Now you have a conversation!" when she introduces me to people. Or she'll say, "You are in China, and you learn Chinese." Well, I've been working on it, but come on, it's only been a month and a half. Sometimes she'll use this in a good way, like after she tells me I don't start teaching for four weeks, she'll say, "Okay, now you go on a trip and you travel." I'm all right with commands like that.

My campus is located across the great river from what everyone calls "downtown Nanjing." Pukou is in its awkward stage right now. Parts of it are in the process of being developed, such as a huge residential area called Venice River Town. It has large apartment buildings and expensive condos with Italian architecture and colors. It comes complete with fountains, fake animals, canals, and gondolas. It even has a building that I believe looks similar to the Colosseum and doves that I'm pretty sure were imported from somewhere. Then there are the parts of Pukou in the process of being torn down. I saw half of a building torn down by a large jackhammer in less than five minutes. I also saw a very big Ferris wheel standing in the middle of a field of rubble, don't know if it's coming or going. Then there are the parts of Pukou just waiting to be torn down; my campus is surrounded by one of these areas.

Walking outside the front gate of the university leads you to a variety of options. You can play pool under a tarp if you go directly across the street. You can get some noodles, machine parts, or lumber if you take a left. If you take a right and walk far enough, you can find the gem of a restaurant that is the only one I eat at right outside my campus. (Except don't order the chicken bits.) However, you cannot reach this restaurant without passing at least a dozen little roadside rooms lit up by a red light. Inside these door-less storefronts are scantily clad women sitting on couches and watching TV. So I guess I get to live yards away from the biggest cluster of brothels I have ever seen anywhere.

Needless to say, there is not much of anything around my campus except for the glorious bus stop that I would not be able to survive without. If you take the bus one direction you can get off in about four stops at a large parking lot filled with scooters and tents and tents of street food. The street food is fantastic! I like to start off with some stir-fry or a soup of my choosing.

Then I move on to the best meat on a stick imaginable. I like to finish the meal with garlic bread on a stick and a refreshing beer. Sometimes there are child acrobat shows going on to entertain me while I eat. However, it is disturbing when the five-year-old boy puts a box on his head while a nine-year-old girl sticks magic knives into the box.

If I take the bus in the other direction, it takes me all the way across the famous bridge and in to "downtown Nanjing." So I am very lucky that the public bus system is very good in Nanjing. I've enjoyed learning the bus system through trial and error. I have figured out how to get to every other university to see the other teachers. I have no problem getting around, and actually kind of like it, except when it's rush hour and I feel like a sardine or when some little kid can't hold it any longer and pees where I'm standing.

Overall, I think Nanjing is a really great city. I have climbed Purple Mountain, eaten at delicious restaurants featuring food from all over the world, drank at bars from the hole in the wall to the all-night dance club, and explored the islands of Xuanwu Lake. Did you know there is one of those ridiculous game show obstacle courses on one of the islands?! That is all just the tip of the iceberg; there is much more yet to do in Nanjing.

My apartment is not the biggest, so let's just say I won't be having too many guests over. However, I think that it's enough room for just me. I got a new air conditioner courtesy of the university. I live high up on the fifth floor, so for safety precautions the air conditioner installer tied a rope around his waist, tied it to the window frame, and climbed out the window. As he hung there and dismantled the old unit on the side of the building, I couldn't take my eyes off of him. I don't think it's really worth it to fall to your death so I'm not hot at night. Overall, not too many complaints about the apartment. It almost feels like home. Maybe I could complain about the man who shouts/sings very loudly outside my building every morning at about seven. How do you say, "Could you please shut your mouth?" in Chinese?

☯

**Jennifer Bulmash**, Nanjing
September 2009

*Ni hao* Alice!

It's hard to believe that I have been in China for almost a month and a half! Even typing that is a surreal feeling. You know, just the other day I planned to take a bus around Xuanwu Lake to visit another teacher at his apartment. I was with a group of friends. As we neared the bus stop, we saw our bus fly past us. We took off at full sprint to reach the bus as it slowed to our stop (or rather as it plowed in at full speed and then slammed on the brakes mere milliseconds before hitting another stopped bus, which seems to be the preferred method of braking for all vehicles here in China), and we barely made it in through the packed doors. I remember glancing around to see dozens of pairs of eyes focused on us as we squeezed down the crowded aisle searching for some breathing room and the elusive empty space on a handrail. Much to our surprise, no one got off at the next stop but several more did manage to pile on, which pushed us deeper into the swarm packed on the back of the bus. I clutched the zipper of my bag into a tight fist, my mind playing the repeat warning of "If they're good thieves, you won't even notice your wallet is gone." My tee shirt had already begun to dampen with sweat. The stifling Nanjing heat combined with the experience of being sardined between fifty to sixty Chinese people (and four sweaty Americans) turned the bus into a unique kind of public, involuntary sauna. Fortunately, I was standing under one of the bus's emergency exits, which was propped open to let air in. When the bus rumbled into motion, I was treated to a luxury the other passengers weren't able to appreciate, a lovely breeze that funneled directly across my face before disappearing against the wall of people behind me.

Why am I telling you all of this, and so dramatically? I guess because it feels like that bus ride is representative of my experiences in Nanjing thus far. In the two weeks I've been without the protective wingspan of the orientation in Shanghai, I have been more frustrated than I have been in a long time. I have also been, however, incredibly pleased and blessed to be living in this very foreign country. Each and every day I do something that makes me proud of myself. Whether I am successfully communicating to a waitress that I would like "fried tofu" or peering out of a taxi window and realizing that I am starting to learn my way around Nanjing, I understand more clearly the value of this experience. Already, there have been days when I wanted to leave. From anger over government red tape (that whole issue with our *waiban* and residency permits) to other personal offenses (did you know China has no ranch dressing?!?!), I have run the gamut of frustration here. It feels as though nothing can be done unless it is made into a huge production. There are always many, many people involved in the simplest tasks (I am told this is an effort to keep unemployment numbers low) and having such an extreme language barrier only exacerbates problems. From what I understand, China is a giant catch-22. There are many rules and regulations to keep order, but it often seems that one does not find out they are committing an offense until after the rule has been broken. It is not hard to see why so many people warned me that China would require patience.

You know, Alice, I believe this country is greatly indebted to its odd charm. Despite all of its annoying tendencies, I have already fallen in love with this weird place. I love city lights at night. You could drop Nanjing's Hunan Lu onto the Las Vegas strip, and it wouldn't appear out of place. I love that people cannot help but stare when we attempt to acclimate ourselves to Chinese life. For every waitress who seems aggravated by my inability to speak perfect Chinese, there is another who is more than pleased to decipher my American Chinese—even if it involves a ridiculous game of charades and a lot of pointing.

I love the taxi drivers who assume that tunnels are places where speed is just a number and other cars are mere competitors in a race to the light at the end. I love that we can decide one day to wander across the lake near our university only to discover a series of connected islands that house, among other things, a small Disney World rip-off of an amusement park and a temporary game show obstacle course. I love that the entire time I've been in this coffee shop typing emails, I have been listening to the same Dido CD (circa 2000) on repeat. This is the third round, I believe. I love that in China it does not matter if I wear a black skirt with brown shoes because I will inevitably see someone else wearing a brown and orange plaid dress with black tights, purple sequined high heels, and a lime green headband with Winnie the Pooh on it.

I love street food made on dirty grills (scallion pancakes, where have you been my whole life?!), and I love Chinglish (a mix of Chinese and English). I love spotting other expats and trading the mutual smile of our shared experience. I love the colors and the sounds and even occasionally the smells of this place that could not be more opposite Olathe, Kansas, if it tried. In answer to the question regarding whether I am enjoying my experience: yes, I am enjoying it immensely. I won't deny that there have been parts of China that have been hard to accept and parts of the USA that have been hard to forget. The moral of my trials here so far has been that I just need to keep moving. Things might be unfamiliar, but that does not always mean they are bad. Life here rarely makes sense to me, but it seems to work for the millions of people with whom I currently share a city. I'm trying my hardest to be open-minded, Alice. Things are often not what I want them to be, but that doesn't mean they're wrong. China is a lot to get used to, but I like it so far. One of my high school teachers liked this Albert Einstein quote: "Put your hand on a hot stove for a minute, and it seems like an hour. Sit with a pretty girl for an hour, and it seems like a minute. That's relativity." I can't help but think about how well it applies to China. There are days when this year feels like it will never end. There are days when I look around and cannot believe all that I have seen and done already.

*And some teachers stay in Shanghai to teach.*

**Carl Siegel**, Shanghai
December 2004

The Carnival Allegory: Flashing lights, loud music, loud conversations, crazy outfits, and vendors selling cool, useless stuff for cheap. Snacks everywhere—food on a stick, food in a bag, food killed just before you eat it. Transportation is an adrenaline rush. Taxis are roller coasters; my heartbeat only slows at red lights. Or for a less hair-raising ride take the subway, where I can witness musical chairs in tight quarters. The rule of the street: bigger is better. This applies to size or quantity. I once saw one woman try to exit the train against a crowd entering only to get rucked over like a quarterback out of the pocket. But it is always fun. The people are the nicest in the world, money is for spending and everyone's a winner! Welcome to the carnival!

**Hélène North**, Shanghai
October 2007

**Street Life**

Good morning, China!

It's seven o'clock, not too hot yet. My street is abuzz with the usual goings-on. After all, it is one of the major thoroughfares of Jia Ding (a suburb of Shanghai). The horn recital that started at dawn is reaching full blast. The news vendor is raising his metal curtain. The construction workers—sort of permanent fixtures of the neighborhood—are having an animated conversation on the sidewalk by the traffic light; they leave a couple of boxes there every night, full of tools, possibly hoping that they might disappear by accidental theft! They've been actively hoarding the sidewalk space for the past

*The Bund at sunrise, Shanghai. Photo by Ken Driese.*

week or so, seemingly entrusted with the renovation of an entire side of the market street. In reality, they've simply added to the existing confusion of life on the margin of the street. Not only does a pedestrian have to dodge semi-permanent pieces of furniture—chairs, couches, tables, stools—that enhance male social interaction (you know, the never-ending card games with money going to the winner), but also shaky toddlers, yakking grandparents, piles of trash (ideal playground for the shaky toddlers!), illegally parked bikes and mopeds and now, the construction workers! But it is too early for that today.

It's a nice morning; the sky has a hint of blue. I am going wherever my feet will take me; I have a little bit of time before school starts. My street is very wide and grand-looking. Its nickname is Bank Street. For an entire block, it's just banks, on both sides of the street! All of them are vying for visibility and respectability, asserting their solidity and power through the display of columns and massive flights of steps that lead to huge glass doors. All of them guarded by a pair of enormous stone lions with gorgeous flowing manes. Needless to say, I encounter lots of serious-looking uniforms and glares along the block. Now, the intersection. I have learned to patiently wait for the end of the countdown and the little green man before I cross the street.

I make a left onto a commercial road. There is a supermarket on the corner. No need for huge parking lots here; most people don't have cars. They take their bikes to go shopping. However, the bike area seems larger than usual, probably because it is empty. I notice for the first time a really nice flower bed and can even smell the fragrance of the marigolds. The road is quiet. In front of the shop, a group of women is practicing *tai ji*; they must be the shops' employees, judging from their red and white uniforms. I still find it amazing that older people practice dancing and *tai ji* in public places without the slightest touch of embarrassment; they are focused and totally absorbed by their art. A woman with heavy makeup and an impeccable hairdo walks up to the leader of the group and asks for advice. The expert models a posture that appears incredibly complex to me involving a specific way of holding her head and shoulders, hand motions and feet position. All this in absolute silence, on a street corner that soon will turn into total bedlam, but which for the time being provides these women with a space to refresh their inner strength, as well as enjoy convivial support.

I walk past small shops that are getting all spiffed up for the day amid an air of busy laziness. Doors are wide open to let the breeze dry the newly mopped tiles. The straw brooms and mops are neatly propped up against the outside walls. The street has put on its morning coat. Indeed, magic is the night.

I recall last night's foray into the neighborhood to assuage a late pang of hunger. I sat at a little street stall in front of a huge bowl of noodles and steamed vegetables. There was hardly anyone in the street. The vegetable and fruit vendors had gone home leaving behind the smelly and gooey remains of the day: burst zucchinis, smashed tomatoes, trampled grapes, rotten apples, bunches of limp greens, vegetable parings, broken Styrofoam containers, straws and plastic cups, and greasy packaging. Amid the overpowering combination of stench and heat, I had to seriously practice my keep-your-sandals-gunk-free skills. But by morning, a metamorphosis has taken place.

I turn left again into a little one-way cobbled street along a canal. Not a soul, which is hardly surprising as there are no shops here, just the outside wall of an apartment building. On the canal sits a wide boat, and on the boat stands an old man. I stop to watch him. He sees me; we smile at one another. He has a weathered face and a long, pointy white beard. His clothes look worn. He is holding onto two very long bamboo poles with one end in the water. When he raises them, I realize they are attached to a huge black bladder that he opens up and compresses to suck the muck from the canal floor. He lifts his contraption, empties the bladder into the hull of the boat, and then dips it again into the canal. I hear nothing as he smoothly lifts it again and empties its contents. He repeats the same gesture time and time again, absorbed by his task, and bathed in the haze of the rising humidity. I say good-bye; he just nods in reply without even looking up, the unsung magician of the muck!

Oops, the street suddenly ends and veers into a narrow passage that hugs the corner of the building and takes me to another cobbled street over a baby canal. I am not far from the market street now. A couple unloads some watermelons onto the sidewalk; a woman organizes neat little piles of greens. More dripping mops look on. How different from last night! The cement still bears the marks of the brooms. Not a tree leaf, not a stray twig. The street fairies in blue uniforms did their job. A fresh slate.

I pass the gate of an elementary school. It is seven thirty now. Kids are being delivered from the back seats of mopeds. Eight children stand by the gate, four on each side, wearing their blue and white uniform and a red scarf around the neck. They look very official with a red banner across their chest, and as students walk in, they raise their arm and shout some welcome! Hey, I wouldn't mind starting the day with a hail from my personal welcoming committee. Well, actually, I too am greeted by officials every day. The guard by the campus gate usually acknowledges me with a discreet nod.

I must hurry now. Here is my favorite bread shop. I buy my usual bun for one *kuai*, thirteen cents. The lady knows me; we go through the same salutations every day. I am now standing by the news vendor, across the street from my hotel. He too knows me. This morning, he welcomes me with a large grin and waves the *Shanghai Daily* at me. Most days, I come too late, and he just waves me away before I can ask. I give him two *kuai*. Thank you, good-bye.

The light turns red; I run across. The guard sees me and breaks into laughter. I am hurrying, still in my shorts. He knows! I am late. When I saunter through the gate a few minutes later, my hair still wet, my school bag in one hand, but definitely dressed to address the Chinese standards, he gives me a cheerful nod. Good morning, China!

*From bank accounts to bus rides and markets to malls, the teachers are engaged in Chinese society. And even when it "rarely makes sense," most go with the flow. With the help of Alice, the* waiban, *and the support of the other foreign teachers, settling in is mostly exhilarating. Next, the teachers meet their classes.*

# 2

# Teaching

*A Seriously Exhausting Endeavor!*

At two o'clock the curtain rises, and I start to impersonate an English teacher.

—Brian E. Lewis, Tianjin

*These emails loosen a brick that enables us to see both into Chinese university life and into our own preconceived notions of how things should function. From vignettes of life inside the classroom to recaps of missed communication and descriptions of relationships with students, administrators, and other teachers, it is apparent that the foreign teacher must be prepared to teach and learn. Christopher Angell writes from Nanjing, "I think I will be receiving a first-class education from my students in how misinformed I am about what they and China are all about."*

*The majority of individuals who travel to China to teach English as a foreign language are recent college graduates, not trained teachers. Their qualifications include an interest in China and some tutoring, coaching, or camp counseling experience. The abrupt role reversal, from college student to head teacher, feels a bit like acting as the opening quote suggests. Other older individuals and couples have taken sabbaticals of sorts from their US work lives to teach in China where the primary qualification is being a native English speaker with a BA from a good US school. Even for experienced teachers like Chris Angell, Lisa Johnson, and Hélène North and university professors like Ken Driese and Jeanne Phillips, teaching in China presents numerous unexpected challenges, but benefits too. Lisa Johnson, a teacher transplanted from Colorado to Tianjin writes, "It is nice to have a completely different lifestyle from the States, and I didn't come to China to work all the time as I do at home, right?" The opportunity to study Chinese or learn* wushu *(martial arts),* calligraphy, tai ji quan, *or a traditional Chinese instrument like the* erhu *provides even more opportunity for cultural immersion.*

*But first, the foreign teachers have to concentrate on the classroom. In the beginning, the discomfort of both teachers and students is apparent in nervous laughter and technical difficulties.*

## TEACHER IMMERSION

**Brian T. Vick**, Tianjin
December 1996

For the first two weeks of class, the students just stared at me intensely and giggled. Then when I spoke some Chinese, they burst out with laughter. I entertain them and make them laugh a lot. I just hope they are learning something in the process. Speaking some Chinese often helps to clear up misunderstandings in meaning, and it puts the students at ease. They see some big white dork trying to speak Chinese, and they can laugh and don't feel embarrassed about trying to speak English. They can correct me on my tones and pronunciations, and I think this also helps reduce inhibitions. The students seem so young compared to US college students, but their intelligence and knowledge of English is astounding.

In my American and British Literature course, we have read and discussed works by Flannery O'Connor, Langston Hughes, Eudora Welty, Carl Sandburg, H. G. Wells, Katherine Mansfield, Bertrand Russell, and several others. We have discussed and performed role-plays based on interviews with Malcolm X and MLK's "I Have a Dream" speech. I have given lectures on the 1960s, racism, sexism, crime and violence, marriage and divorce, plastic surgery, and politics.

**Ian Clark**, Nanjing
October 2000

My classes provide a stoic stage with fifty vibrant audience members. Each session sounds like an extremist sitcom with all the teens whooping, laughing, gasping, sighing, bustling, and shifting entirely in unison. I walk in, and the class laughs boisterously. I say, "How are you?" I am greeted with instantaneous laughing and then boisterous applause. It's so emotional and hilarious. I'm performing like a comedian, actor, motivational speaker, singer—everything.

Among the students' customs of standing to speak and modesty is an impatience rivaled only by static electricity. They don't allow time for each other to think while speaking, and they laugh wildly with the slightest mistake. They all seem to make the same mistakes, yet they all laugh at each other.

*Students in China begin learning English in first grade. Most university students in China have a good grasp of English vocabulary and grammar. What few students have had is an Oral English class or a class taught by a native English speaker. This is at least part of the explanation for the self-conscious student laughter in the classroom that both Ian Clark and Brian T. Vick describe. Most Chinese university students have not been encouraged to speak up in class; Chinese students expect the teacher, the expert, to do much of the talking while students respond when called upon.*

**Christopher Angell**, Nanjing
July 2007

So far, my biggest problem teaching is in the technology area. Most classrooms have a computer and computer projection screen with a nice power panel full of buttons to work everything, but the labels are all written in Chinese so there is a lot of guesswork involved in such mundane tasks as turning the computer on and off. Of course, I could ask a student to help me, but as a compulsive do-it-myself-er, this has proven quite impossible. So the class is usually treated to the mechanically deployed projection screen going up and down at least five times a class, PowerPoint presentations that run backwards, or my collection of acid rock suddenly starting to play for no apparent reason. The kids seem completely unfazed by these little quirks. Maybe they're thinking, "If this is the best the Americans have to offer, we're definitely taking over the world!"

☯

**Adrian Neibauer**, Chengdu
September 2003

Yesterday, Ellen and I had our first day of teaching at the University. My class was great! The students are only a few years either younger or older than me with one older man in his forties. Everyone is a post-graduate of some sort and has been a part of the workforce for some time. All of them decided to take time off of their work in order to improve their English skills, so the motivation is very high. They all feel it will benefit their jobs to learn English. I have two flight attendants from Air China, a lawyer, a travel agent, and a few early graduates. I am very excited to help them with their English!

☯

*Brian E. Lewis captures the before, during, and after experience of the first day teaching.*

**Brian E. Lewis**, Tianjin
September 2002

The days are just packed. I teach English in the General English Department, which for various unknown reasons is different from the Normal English Department. This department is located on the fifth floor of the Main Building, the imposing, towered structure which is the official face of the university. Like all auspicious buildings in China, it faces south. In *Feng Shui* (fung shway), traditional Chinese geomancy, facing south has important benefits and is highly symbolic; the emperor's palace always sits in the north and faces south, and in Classical Chinese works "faces south" is often an expression for lordship and mastery. In front of the building is a small park with a large white statue of Zhou Enlai, one of China's original revolutionaries, architect of the opening of China to America during Nixon's presidency, and the man who generally can be said to have started China down the path of reform after the Cultural Revolution. He is one of the few truly admirable men of Mao's time and is counted almost universally by the Chinese as one of their greatest statesmen. He would no doubt be amused to see his benevolently stony gaze greeting returning students at the south gate.

Like much of the university, the main building is impressive on the outside, but the inside resembles a Colombian prison. The halls are damp and sparsely lit, the smell of ammonia (from the poorly drained toilets) spreads its tendrils throughout the entire building, the desks are bolted in place like in a political prison, and the ventilation system has been boarded up to prevent any students from escaping. Still, if I look out the window of my classroom, I can see Zhou Enlai waving at me, and I know that it's all for the best. Actually, although the facilities here are often decrepit, I shouldn't give the impression that this bothers me, because it doesn't. I didn't want Club Med, and I ain't gettin' it, so what is there to complain about?

On Tuesdays and Wednesday afternoons, I teach from two to four, the same class but different sections. The class is Oral English for English Master's Degree Candidates. When I arrive in room 535, there is a rather sour middle-aged woman at the door who hands me a class list. On it are about thirty names in Chinese characters, which except for one or two are more or less incomprehensible. She waves her hands, mutters at me, and hands me my textbooks, which are completely different from the ones I was told we would be using. I thank her, though I'm not sure why, and go to the front of the class. Just in case I didn't feel self-conscious enough, they have thoughtfully placed a raised platform along the chalkboard, so I can truly tower over all the seated students. There is a small podium in place, and I proceed to hide behind it as best I can, in part to steady my nerves. Stage fright? You betcha. Showing up for my first day of class is like showing up to opening night of a play, only they hand you the script when you get there and tell you to break a leg. I don't know what role I'm playing, what it's about, or when it's over, but by God, the show must go on.

At two o'clock the curtain rises, and I start to impersonate an English teacher. A few students in the back are grinning at me, the grin that little boys have when they're about to throw rocks at cars on the freeway. I introduce myself to them, and tell them that I will use English names for them in class, but that I will learn their Chinese names as well, as a sign of respect. That means a lot of memorization on my part, as each class has about thirty students. I explain to them that if any of them feel a little embarrassed about their English, then I will speak a little Chinese to them, and they will feel much better about their English. This gets an appreciative laugh. Then I tell them a little bit about myself: about Denver, about my studies, my hobbies, and my family. The part about my parents divorcing when I was about one always gets a lot of sympathetic looks or downright wincing. Divorce happens in China, but it remains rare, and the Chinese are largely shocked and saddened by American attitudes towards it. That's partly why I mention it, because they find such distinctions fascinating. Then I tell them about my experiences so far in China, and how I prefer Tianjin to Shanghai, which appeals to their community spirit, though I find that only about half of my students are native born Tianjiners. Usually at this point I spring a little

Chinese on them; they gasp and then laugh. I find that speaking Chinese to them, though I keep it very limited, helps relieve tension because they invariably think it hilarious to see a "White Devil" speak their language, even if I speak the words correctly.

Then I have them ask me questions. I got some very thoughtful ones. One girl, Ginny, asked me why I study Chinese philosophy and what makes it different from Western philosophy. That one took a while, but I gave as thorough yet efficient an answer as possible. Usually, I get some variation on my feelings about China and China's place in the world. One sensitive question I got was how I felt about Japan. Many Chinese virulently hate the Japanese, so I tried to be tactful. Essentially I said that though I admired many things about Japanese culture, Japanese history has some very unfortunate episodes. And I let them know that I knew about the Chinese feelings about Japan, which I think they appreciated because it shows that I'm no dilettante.

After this, I have to find out who has English names and who doesn't. That's when I find out that not only are these not graduate students, they aren't English majors either. I guess the eleven-year-old girl in the front row should have been my first clue. Her English name is Mary, and somehow she got permission to audit the class. Her feet don't reach the floor when she sits at her desk. Anyway, finding out who doesn't have an English name is a Herculean task because of the famous reticence of Chinese students to speak up or volunteer in class. At this point, I give a five-minute lecture on the virtues of raising your hand, which I usually need to repeat twice, as they don't take to this very well, preferring instead to stare blankly at the teacher when he asks if they understand him.

I have the class give suggestions for English names for the uninitiated among our classmates, and then move on to the information cards. I like these because I can find out useful information about my students. I have them write their English name, their Chinese name, hometown and province, major, number of years studying English, reasons for said study, and hobbies on a piece of paper and hand them in. I then match these to the class list and add water. The Name Game follows, but because I have too many students who are too shy to speak, I'm the only one who plays. Each student says their English name when I point at them, and I have to say their name plus the name of all the students before them, which means that by the time I get to Woods in the back, I have to say about thirty-two names. Invariably, I find one or two who still don't have English names, even though I took fifteen painful minutes to root out and disperse English names for everyone. "Where were your hands?" I ask them. I try to make it a joke, and that relieves the frustration. My favorite example of the refusal to raise hands occurred during the filling out of the info cards. I usually walk around a lot, to circulate through the class, and after about five minutes of info writing, I noticed two guys in the back who weren't writing. Turns out, they had no pens. Just when were they going to say something? I suggested to them that they were fortunate this wasn't a test. I am happy to report that my students are becoming avid hand raisers, so my relentless beatings of offenders have apparently not been in vain.

As for the names they pick, most of them are very safe, ordinary names, though there are some more innovative ones, like Zoe and Lynch, who seemed embarrassed when I disclosed what it means to lynch someone. I told him to tell people that he was named after a famous movie director, David Lynch. The name game is fun because they can't wait for me to screw up. And it is pretty difficult sometimes to remember their names. I exaggerate a little for their comic relief. Chinese students learn principally through memorization, a millennia-old practice in Chinese education. Imperial scholars were required to know the Classics by heart, which meant memorizing dozens of books. So they take great pride in their memory skills, and rightfully so, as they are quite impressive. I usually make it through with only one slip-up, and they applaud my performance. Afterwards, I make a point of using their names to call on them. After the memory game, I use chain questions to get them used to their names. For example, I call on Lydia and say, "My name is Brian. What is your name?" Lydia then has to repeat this question to another student, who asks another, and so on. Afterwards, I spend some time talking about the direction of the class for the semester and my general expectations, which are fairly small. I give them my contact information and make sure they understand that I am available to help them.

Next activity: discussion. I planned this activity to help me diagnose their English ability, which varies quite a bit from student to student. For this, I use a quote from Ralph Waldo Emerson. It reads:

> To laugh often and much; to win the respect of intelligent people and the affection of children; to earn the appreciation of honest critics and endure the betrayal of false friends; to appreciate beauty, to find the best in others; to leave the world a little better; whether by a healthy child, a garden patch or a redeemed social condition; to know even one life has breathed easier because you have lived. This is the meaning of success.

I like this quote, and I feel that it makes a good discussion point because success, however defined, is of utmost importance in China now. Being in China currently is a little like being in America in the 1980s: it's the Me Decade. With China's newfound openness and the economic reforms which have accompanied it, the chance to cash in and improve their living standards lures many young Chinese. One student, Michael, disparaged Emerson's idea as being too abstract, and that having a good career and a lot of money is more concrete and thus more successful. Most felt that Emerson's idea was virtuous and that such a person would be both good and successful, but that it was very difficult or even impossible to attain. One girl, Chris, felt that having a loving family and a peaceful life was a kind of success. Through a kind of Socratic questioning and answering, I was able to persuade them that becoming the kind of person Emerson describes involves much hard work, which many of them felt was a prerequisite of success which he had left out. All in all, we were able to have a pretty high level and, dare I say it, philosophical discussion about success, where they did much of the talking.

After my Wednesday class, many of my students stayed after to chat with me or ask questions. Some of these questions were hard-hitting, others unusual. Woods asked me about 9-11, which has been all over China. I gave a truthful answer, but one which I hope was tactful and diplomatic as well, as American foreign policy is generally abhorred outside the States. What I said is not really as important as how they responded. I think most Americans would be surprised by the deep affection and friendship with which Americans are viewed here. Our government is often criticized, but the Chinese people really like Americans, and the general feeling towards us is goodwill, and that the 9-11 attacks were completely undeserved. There is a deep sympathy for this day in China, and the bookstores are glutted with Chinese-authored materials about it, some of it rivaling American coverage in its sentimentality. The same student then asked me what my first impression of him was, which is a fairly bold question for a Chinese student. I told him that we just met, so I can't form a real opinion about him, but I see he dyes his hair, so he is a very individualistic person; that he sits in back, so he wants to observe without being observed; and that he asks hard questions, so he is very thoughtful. But, I added, I don't know yet if he is a good

*Art student. Photo by John McGee.*

student. This made everyone laugh, and I think I preserved my face, as I think I caught something in his question that was designed to challenge my authority. Later, after I read his info card, I learned that he majors in Chinese Calligraphy, which explained a lot: he has an artist's temperament.

Other students were more curious about my experiences in China, my impressions of the Chinese people, why I decided to come here, etc. When I mentioned my interest in martial arts, and that I was taking a martial arts class here, my student Angie offered to give me her sword that she was no longer using. I thanked her profusely, but told her that it was a very extravagant gift and that I couldn't accept it. Later, after everyone left, she came up to me and said, "I hope what I said did not make you angry." I had to explain that a sword is expensive, and that while I appreciated the gesture, it would be wrong of me to take advantage. She was much relieved that I was not angry and that it was just a cultural misfire. In this case, it was a sort of reverse culture problem: she made the offer seriously and in a way that an American might, while I assumed that she was making a polite offer which she did not really intend to fulfill, and I made a polite refusal in the Chinese style, in the expectation that she would offer again. We decided that getting me the name of her *tai ji* instructor was a far better show of friendship than a sword. All in all, my students stayed forty-five minutes after the end of class just to talk with me, which was gratifying, amusing, and humbling all at the same time.

It had been grey, cold, and drizzling all day long. A student, Summer, suggested that the weather expressed the feelings of all China in remembrance of September 11th.

*Despite a work schedule that sounds light, fourteen to twenty hours a week, the accompanying lesson planning and grading of assignments adds significantly to the workload, especially at the beginning.*

**Tim Lehmann,** Nanjing
September 2007

Teaching is a seriously exhausting endeavor! I have more than three hundred and fifty students; I have eight classes a week with anywhere between thirty-five and fifty students in each class. They are all post-graduate students, and the classes are all required Oral English. Most are either my age or older. I have fooled them into thinking that I'm in my late twenties—a much needed edge. Many are skilled and quite disciplined. They simply lack experience with class participation. Such is the Chinese way. I am trying to break them though, or rather, steer them toward the beautiful logic of speaking in an *Oral* English class. They are getting the point, I think; I hope.

**Mary Barton**, Nanjing
September 2003

My free time is limited right now until I get the hang of my schedule and more experienced at teaching. I teach two classes. Both are double degree students, those who have their undergraduate degrees and will be graduating next year with either a major in International Trade or International Finance. The Trade class is really big with thirty-six students, while the Finance group is sixteen students, much more manageable. They are great students and a pleasure to teach. I have each group twice a week for three and three-quarters hours each. That is a long class!

My classroom is not air-conditioned. It has two ineffective fans on the ceiling. I have a blackboard and chalk. Without a computer, I have to be more creative. My monitors (assistants in the class) arranged for a different classroom last class in order to watch a movie. Since they are trade/finance majors, we watched *Catch Me If You Can*, and my classes are designed around the money theme. These students will be with me for four weeks on an accelerated program. I don't know what my schedule will be after that, or if I will have a classroom with heat for the winter months.

**Catt Stearns**, Wanzhou
September 2009

I have been teaching for two weeks, but only three days a week with four-day weekends! Lesson planning is the hardest part. I rack my brain for hours trying to figure out the most fun, yet educational activities to do with my class. There's always this fear that one class will go horribly wrong, the students will hate it, think I am lame, and never want to attend my class. Man, there's a lot of pressure. Luck has been on my side, though, and I haven't had any major teaching fiascos, but I'm sure they're on the horizon.

My students are actually really great, incredibly keen on learning English and all about America, and have offered everything from erasing the blackboard to being my new best friend. The first homework assignment that I gave them was to spend time with me, so for the next week I'll be busy having meals and going on excursions around the city with my students. This assignment works two ways: they get to practice their English and up their participation grade, while I get more of an insider's view of the city, learn about more delicious Chinese food, and practice learning my students' names.

November 2009

Going to lunch or dinner with students can either be a grueling task of getting these kids (ok, not kids, college students) to say something, which is the majority of the time, or answering rapid fire questions about myself, America, college in America, high school in America, music in America, American sports, American presidents (you get the picture). About two weeks ago, I was finishing up lunch with some of my chatty freshman students, and their final question went a little like this:

*Students:* Miss Catt, are your parents high?

*Miss Catt:* I'm not sure what you mean. (laughing in my head)

*Students:* Oh, I want to be high like you! How do you get high?

*Miss Catt:* (thinking hard, and trying not to laugh) Oh, oh! You mean tall?!

*Students:* (giggle, giggle, not understanding the true translation) Oh yes, of course, tall!

**Clio Goldsmith**, Nanjing
September 2009

For my first lecture topic, I just did a big introduction of myself: my time at the Olympics and my senior thesis project about reusing plastic bags into products. I have to admit that it may have been a bit narcissistic, but the students liked to hear about the Olympics, and then I did a demonstration of how I melted the plastic bags with an iron. Since most of my students are engineers, the products that I presented struck up some interesting conversations like, do I have a patent yet? And do I want to manufacture and sell them commercially? When I plan out my lecture topics, I make sure that they are a little out of the ordinary, something the students wouldn't know to ask about American culture, for example, "The American Road Trip" or "Volunteering and Community Service in America" or "How Chinese People Are Portrayed in American Movies and TV." These are topics that I am very interested in which helps make my lectures much more interesting and might not be the mainstream information all the students usually hear about America. They know about all of our holidays; they have a general idea about the education system and political system, yet when I ask them what they want to learn more about American culture, the most common answer is, "the American education system." So my mission is to mix it up a little bit, add some spice, and entertain them. Because, after all, the class I teach is in addition to their regular English class with English-speaking Chinese teachers. My time teaching so far hasn't always been a walk in the park, but I am learning a lot about how to teach the classes better, and I love all the free time I have!

**Elizabeth Phelps**, Nanjing
September 2004

Teaching (especially the planning part) is so much work! Another teacher from Wellesley and I have both been spending most of our time the past two weeks preparing for classes, grading homework, and teaching. Fortunately, we do have four-day weekends, so we've had some time to enjoy ourselves too and see a little bit of Nanjing. Despite all the work, I'm finding that I really like teaching. We're teaching all English majors, which helps, since they're all moderately motivated to learn and have a fairly good English background. We're teaching oral, writing, and reading to mostly sophomore students. One of my favorite parts has been getting to know the students, both in person and through their writing. It's especially interesting to read the writing of students who are very quiet and unemotional in class, but who reveal so much in their writing. Some of the essays have been quite personal, almost as if they had no one else with whom to share their feelings about certain things, such as a difficult economic situation for the family. My colleague has been asked (through writing) for advice on one student's love life!

**Lisa A. Johnson**, Tianjin
September 2000

Classes continue to go well, and I can't believe that it is already week five and that I must soon prepare midterms for my graduate students, all 650 of them!

I leave tomorrow night for a five-day adventure north into Inner Mongolia. We have the whole week off for National Day, but I did have to teach on Saturday (yesterday) and will have to teach on Sunday (next week) to make up for the days off—figure that one out.

You were right about the numerous contacts. I must get two or three calls a week from people who want me to teach. I have said, "No." I am enjoying my work here at the university and with the one group I teach from the pharmacy school on Thursday evenings. I am studying Chinese two to three nights a week with a friend from my department and that is enough. It is nice to have a completely different lifestyle from the States, and I didn't come to China to work all the time as I do at home, right?

February 2001

To be honest, these huge classes are a bit much and I really question their "use" of me as a native speaker. I suggested a different way of teaching, but it seems more important to them to have their students exposed to native English rather than practice speaking. Of course, the students want the complete opposite. They want to talk and to have someone correct their pronunciation. Funny, just like in the States, the students often want something different from what the university has in mind.

*While most teachers teach university students, I had the pleasure of also teaching several classes of high school students at the foreign language school affiliated with the university, which attracts students from throughout Yunnan Province.*

**Mary Beth Ryan-Maher**, Kunming
September 1999

The English skills of my students are quite good. The school here divides the studying of English (I am not sure about other foreign languages) into many separate classes: listening, intensive reading, extensive reading, writing, and oral English. Not exactly an integrated approach, but it seems to work. What is the difference between intensive reading and extensive reading? Well, I asked that question too. Intensive reading means line-by-line analysis of a text; extensive reading is a more holistic analysis of a work. Again, I am not sure why these are separated, but my American Literature students also have these two classes, and German, as part of their curriculum.

My American Lit students are college seniors, and based on some writing I have given them in an attempt to learn more about them (there are sixty students in the class) it seems as if many are not very optimistic about their employment prospects. This is a time of rising unemployment in China, and Yunnan is one of China's poorer provinces. They are very earnest and disciplined, and most were as horrified as me last week when one student's cell phone rang in the middle of class. (No metal detectors or security to confiscate these items here like in New York City.) My student was greatly apologetic, and I think we will all forgive her.

Additionally, I have 120 sixteen-year-olds for Oral English. Many of my students are from outside of Kunming, so they live in the dormitories on campus too. Last Thursday night, Bella and Pauline came over to ask me to play ping-pong (I thought). We ventured off campus quite a ways and went into a small alley and up some stairs to a large, neon lit room with music blaring. It was a roller-skating rink! Panic. What happened to ping-pong? Well, no one was roller-skating, and they told me that the woman at the desk said that the place was closed—forever. Whew, I thought. So instead of ping-pong or roller-skating, they took me to visit their dorm.

They live eight to a room. Bella and Pauline's room was on the sixth floor (no elevators; Rob and I live on the fifth floor so I am fairly fit when it comes to stair climbing). So in addition to me, and the eight girls who live in the room, several others crowded in to visit. The small room had four sets of bunk beds that also served as drawer and storage for each girl's personal items, and a narrow table in the aisle between the bunks where they eat and do homework. They offered me a pear. I accepted and suggested that we cut it up and share it. A big no-no. Pears cannot be cut. They symbolize unity. So they peeled the pear, and I ate it. A good lesson. These girls are in their second year at the school, so they are not so homesick, but several were certain they would return home after they graduate; others wanted to stay in Kunming.

My middle school classes are basically tracked. I have one college-bound group, one group specializing in tourism, and one group studying secretarial skills. As you can guess, the English conversation and comprehension level is from high to low. My secretary class is quite shy, tourism is a mixed bag but definitely more playful and less self-conscious, and my college-bound group is the most outgoing and confident. Basketball, soccer, and volleyball are the favorite sports. The boys and girls play on the same basketball team, everyone with his/her class. The students here are very close. They go to school with each other for all three years, and many live together in the dorms. They are not mixed with other students from other classes. They know each other very well. This is also true on the university level. You begin university with a class, and take all your courses with these same people; there are not very many electives. So far, I don't detect a lot of the cliques that we find in US high schools. Mostly, I am struck by their true affection and caring for one another. There is a lot of effort at developing class spirit and unity.

*First impressions, of course, are not always positive. Some teachers begin a little more skeptically.*

**Ken Driese**, Lijiang
October 2005

Teaching here is more challenging than I had imagined. Not that it is hard to get through a week of classes, but it feels somewhat futile as the students don't really seem to improve. Classes are huge (sixty students) and diverse, with students ranging from those who speak essentially no English to those who are relatively conversant. And none of them could write themselves out of a paper bag. So we plod forward shifting strategies and trying new things, but it feels frustrating to me now. I'm not used to teaching without seeing some results. Some kids actually turn in writing assignments on Post-Its!

**Ellen Axtmann,** Lijiang
October 2005

As Ken reported, the students are disappointing. The only hard thing about being here is wondering if we are accomplishing anything. We are certainly loving the area and learning about China and enjoying ourselves, but one wonders whether spending two hours a week with sixty students trying to teach them Oral English has any effect at all. Sigh.

There are some shining lights among the students. I had a very heart-warming letter from one student who is desperate to improve his pronunciation and works really hard. Unfortunately, we have started to refer to him as "the stalker" because he wrote me a note asking me to hike with him this weekend and then showed up unannounced at our door last night! I think he is genuinely interested in improving his English, but I need to have a talk with him and let him know that weekends are my family time! Many students seem to want to follow me home to practice their English. Thus far, I have gotten away with telling them I can't give them my phone number because I don't know it (this *is* true). All part of the package, I guess.

*Other than a two- or three-week crash course on teaching provided by the Colorado China Council in August each year, most new teachers will receive virtually no other guidance from their respective schools.*

**Dana**, Hangzhou
April 2001

The university has forty thousand students, and it's hard to tell how we fit into this giant bureaucracy. Two years ago, four universities merged into one enormous university. Administratively, it's a nightmare, and the foreign teachers are often lost in the shuffle. Although the Foreign Affairs Office hosted a welcome banquet and a holiday dinner for the teachers who live in our building, we don't feel integrated into the university. In fact, I've never even met anyone in my department, nor can I get a straight answer as to exactly which department I'm part of. Brian's part of the foreign language college, but he's never formally been introduced to any colleagues or invited to any meetings. We heard through a foreign teacher that the department head did not even know Brian existed and that was in December. We have met with the dean only twice, on our initiative, and have practically no contact with any other Chinese person on faculty or staff. The exception is the man who pays us. We call him our handler. He's got a good heart, but he's incredibly overextended and quite frankly is not all that helpful with our administrative needs. In fact, the first week we arrived, he drew a map of the campus for us instead of giving us a tour as we suggested. Despite asking repeatedly, we've just now found out from him where to go to make copies. Basically, he picked us up at the airport, dropped us at our guest house, gave us our schedules, drew a map, and we've been on our own ever since.

Although I originally found this treatment surprising and a bit inhospitable, both Brian and I are comfortable with it. It gives us lots of freedom to do the things we want because the university places absolutely no demands on us. (When we first asked if we were expected to follow any curriculum, the man who pays us said our only job was to make sure the students have fun.) I think this situation might be difficult for someone who prefers a little more hand-holding.

In short, we like our jobs despite the isolation from the university community. We live with about eight other foreign teachers with whom we exchange materials and advice about teaching. We also get together with them once a week for dinner in the newly renovated dining hall in our guesthouse. But the best part about teaching here is the students. They're extremely bright and sophisticated and accustomed to learning from foreigners. They're responsive in class (especially the freshman) and have definitely made my job as a first year teacher a lot easier than I expected!

*And while most foreign teachers operate quite independently, some face a little more scrutiny. Here's a unique account of a hands-on administrator.*

**Patrick Tartar**, Lijiang
June 2008

The department head is a scary man. Although he can't be taller than five feet six inches, he absolutely terrifies me. (He would make an excellent James Bond henchman in a movie.) He rules his kingdom with an iron fist. Our first taste of his leadership style came at a department meeting held after the first month of class. In front of the entire English teaching staff (i.e., one hundred teachers), he called out each foreign English teacher by name and read a list of their perceived shortcomings:

"Bonnie! Very unorganized. Your accent is difficult to understand."

"Ellen! You are not doing a satisfactory job; your classes are very boring."

"Peter! You don't look like a teacher. You need to dress like a teacher. Many of you need to learn to dress like teachers."

"Patrick! Very good teacher. So young. Very professional."

"Heather! Very young. Very professional. Beautiful. Good teacher."

"Adam! Your students are very unhappy. You say the book is rubbish. The book is not rubbish! *Use the book dammit!!*"

Heather and I were the only foreign teachers not raked over the coals.

I didn't land on his good side by accident. I came to China ready to play his game. At the first English Department meeting I handed him an expensive coffee-table book from Seattle, the first of several gifts this year. At the National Day banquet, I made a point of entering the private room where the Deans, Vice President, and President were sitting and toasted them all in Chinese. At the Christmas party, I respectfully presented him a very nice bottle of red wine. In China, blatant brown-nosing, even bribery, can be good for your career.

Public humiliation is his greatest pleasure. Earlier in the year, one of our students dyed his hair platinum blonde. The chairman didn't think this appearance was fit for a representative of his department and made him dye it back to black. Then, at lunchtime, he made the now steely blue-haired student stand at the flag pole in the center of campus. All of the senior English students were made to surround him and shout insults and derogations. The scene was a complete throwback to the tactics used by the Red Guard in the 1970s [*during the Great Proletarian Cultural Revolution, 1966–1976*].

The entire department is permanently in fear of tongue-lashings or worse. In the third month of the term, he decided that the Chinese teachers weren't meeting his expectations and decided to dock their pay. He lowered their contractually guaranteed salary by twelve percent every month—double the cost of rent. There was nothing the teachers could do if they wanted to keep their jobs.

At a meeting in the fourth month, the chairman announced to the entire staff that Julian was the worst teacher in the school and would be fired during the holiday break. Following the break, he announced that Julian had come to him on his hands and knees, crying, and begged to keep his job. He would now be fired at the end of second term. Julian had officially been rendered a joke to all of his colleagues.

## ADMINISTRATIVE DETAILS
## AND DEPARTMENTAL DIFFICULTIES

**Julie**, Tianjin
March 2005

I started my second semester this week. This semester I am teaching all freshmen and one Oral English class for history graduate students. It should be another great semester despite a slightly rocky start. My department gave me the wrong books, the wrong schedule, and told me to go to the wrong building. How delightful. I think they were just trying to test me. Apparently, they posted a revised schedule all over our offices in *Chinese*, and then forgot to tell little ol' me. Anyway, I barely made it to the correct classroom on time only to discover that my students all had different books than me. No worries. Plan B. It ended up being a rather successful Oral English class even though it was supposed to be reading and writing. Such is my crazy life in China. Happy Year of the Rooster!

**Brian T. Vick**, Tianjin
October 1996

My Chinese advisor said I could use whatever materials and texts I wanted, and then proceeded to order and insist the students purchase texts he felt appropriate. (This was, of course, after the students purchased the texts I had instructed them to buy.)

I genuinely feel that one piece of advice I would pass on to future teachers is that no matter how much stress and difficulty is dished out on your plate, always think of your students. If you can realign the messiest situations to benefit your students, it will pull you through the strife. Also, if you can channel any departmental confusion or negativity away from your students and classes, you will save yourself and maintain your sanity. Besides, the students make it all worthwhile, and they shouldn't suffer any backlashes of your frustration towards the administration. I try to do everything I can for my students. They are smart, kind, compassionate and respectful. They expect a lot and crave the extra nurturing element that I feel is lacking in American school systems. They desire assistance not only with education but also with life in general. They will soak up as much as you're willing to give.

The other aspect that impresses me most about the Chinese students is their attitude. The ones I have spoken with in depth feel that helping China solve its problems and contributing to its overall well-being is more important than making lots of money.

**Patrick Tartar**, Lijiang
June 2008

The work week is never dull when you're employed by a Communist university in the backwoods of southwest China. The last two weeks were no exception.

Last week, I entered the listening building and found myself shrouded in a thick cloud of smoke that smelled like burning garbage. The smoke followed me up to the third floor and into my classroom. About ten minutes into our DVD, the computer screen started to twitch and soon the power failed. The now billowing smoke in the hallway was coming from an electrical fire which had burned through the wires for the entire building. Needless to say, class was cancelled.

Irreparable damage had been done to the two rooms where I hold most of my listening classes. I received an email from our handler telling me my Wednesday class was now in room three. On Wednesday, I went to class with my mom who planned to observe. No one was there. We waited fifteen minutes, checked the building, and left. I was unable to get a hold of our handler, my one and only resource in these situations, and was clueless as to what happened.

Eventually, I was informed that not only had my class been moved to a new room, but it had also been moved to a new time, four thirty. This meant that my class had shown up, but I hadn't.

One week later, I go to teach my listening class, and again, no one is there. Exasperated, I track down our handler at five o'clock and demand to know my schedule. She said that she would tell me at the start of English Corner at seven that evening.[1]

English Corner rolls around, and of course, she doesn't show. I call her several times on a student's cell phone, but she doesn't answer. At eight o'clock I'm entrenched in conversation with a flock of students when a group from my MIA listening class comes by and asks me why I'm not in class. Class?

Apparently, my new class time was seven thirty. For the second week in a row my class thought that I just didn't show up. I had to explain the situation to several groups of students who came by English Corner. The whole process caused me to lose face because I didn't know my own class times.

Perhaps the administrators at my next job will have a little better handle on things. But of course, that wouldn't be nearly as entertaining.

## IN-CLASS ASSIGNMENTS

*As curious as Chinese students are about their foreign teachers, teachers are also eager to learn more about their students. The classroom provides many insights.*

**Eva Tam,** Fuzhou
February 2007

The second-year students in the Business English Department had a drama performance in late December. Since I teach all of these students, I helped them edit their skits and rehearse. I'm at an all-women's college, and it was funny seeing my students play male parts and dress like men. A majority of the skits were violent and involved at least one person dying. I was surprised because I was expecting sweet fairy tale stories about love, but instead I got stories about murdering lovers or other sad stories about misfortunes falling on people who then died tragically. But this is also the group of students who told me they want a lesson on sex. One student even said, "Love is boring. Let's talk about sex. It's more interesting." I suppose I shouldn't have been that surprised.

**Karen Raines**, Shanghai
April 2008

I had an interesting experience in one of my classes today. In class, the students were giving group presentations on the topic of their choice. One of my groups decided to discuss the protests during the Olympic torch relay in France. They mentioned the text messages many students received to boycott Carrefour, a French superstore much like Wal-Mart. The group called on various students to state whether they agreed with and would actively support the boycott. The first three students responded, "Yes, of course," and they were promptly congratulated by the group leader for being loyal Chinese. The fourth student I called on, a very bright young woman, responded that she wanted to know where the text messages came from. The class grew quiet with this deviation from the script, and the silence prompted her to explain. She wanted to know if the text messages came from people with Chinese interests at heart or from people at Lotus (one of Carrefour's competitors). She wouldn't participate in the boycott, she concluded, if it was to make a business, even a Chinese business, more money. The group leader simply said, "Okay" in response and kept going with the presentation. I was, however, struck by the individualistic, analytical, and brave ideas the lone dissenter displayed. It's amazing to see someone stand out as an individual in a society that values conformity. A proud day for any teacher.

**Barbara Gambini**, Shanghai
February 2001

Last week, I tried to have my students compose limericks. First, I wrote some famous examples on the blackboard; then I explained what a rhyme is and how the basic scheme of a limerick works. Here are two they came up with:

Barbala looks like a banana
Banana looks like a Barbala
Barbala likes to eat banana
Banana is liked to eat by Barbala
Both sweets

On top of the fact that they mucked up my name once again, the rhyme Barbara-banana had been tried by some other students in the first term. Wounded in my literary pride more than anything else, I offered profuse explanations as to the real nature of a rhyme, the difference between rhymes and assonances, but they stubbornly persist in their mistakes.

There was a president in Washington
Whose name was Colinton (they wrote Colinton!)
So to make a piece of news
He cheated the civilians

I do not wish to sound paternalistic, but I prefer to run that risk and still say what I think. Chinese students are behind their western counterparts in some aspects of their emotional maturation. An infinite list of taboos that operate both vertically and horizontally (i.e., between generations, but also among peers) protects them from any sensitive or obscene topic. Censorship on TV and the press adds to this. Therefore, at age eighteen or nineteen girls still walk around with soft toys, teddy bears, and Hello Kitty stickers, and they speak with a fake voice that's somewhere between whining and childish, but which I suspect is a deliberate affectation because I've heard it among other young Asian women before.

What's more, students come up with some positively absurd arguments in defense of their theses. Here are some examples: A twenty-year-old student said she'd learned from *Home and Alone* that the weak can overcome any difficulty if they use their wits. In a composition on the differences between genders, a boy wrote that the movie *Braveheart* proves how men's proof of courage remains unparalleled by women; a girl commented that if, in *Titanic*, it had been Rose to die instead of Jack, the latter would not have been as strong as she was in overcoming the loss. Their opinions did not sound unworthy; it seemed a pity to deprive them of all credibility with Hollywood-esque arguments. The fact is that they're not used to employing logical arguments in their discussions. Some of the most renowned scientists on earth are Chinese, yet the Chinese are not taught to use logic in diatribes or debates. They did not invent diatribes and do not seem too happy to take part in them. They prefer the *ipse dixit*[2] model; I advised them to quote more authoritative sources.

☯

**Christopher Angell**, Nanjing
June 2007

First, I have some general observations. The students are almost identical in their approaches to school as US students. There are some kids who are extremely attentive, hanging on your every word. Most of the rest hang on your every third or fourth word, and there are a few who are hanging more on the words uttered to them by their girlfriend or boyfriend last night, and what *that* meant, than what I am saying. They are respectful, sometimes standing up to answer when called upon to respond to a question, and they want to please. None of my kids are English majors, but their understanding of the spoken word, their vocabulary, and their ability to read English are surprisingly good. Their weakness is in speaking the language, for the obvious reason that they don't get to practice much. And they are like American students in one other way: they don't always show up for class!

I think I will be receiving a first-class education from them in how misinformed I am about what they and China are all about. Let me give you one or two examples. They are interested in, but not awed by America, and I wondered aloud if they might want to discuss how Americans view China. This suggestion was a big hit, and I began by asking each member of the class to name a famous American. After I heard the first answer, Martin Luther King, Jr., you could've knocked me over with a feather. MLK was followed by the usual suspects: President Bush, Abraham Lincoln, JFK, and Michael Jordan, among others.

Then I asked them how many famous Chinese people they thought a typical non-Chinese-American student could name. I suggested most such Americans could probably name two, and I asked them if they thought they could tell me which ones they were. After smiling knowingly, as if American ignorance of China was to be expected, they gave the answers I would have agreed with: Chairman Mao and Yao Ming. For those of you who are not basketball fans, Yao Ming is now a superstar player in the NBA who was selected the number one pro draft pick in 2002, even though he had played only in China and had never set foot in the United States. By the way, he is seven foot six!

I used this chat as an introduction to a documentary I have on Yao's first year in America, when he spoke no English, knew almost nothing about American culture, yet had to act as essentially the first ambassador of the Chinese people to America in fifty years. I was a little wary because the first section of the video features some film and commentary on the Cultural Revolution and Chairman Mao, and I wondered how the students would react. To my surprise, when the shots of mass demonstrations complete with shouted slogans and arms being waved in the air simultaneously came on, the kids started laughing! It wasn't a disrespectful laugh, more of a "I can't believe people used to act like that" sort of laugh. My first thought was, "The Red Peril just ain't what it used to be!"

## DORM LIFE AND OTHER COMPARISONS

**Christopher Angell,** Nanjing
September 2007

In a typical dormitory here, there are six to eight students in each room, which is about the size of a typical US college dormitory room. This squeeze is accomplished by putting bunk beds along the wall on either side of the room. Then a "common" table is usually put in the middle of the room for studying (although for obvious reasons, this is most often done in the library). There is no hot water in most of the dormitories, and students usually send one roommate downstairs to the hot water outlet to fill a basin if they all want it. But often they don't bother. There is no air-conditioning and no heating in the dorms in a city that is known as one of the "Three Furnaces" of China. In the winter, the temperature here often falls into the forties. There are no clothes washing machines available to speak of (there is a "laundry station" but few use it because it is expensive and "not clean"), so

*Dormitory. Photo by John McGee.*

students wash their clothes in basins in their rooms and then hang them to dry either on poles stuck outside their windows or in the rooms themselves. This gives many dormitories the look of gigantic concrete clotheslines, both inside and out. I can only imagine the bobbing and weaving that must take place inside the rooms to navigate the underwear obstacle course!

The university facilities for student activities include at least thirty basketball courts with no nets and bent rims, twenty badminton courts, two soccer fields, and twenty ping-pong tables. There is also a dark, overused weightlifting room and surprisingly, a very popular indoor in-line skating floor. Almost all of these are in constant use after classes let out. There are several school cafeterias sprinkled around the campus where the food is inexpensive (less than a dollar a meal) and a special cafeteria for Muslim students.

I've heard that many Chinese universities are renovating and expanding their campuses so that there will be as few as four students to a dorm room. The rumor is that some of the new ones even have elevators, truly a luxury in a place where it is common to carry all your groceries up four to six flights of stairs!

Chinese university students have a hard life compared to their American counterparts. Yet they are, for the most part, happy to be here, enthusiastic about learning, and very civil toward one another. One might suppose that since they may have known little else but crowded facilities during the educational process that they would be naturally more content under these kinds of conditions than the average American student. I have been surprised to learn, however, that they are very aware that things could be better. This is in part due to access to the Internet and American movies, and in part due to their own imaginations.

The students here complain a lot, at least amongst themselves, but bear their burdens with a certain blend of stoicism and recognition of the realities of their country. Most have worked extremely hard to get the chance to attend a university, which is seen as the "big ticket" to a better life, and so they are willing to put up with the inconveniences now in order to get the payoff down the road. If you ask them their opinion about their university lives, the answer that is most often returned is that they know China is a developing country, that there are "many people" here, and that it will take time for university life to improve.

November 2007

In some ways, the students here are far out in front of their American counterparts. In particular, their work habits are outstanding. This has been ingrained into them since primary school, where many students attend "after-school" classes to stay ahead or at least even with their classmates. When they reach middle school, Saturday and Sunday classes are not unusual, and I regularly see students still at school on weeknights until eight or nine. Why? The competition for jobs here is fierce. In a nation of 1.2 billion people with a developing, rather than a developed, economy, parents believe their children must do everything possible to get into a good high school and then a good university. The pressure is palpable on all concerned: students, teachers, and parents.

Here at the university, it is not unusual for students to have three to four, two-hour classes a day. This does not occur every day, but perhaps twice a week. On the "off" days, two classes a day is probably the norm. Many kids also attend classes on Saturdays and Sundays. Despite the workload, my typical student is enthusiastic, extremely well-behaved, and relatively happy.

In class, they are marvels of educational engineering. When I ask them to perform a task in class, they get to work immediately. The classroom is quiet, and they continue to work until either the bell rings or I tell them to stop (this happens when I get spooked and begin to think I'm living in a Stepford Wives reality). I often divide them up into different groups to work together to solve problems. Sometimes they work in pairs, other times in groups of four or five. In my American experience, this could lead to veiled complaints about who was matched with whom or to some trouble getting certain students to work with one another. Here, it seems like no matter who they are asked to team with, they get right to work and work well with that person. I'm sure there are personality conflicts here, just as there are everywhere else, but the Chinese kids don't seem to let that interfere with what they must do or at least they are able to hide it, or both.

Where the Chinese student is behind the American student is in independent thinking and social awareness. I am teaching a course in argumentative writing, and I can see that the kids are not used to expressing their opinions. I know that the Chinese educational "powers that be" are fully aware of this and see the advantages of a more liberalized educational system, but with such huge numbers of people vying for entry into the universities, many people here believe that the only fair way to select students for admission is by means of the high-stakes standardized test. This creates a domino effect in which teachers down the educational line "teach to the test" at the expense of a more exploratory teaching style. In other words, teachers and students are chafing under the present system, but no one seems ready or able to make any significant changes until there are more opportunities for university admission.

Socially, the students here have spent so much of their time up to now either at school or at home studying that there is practically no time for any social life. As a result, their social skills seem relatively unsophisticated. More than a few students, for example, shy away from dating as an activity that will detract from their true purpose for being at school. Others who do date seem to be more attracted by "puppy love" than by any prospect of a lasting relationship. In fact, many girls here are frank about the fact that their university loves will be temporary because when they are ready to marry, they will base their decision on more practical considerations than just love. Their parents will often have great influence on who they choose as a partner, and most girls say the most important factors in choosing a husband will be whether he can provide a house, a car, and of course, a steady income. This shocked me at first, but then as I turned it over in my mind, I realized that in a society like China's, alongside tradition stands the fact that there is a very large gap between the "haves" and the "have-nots," and no matter how deeply in love you might be, being a "have-not," romantic idealism aside, can make anyone's life here extremely difficult. This is not to mention that if the eligible bachelor or bachelorette is an only child, the parents' future retirement income might be riding on who the child chooses.

**Patrick Tartar**, Lijiang
June 2008

My students live quite a different college life than I did, and it is mostly because they are not allowed to move off campus, and must live in the dormitories for their entire career. This is no small imposition considering the state of these dorms.

Six students share a room that is little more than a long hallway. Bunk beds line the two long walls head-to-toe. There isn't an inch of free space. A narrow walkway runs between the desks from the door to a small deck in back. The deck holds a sink and a little closet. Inside the closet is a single squat-toilet with a shower head hanging directly over the "toilet."

The boy's dorms are on the end of campus property far from the library, classrooms, cafeterias, and most importantly, the girls. Each dorm building is enclosed by an iron fence with a security office at the only entrance. A "dorm mother" sits inside the office and restricts all access to the building.

Boys may only enter a girl's room between ten in the morning and three in the afternoon and can stay for a maximum of ten minutes. Furthermore, the boy must leave his ID card at the gate. If he exceeds the ten-minute limit, he will be rounded up and escorted out of the building.

At night, all of the students must be inside their rooms for the eleven o'clock curfew. There is a rotating schedule of students who act as dorm monitor. These students go from room to room, taking attendance of who is in by curfew, and who is not. If you miss curfew, your name gets put on a list. If you miss curfew three times, your name gets put on the "Poor Student" list, which is posted in every dorm building and outside several of the classroom buildings. Other members of this list include students who skip class, and those with the lowest grades. When a new version of the list is posted, students can be seen huddling around it, laughing and pointing.

At eleven thirty, all electricity to the dorms is cut off, even on weekends. This is a huge problem for most of the boys because most of them have serious computer game addictions. My students tell me that they often read by flashlight after the power goes out.

In addition to the electricity shortages, there's no heat. No heater is provided in the rooms and they are not allowed to use space heaters or electric blankets, which are confiscated upon discovery. This is obviously a major problem in the winter, when at eight thousand feet elevation, the nighttime temperature is regularly below freezing. This winter, nearly every one of our students had "chilblains," a red itchy swelling caused by exposure to cold, all over their hands and ears.

One of our wealthier students once indignantly said, "My father would just buy heat for our entire building, but the school won't let him! He is very unhappy about this." I would be too.

❧

**Eric Fish**, Nanjing
October 2007

Teaching is the hardest thing I've ever done, and I now definitely have a greater respect for teachers. As hard as it is, I still have one hundred percent smart, respectful, and motivated students, and I'm paid very well. So for teachers throughout the world who aren't this lucky, I can now sympathize and am regretting the hard time that I gave some of my teachers when I was in school.

One of the greatest challenges here is getting students to be confident. The biggest difference between American and Chinese students that I've noticed is a social difference. Boys and girls in their freshman and sophomore years of college here are going through the same social adjustment as American kids do when they're in sixth or seventh grade. The boys and girls are terrified of each other, and unless people are dating, there are seldom meaningful friendships between boys and girls. I asked a student about this, and she said that up through high school, boys and girls are often kept separated because teachers and parents think they would be a distraction to one another's studies. Hardly anyone is allowed to date. If a boy and girl start talking to each other too often, the teacher or parents will assume there is funny business going on and forbid them from seeing each other. Boys and girls who like each other and want to be friends won't talk to each other, because if they do, they will be forbidden from talking to each other. It's a vicious cycle. So by the time they get to college and are allowed to socialize with one another, they often are too shy. Everyday situations become like an awkward junior high school dance.


November 2007

I'm learning more about China's culture, especially when I grade students' papers. I've found that they are incredibly candid in these essays. There have been two big things I've learned from these papers. First is the importance of family here. Not that family isn't important in the States, but it's at a whole new extreme here. In America parents tend to want their kids to be self-sufficient and support themselves. Here the parents fully support their kids so they can study and not work at all. Then they expect to be completely supported when they are old. The paper that illustrated this the most was a girl who wrote about her father. She said that growing up he worked thirty miles away from home so he could earn enough to send her to college. He could only afford to take the bus home once a month to see her and the family. She started becoming interested in studying English and one day her father, while away at his job, bought an English book for her at a real bargain. He was so excited to give it to her that he couldn't wait a few more weeks to take the bus home so he *walked* the thirty miles to give it to her. When he got there she realized the book was French and that he had been ripped off, but she never had the heart to tell him. After reading that, I really had an "oh shit" moment. That's the kind of thing that happens in movies and tall tales, not real life.

The second thing I've learned is not as intense, but still interesting. Many students talk about the social effects of the one-child policy on people they know. The second generation of one-child families is growing up which means because their parents were only children also, many kids today have no siblings and no cousins. Most families are two sets of grandparents, the parents, and one child living together that means there are six people spoiling one child. This has led to the rise of what the Chinese call "Little Emperors" or "Greenhouse babies." These kids are raised without having to share anything and having grandparents that are basically glorified butlers to them all day. By the time they go to college, they can't get along with other students because they have to have everything their way. It has become a major social concern that the government is even starting to discuss. This was one of the last problems I expected in China, but I suppose it makes sense.

## "CHEATING"

*Patrick Tartar writes, "I have seen every type of cheating strategy imaginable— from students literally hiding under desks with dictionaries, to furiously writing vocabulary words on desks, to the old-fashioned 'big yawn, arm stretch, and peek at the paper next to you' move." These maneuvers are familiar to teachers in the East and the West; the difference is that in China the motivation is about "saving face" and not necessarily your own. Some more unexpected maneuvers include blatantly whispering answers or switching seats to translate for a classmate. This is reprimanded in the United States. What about in China?*

*In the Chinese classroom, the mind-set is that one student's failure reflects badly on the whole class. The students feel a bond and responsibility to help one another. This is a completely alien concept to Westerners, who can easily become frustrated with students whispering answers to one another, as we are oriented to measure individual mastery and knowledge. How are foreign teachers supposed to assess students who won't readily or voluntarily answer questions in class, who share answers when called upon, who "cheat" on tests, and turn in papers that seem purely plagiarized? The irony is that while teaching English to Chinese students, who are eager to learn about US customs, they simultaneously appear to be flagrantly breaking cultural and academic rules as we understand them. In this case, it is the foreign teacher who feels, as Carl Siegel would say, "rucked over like a quarterback out of the pocket." Perhaps the greatest academic taboo in China is the class "losing face." And while the foreign teacher may encourage class participation, discussion, and hand-raising, an understanding of the class spirit of cooperation and determination to "save face" will prevent much aggravation. There are many ways to evaluate students and designing cooperative activities and in-class assignments will reduce this tension for students and teachers alike, especially for Oral English classes. El-len Axtmann encountered this in her first semester teaching, and her husband, Ken Dreise, battled with grading student writing.*

## Ellen Axtmann, Lijiang
December 2005

The semester is quickly drawing to a close, which is good because both students and teachers are tired of the whole drill. I actually reprimanded one of my Tourism classes (Oral English) last week. They are my worst class, and my last class of the week. Complete slackers. I finally lost it and ranted for about five minutes. I suspect most of them didn't have a clue what I was talking about, and I'm not sure it made me feel any better or will change their behavior. The tourism classes are the hardest because the students barely speak English and most are not interested.

December 2005

Ken is pulling his hair out right now. He is grading his writing classes' research papers. He is spending all of his time on Google, finding out from which sites his students have plagiarized. He says that two out of three papers are copied word-for-word from the Internet. I am urging him to not bother grading them (it was just one assignment among many), but he feels he should reward the students who didn't plagiarize so he has to grade them all (and hunt down the sources for all the copied papers). He is under a mountain of writing.

*Like many other things, the concept of the research paper is not necessarily the same in China. Most US teachers expect papers that are a blend of original student writing and quotations properly cited in footnotes or endnotes. What they will find is that an excellent student may copy a source without quotations or citations. The roots of this may be the practice of rote repetition throughout the student's educational experience where the value is not in original interpretation but in precise regurgitation. Another source may be the prevalence of communal beliefs, values, and ideas. In Chinese culture, the concept of individual ownership of ideas is still peculiar. It's another area where US teachers must suspend judgment and alter their teaching strategies and assignments accordingly.*

*While admission to a Chinese university used to be entirely determined by the National College Entrance Exam or* gao kao *(pronounced gow kow), a nine-hour test administered over three consecutive days in June, now privately paying students may also enter university. Ellen Axtmann and Ken Dreise are teaching at one such college.*

**Ken Driese,** Lijiang
March 2006

Our college is an unusual product of China's changing society in that it is a privately managed business. Students here have had the misfortune of failing their college entrance exams, and therefore, losing the opportunity to attend first- or second-tier colleges in bigger cities. Teaching English as a Second Language at a school like this is a little like trying to get George Bush to use big words correctly.

The system itself is self-defeating. As an Australian colleague put it, only half-jokingly, before he left, "Student grade sheets have three columns: the student's academic mark, their parent's income and their final grade." Cynical, but not far from the truth. Students who pay the tuition *do not fail* no matter how poorly they do academically. Students who never attend class and fail are given the opportunity to take a five-minute makeup exam (oral) by a different teacher from the one who failed them, and if they survive that, they pass the entire course. If they fail this makeup exam, the school *still* has the ultimate last word, and the kids are almost always passed. The system amounts to a pay-for-a-degree program requiring four years of tuition. Merit is not crucial. As a teacher, it can make you crazy.

In China, failing the college entrance exam usually means not only no college but also a bad job. Unless you can find a school like ours that, though not high on the academic totem pole, accepts students who cobble together the extravagant tuition and buy their way in. Ten thousand *yuan* a year (about US $1,250)—a small fortune for many Chinese—is the cost for one year at our school, compared with much lower fees at academically better, state-run institutions in big cities like Beijing, Tianjin, or Nanjing.

Not all of the students here have rich parents. Some come from poor farming families who struggle immensely to send their kids to this college. It is to protect these students that we come down harder on the insolent kids that don't apply themselves. Also, unlike George Bush, many of the students are genuinely nice, and it's often the poorest students, the ones whose families are living hard so that their child can get a better education that are the most generous and motivated.

The educational system is much different in China. To some extent, one understands the predisposition for coasting among students who, as children, attend primary school from seven thirty in the morning until five o'clock at night, and then stay up until nine or ten at night doing mandatory homework. College for many of these kids is a time to relax and have fun, far from the pressures of senior middle school (though they are often homesick).

My understanding of education in China is that students struggle through primary, junior, and senior middle school in anticipation of the feared college entrance exam which is taken during their senior years. The entire system focuses on preparing the kids for a battery of standardized tests that they take periodically throughout their school years. It's no wonder that kids are sick of study by the time they reach college. As one of our Chinese friends here put it (while her ten-year-old studied), *"Nobody here likes the system but nobody changes it."*

Teaching here is a daily struggle between a sense of ineffectiveness and frustration on the one hand and responsibility to the twenty percent or so of the students who are motivated to learn on the other. For Ellen and me, being here is enough of a reward, and teaching is the price we pay, so we make of it what we can. There are good days and bad days. As students have said in "position" papers, *"Every sword has two blades."* (??!!)

*In terms of the sheer numbers of children going to school in China, the Chinese Ministry of Education reports primary school enrollment of 100.7 million in 2009. That number dwindles to 54.4 million students enrolled in middle school, and 24.3 million in high school. Less than half of these students will take the college entrance exam, and only about 6 million students will receive a university spot based on the exam.*

**Theresa**, Tianjin
September 2007

As we head to the end of the semester, and I've had my students for over three months, I can say that I adore almost all of them. They have befriended me with hours of talking and strange Chinese meals after class. The more I learn about their outlook on life and pressures to succeed the more I understand about what American privilege really means. To have things like after school activities and "fun" is a luxury that young American students don't really think about, at least I didn't. Before the college entrance exam, the Chinese students spend months of twelve to fifteen hour days studying. And I don't mean let's go to Starbucks and listen to iPods study. I mean intense, mom will feed you, because you don't have time to waste, studying. Their motivation to work hard is inspiring and something I hope to learn more about. I hear that getting into a good college can mean a difference of being a construction worker making sixty dollars a month to being a teacher and making four hundred. Right now, my students are in the middle of my "final" exam. I had them each make a personal flag—essentially a poster that has five elements about who they are and what they stand for. Hearing what each of them has had to say about their own lives at a personal level has been another highlight of my trip here.

*For those who enter university, the next major goal is often to study abroad.*

**Carl Siegel**, Shanghai
September 2005

Work this year for the first term means early mornings teaching "Preparation for IELTS (International English Language Testing System)." Essentially, it's a test prep course, but it's a biggie. If they do well enough, my students get a double-degree from the University of Technology, Sydney, our Australian joint venture university, which significantly enhances a Chinese diploma in most areas. A good score is the only ticket to study abroad as well. This is an exam-based culture with rigorous expectations, throw in some unchecked anxiety, and pass it on to me. And of course, the test is insanely difficult and not all my students are going to pass.

The bright side is my students are angels. And the test is an overall proficiency for speaking/listening/reading/writing, so no matter their IELTS score they get something from the course. The other bright side is our faculty is fabulous. There are five of us: three American guys, one Australian woman, and one Romanian woman. And my new campus is enormous like a space colony with over thirty thousand students. I don't even know my way around. Walking to class I pass two underground levels of just bicycle parking.

*And while the writers' appreciation for their students shines through in many of these emails, a student of Kimberley Te Winkle in Tianjin offers a Chinese perspective on foreign teachers.*

April 2000

Luckily for me that I have courses taught by foreign teachers almost every semester. In class, they solicited creative input from us, including opinions, criticism, and debate. Whatever we thought merited their consideration. This more spontaneous student-active approach to teaching impressed me deeply. Their diverse background made the lesson not only dynamic and enriching for me, but also imbued me with a liberal mind. Through both formal and informal contact, I formed valuable relationships with my foreign teachers and improved my understanding of Western culture, English, and the role that teachers play in Western education. These teachers have opened a new window to the world for me, and I just hope that I may have the same opportunity to broaden this window for more people.

## REFLECTION

**Catt Stearns**, Wanzhou
June 2010

For the past ten months I have been living in the middle of China as an English teacher. I came to China because I didn't want a "normal" job, I didn't even know what kind of job I wanted or what exactly I wanted to make out of my post-collegiate life. I just knew I wanted to travel more. During the past year, I've tried to answer the myriad questions the Chinese have thrown at me: Why are you here in China? Why didn't you find a job in the United States? Did you teach before you came here? Will you be a teacher when you go home? Then one guy put it plain and simple, "Did you choose to become an English teacher in order to fund your traveling?"

I was hesitant when answering this question. The way it was phrased made me sound like I was self-centered and not here for the right reasons. It was like I came to China for myself never thinking of the impact I would make on the students and the people I met and worked with while here. I came to China to travel (not necessarily teach), but it's the teaching part that allows me to do so, and it's been the teaching part that has had the greatest impact on me throughout my year in China.

As I start to wrap up my time as an English teacher, I find it rather difficult to really put into words my accomplishments, my downfalls, and the lessons I learned within these past ten months. Part of me is proud, part of me is disappointed, but the biggest part of me is completely grateful to have had this experience.

There were days when I came back from class completely discouraged. I could see the blatant boredom, confusion, and total lack of interest on the students' faces, and I wished I could fake ill and end class early in order to save myself and the students. I often wonder whoever thought I could actually teach should never have put so much responsibility and trust in my hands. I mean really, I was taking college finals less than two months before I started this job. Now, I am on the opposite side of the spectrum with no experience and just a Bachelor's degree and the ability to speak English. I wouldn't even hire myself.

Fortunately enough for me, as well as the students, not all of my lessons ended up being a waste of time. The students would never exactly say, "Great lesson, Catt!" or "Wow, you just taught me so much!" It's more of the communal feeling that seems to form between my students and me after a class I know that they actually enjoyed (and I enjoyed teaching) and from which they know they actually gained something. When this happens, students don't feel such a need to rush out of the classroom in order to avoid speaking English to that no-good foreign teacher. If I'm lucky, and actually good at teaching that day, they'll stay behind, maybe help me erase the chalkboard, take time with their good-byes, and possibly have somewhat of a normal (although slightly forced conversation) with me.

One of my favorite and most successful lessons was a debate on globalization that I assigned my sophomore students. Practically all of my students saw the process of globalization as completely beneficial. How could it not be? They wondered how we could have a debate on this. The most popular comment was, "Look at how globalization has benefited our China!" It is hard to wrap your brain around the changes that have happened in China in the past twenty, even ten, years. The fact that Chongqing used to be some backwater town with nothing more than five-story buildings just fifteen years ago and is now one of the biggest cities in China (and in the world) with multiple sky-rises and endless high-rise apartment buildings stands as a testament to the changes that China has seen and endured. And according to my students, it was the process of globalization and China opening itself up to this process that has made cities like Chongqing rip from the seams and give their population a better life. The motto of the 2010 Shanghai World Expo is "Better city, better life."

While I may not teach English again or even teach in a classroom, I have discovered that there is some sort of teacher in me. I now find it extremely satisfying when my students actually laugh at a joke I make. After nine months, they not only understand my English, but my sense of humor as well. It's a sign that they have come to know more about their foreign English teacher as an actual, living, and breathing person. There have been so many times in China where I've felt the exact opposite. Being the cause of gasps and "what the hell" facial expressions (and who can forget the time I was mistaken for a mannequin in a clothing store) can be more or less a dehumanizing experience. But when the students laugh, not at me, but with me, it's made me realize how much the whole us vs. them, east vs. west mentality can easily be broken down.

☯

## CONCLUSION: I LOVE THIS JOB

**Patrick Tartar**, Lijiang
June 2008

This work year has been filled with many entertaining moments. I'm positive that I will never again have a job that causes me to laugh on such a regular basis. A recap of some of the best moments:

1. We received our teaching schedule and list of subjects to be taught a mere sixteen hours before our first day of classes. We were given our first and only tour of campus in the pitch dark at eleven o'clock at night, just nine hours before our first class.
2. During role-playing skits, students actually smoked cigarettes on stage. One student brandished an enormous butcher knife (real) and repeatedly waved it in the faces of the students he was pretending to "rob." These skits have also included numerous love triangles, suicides, and even a group of evil robots set to take over the world.
3. I had one twenty-year-old student vehemently argue with me for a full five minutes about her wish to be excused from class because she was

*John McGee with his class. Photo by John McGee.*

thirsty and needed a drink. She failed to see the logic in my argument that she was old enough to plan for her drinking needs before coming to class.

4. I've fielded the following questions: Who is your favorite student? Why do foreigners really hate China? What is the most romantic thing you've ever done? Do you love Donald Trump?

5. My students' work group names included "Perfect China," "The Absent Group," "Mr. T," "Sleepless in Seattle," "Without a Clue," "Wild Sexy Man's World," "Edison's Photo," and "Whatever."

6. Two girls in Heather's speaking class performed a wildly dramatic skit where they fought over me. One claimed that I was hers because we were in love, and I had bought her an expensive pair of shoes (which she promptly whipped out of her bag and shoved in the other girl's face). The other argued that I was hers because I had "knocked her up."

7. We've had no less than forty notes requesting a leave from class to get an IV treatment for life-threatening ailments such as the headache, common cold, and sore throat.

8. I've been greeted with screams and roaring applause by a roomful of freshmen after returning from a four-day absence.

9. The sophomore leader of the Communist Party came to take my final exam with an enormous Communist flag hanging from a flag pole stuck in his backpack. He left the final early, claiming he had a duty to go hang the flag.

10. More than many times, I have had random students approach me on campus and say, "You're *so cool!*" before immediately turning around and walking away.

11. I have seen every type of cheating strategy imaginable, from students literally hiding under desks with dictionaries, to furiously writing vocabulary words on desks, to the old-fashioned "big yawn, arm stretch, and peek at the paper next to you" move.

12. I've had students literally fall out of their chairs and gasp in astonishment when watching footage of a gay wedding in a Hawaiian documentary.

13. I've witnessed an entire class of fifty students crying their eyes out at the end of *Armageddon*, boys included.

14. In my personal favorite moment of the year, my girlfriend Heather Bugni's student took a speaking activity to the most unexpected of places. He held up a photo of a beautiful white woman and was supposed to tell her life story. Instead he said, "I will not tell you the name of this beautiful girl, you have to guess. I think that she is the most beautiful girl in China, and her boyfriend's name is Patrick." The class literally shouted, "Bugni!! It's Bugni!!" The student said, "I think she is the most beautiful girl in China, do you?" "Yes!!Yes!!" At this point the entire room of fifty students began to chant, "Beauty Bugni! Beauty Bugni! Beauty Bugni!" And really, what are you to do in this situation?

Some day in the not-too-distant future, I'll be sitting in a cubicle, thumbing through paperwork at a "real job." In these moments, I will always be able to think back to these students, and this year, and smile.

*From the vantage point of their classrooms, these teachers learn firsthand what it is like to be a young person in China; they learn about the rigors and rigidity of the Chinese educational system; they learn Chinese values, customs, and perspectives on education, foreign policy, and globalization; and they are welcomed into the lives of their students. They are truly seeing China from the inside.*

# Cross-Cultural Experiences

*Which Side of the Mirror Am I On?*

跨文化經歷

There are good China days and bad China days. The good far outnumber
the bad, and even the bad have their good side.

—Brian E. Lewis

*Despite our ever globalized and interconnected world, culture shock still exists.
As Dana writes, "It's a lot easier to visit another culture than to live in it." What
she means is that practically everything one thought constant and reliable becomes
upended during a sojourn in China. Answers to questions you thought you knew,
change: Don't all babies wear diapers? Doesn't everyone like cookie batter? What is
cheating? Eric Fish writes, "Things I take for granted as common knowledge (such
as you shouldn't stereotype) can be controversial subjects here." Confusion sets
in, sometimes in conjunction with other typical symptoms of culture shock, such
as anxiety, depression, fatigue, self-doubt, and even paranoia. Can culture shock
be avoided? Not really. No amount of preparation can prevent it altogether. The
Colorado China Council screens for candidates who can survive culture shock and,
best of all, who can adapt to life in China. The Summer Institute seeks to prepare
teachers for the duties of their jobs, but also for the inevitable onset of culture shock.
Although it's a hazard of living overseas, one that causes a handful of teachers over
the years to break their contracts, for most, it is as Brian E. Lewis describes above:
the good outweighs the bad.*

*These e-mails reflect teachers' experiences in dealing with cross-cultural differ-
ences once they have settled in a bit. The teachers are no longer on the "China high,"
full of excitement and curiosity. Instead, they are feeling alone and different. They
perceive cultural differences as warts not wonders. In the depths of culture shock,
withdrawal, blaming, and even unbecoming behavior by US teachers have been self-
reported. Eventually, teachers achieve some level of competence and stability in this
new culture; their sense of humor, autonomy, and independence returns.*

## CHINA BLUES

**Karen Raines**, Shanghai
December 2007

I have heard some people describe culture shock as "China Blues." I, on the
other hand, have feelings of being lost in a dark, smoky, smelly abyss. Culture
shock, to say the least, has reared its ugly head and seems to follow me down
every path I take. I intellectually understand that the homesickness and for-
eignness will not bother me as much the longer I am here, but emotionally, I
am unhappy and I keep thinking about the day I get to go back to America. I
think I have discovered the three biggest culprits: the food; an apathetic class;
and the four S's—staring, smoking, spitting, and split-pants.

The staring, at first, did not bother me too much. I understood that living in the suburbs there would be many people who did not regularly see Westerners. Consequently, I took the staring in stride. However, it started to wear on me about three months into my stay here. People would look at me and continue to stare, twisting their necks in odd positions until they could strain no more. Sometimes I would stare back just as hard, but that did not dissuade the perpetrators. I began to feel like an animal in a cage at the zoo, only (thankfully) no one tried to feed or pet me. It got to the point where I did not leave my room without my iPod or sunglasses. Even in the winter when there was no sun to be seen, I wore the sunglasses. People still stared, but at least I felt more protected behind the lenses.

The smoking and spitting bothered me for similar reasons: both were everywhere and done without compunction. Even Americans, who would probably not even consider lighting up in America without asking if it bothered anyone around, lit up happily and heartily everywhere. I found it especially hard to get used to since I am a native Californian; I can't even remember what it was like to be around cigarette smoke in public. However, I actually detest the spitting more than the smoking. I understand people need to spit sometimes, but it happens more than frequently in China. There is also a whole noisy process in spitting that turns my stomach.

Although I found the children wearing split pants to be quite adorable, I loathed the fact that their parents allowed the children to go to the bathroom just about anywhere. When I returned to China after a short holiday a friend texted me and asked if I was back in China. I responded, "I just saw a little boy pee on the airport floor. I am so back in China!" I used to think people were silly for asking others to take their shoes off when entering their house. Now, I understand—one just does not know how much DNA one is walking around with on the bottom of one's shoes.

Some of my experiences may seem silly or even funny, but my feelings of depression and even resentment lack any lightness or hilarity. I've gotten to the point where I have simply refused to learn any Chinese. It is almost like I blame China for making me feel this way even though it was my choice to come here. I have a new understanding of how immigrants in America must feel. I used to think that if one was going to live in another country, then he or she should bother to learn the language. I used to consider people who lived in America and did not learn English lazy. Conversely, I now see that there is a dichotomy in being an immigrant, being an outsider. An immigrant is both conspicuous and invisible. Conspicuous in that their physical appearance, dress, and language cause them to stand out and be noticed by natives; invisible in that their emotions, obstacles, and even successes are marginalized by superficial concerns and complaints. I have it easier as an "immigrant" in China than an immigrant in America. Although I stand out, most of what I do brings humor to onlookers. Whether it's eating with chopsticks, or crossing the street, or even using a few words of Mandarin, I inspire laughter (mostly kind) wherever I go. I suspect it's different for immigrants in America. Food for thought.

Hopefully, my blues will thaw with the end of winter.

❧

**Peggy Rosen**, Shanghai
September 2003

Not sure what day it is or how much time has passed since my arrival, but I know I have a class to teach later today. I think it is Wednesday. Sometimes I think I am "Alice in Wonderland," but no, you're Alice, and I am Peggy in Chinaland. So much has whizzed by that I can't believe I am approaching a month here. I have one hundred plus new Chinese faces with strange names to learn, a lot of togetherness with new colleagues, an abundance of Chinese Take Out and Sit In, many bicycles, a lot of *Ni Hao*'s, charades, and miles and miles of walking with a new adventure at every turn. These are the ups and downs of being halfway around the world from familiarity and loved ones. Does that sum it up?

On the whole, I see the blue sky here on campus, but I have been told by others, it has not been so blue. When a bad day comes along in China it "packs a whammy." My first was last Friday. I believe it was the equivalent and sequel to the book *Alexander and the Terrible, Horrible, No Good, Very Bad Day*. First, I woke up at about three thirty in the morning dripping in perspiration thinking that I was running a fever. Then, I realized or thought the heat was on. I looked up helpful Chinese phrases to tell the desk staff that my air conditioner was broken. I went to take a shower and realized with lathered hair that there was no hot water; that didn't matter too much because it felt good at this point. (The temperature on my clock registered 29°C.) There was no water pressure. I found out that the air was off in the entire hotel. I probably said that there are hairy toads in my room instead of the air conditioner doesn't work in room 716.

This was also the day that I had three different subjects to teach in a row. I couldn't find my class notes. I decided to wear a skirt that wrapped around; the buttons all fell off while I was teaching. When I asked the class to write to me what they thought I should do in China during my year here, one student said I was fat and should lose weight while in China. (Couldn't go much lower than that!) My second year students helped, and we had a few laughs together in the afternoon.

That was Peggy's Terrible, Horrible, No Good, Very Bad Day. Not so bad a few days later. Last Friday, the university treated us to a banquet for Fall Festival and Teacher's Day.

❧

**Barbara Gambini**, Shanghai
December 2000

On more than one occasion, I have been struck by the disarming frankness of the Chinese, which may be offensive, if it didn't take you totally aback to the point of becoming funny. Everybody here feels it appropriate to ask you how much money you make, how much you paid for a certain item, and they don't hesitate to tell you a certain thing is not worth the money you paid for it. A month ago, I went to the hairdresser. While I was desperately searching for words to explain the haircut I wanted, he quite amusedly observed that my hair was not as beautiful, shiny, and thick as the hair of Chinese women. You may imagine his loss of composure when he noticed my protruding ears, which was a sensational enough attraction for him to summon his colleagues and show them, too, not without a belly laugh.

Another time I was at the tailor's, trying on new trousers. Another customer stepped in, saw me and asked, "How come you have such a thin face and such fat legs?" She didn't even say "big legs," she just said "fat." So finally, all those who year after year have denied that I have big legs are finally unmasked, like those subjects whose hypocrisy was exposed by the innocence of the child crying out, "The King is naked!"

**Dana**, Hangzhou
April 2001

It's a lot easier to visit another culture than to live in it. Of course, living here makes the whole experience that much more interesting, but lately I've been more sensitive to cultural differences and little things make me crazy. In fact, I put off responding to your previous email because I thought it would reflect my mood and not the reality of our situation here in Hangzhou. Fortunately, I'm feeling much better about things and attribute my bout of culture shock to the stress of daily life. I still have a tough time with the language, the traffic makes me cringe, and it's hard for me to deal with the sexism. (The head of the foreign language program didn't even know my name at the end of last semester. To him, I was Brian's wife.) But, now I'm better at going with the flow, and my stress level is definitely going down.

**Jeanne S. Phillips**, Fuzhou
September 1999

My classes begin tomorrow, to my alarm. Luckily, the week will be only four days long with the National Day holiday beginning on October first. It will run through October seventh, but it doesn't come free. At first the holiday was to be only Friday and Monday; then Tuesday was added last week. Then last Friday, it was announced that Wednesday and Thursday would be added to accommodate people who want to use the unusually timed and lengthened holiday to travel. But Wednesday and Thursday were not really holiday time, just a convenience to be purchased by working on Saturday, as if Wednesday, and on Sunday, as if Thursday, making for a rather long following week. The logic of all this was a cross-cultural test of humor. Although our Chinese friends did not laugh as hard as we "big-nosed barbarians" (a commonly used term for Westerners), they too were wryly amused.

**Larry Davis**, Hangzhou
April 2000

A great deal of flexibility and patience is critical. This place is not organized according to Western standards, and it's pointless to compare how things are done here and in the States. Holidays are not announced (or even decided) until the week before. I rarely know exactly what I will be teaching more than a week before classes start, and even then, it's usually about three weeks into the term before my teaching schedule reaches its final form. I have a very good relationship with my academic department, but that relationship is partly based on patience and not expecting anything to "be like the States." On the other hand, I'm sure my colleagues cut me a lot of slack too.

*For Chinese American teachers, like E. H., the experience is even more multi-layered and nuanced. While Chinese students seem to flock to, even "stalk," their foreign teachers who are non-Asian, the experience for Asian Americans is mixed.*

**E. H.**, Tianjin
February 2002

My experience up to this point has been very accurate, realistic. Due to my Chinese face, people are rude to me, budge in line, and I feel I've had to mature and take care of myself even faster than if I lived in New York City alone. Ironically, I don't feel there is any one student I can call a close friend yet. Due to the sheer number of them (last semester, I taught about twelve hundred; this semester, I have over eight hundred), they seem embarrassed to "bother" me, even when I give them my phone number because they know I have so many students. The end result is that almost no one contacts me! I feel very lonely at times, trudging back to my Guest House surrounded by American teachers much older than me. Sometimes I pass those dirty but noisy dorms and am envious. I am hoping that the new semester will bring more personal satisfaction.

February 2002

Some days I hate it here, and some days I love it! For the past couple weeks I've been reminding myself that I'm on that destabilizing curve of culture shock: where the fascination peters out and when one can become critical of one's host country. I've only become slightly critical and have started to miss the lush, upstate New York forest where I grew up. But oddly enough, after a month's vacation completely surrounded by Chinese speakers (I went to see family in Taiwan and Shanghai for New Year's), I feel more uncomfortable speaking English! Even though it's easier to write or pronounce, I feel "foreign" doing so. I didn't expect this to happen, and it feels weird. I wonder if I should have spent late nights discussing ancient Confucian riddles with my uncle, a traditional Chinese medicine expert, and have those monosyllabic words penetrate my head so deeply in the night hours. In the past everything was simple, separate; now, it's all becoming more melded together!

*Since culture shock is unavoidable, the self-awareness of these teachers and the ability to write about and confront such mixed feelings is one way to successfully navigate the rocky waters. Amid the daily cultural collisions, many teachers find some refreshing satisfaction.*

**Eric Fish**, Nanjing
May 2008

Recently, I showed a class an episode of the *Simpsons* where the family visits Japan. It was pretty lighthearted, and I asked the students to name things they saw that were stereotypical or unrealistic in Japan's portrayal in the episode. One student stood up and said, "The Japanese were mean to the Simpsons in the episode. In reality they act very nice, but they should all get the best actor award because inside they are very cruel and want to take over the world." Another student stood up, and rather than answering the question, went on a tirade about how the Japanese deny the past. I've never seen a *Simpsons* episode stir up so much emotion.

These events have evoked in me for the first time what I would consider culture shock. I was warned from the beginning that I would inevitably experience it at some point, but I had no idea this is the form it would take. I pictured culture shock as being utterly frustrated with the language barrier, or some quality of life incompatibility that would send me curled up in the corner crying for mommy. But it hasn't been like that at all. These events made me feel like I was hopelessly surrounded by ignorance. I can argue and reason until my throat runs dry that the Japanese aren't inherently evil. But even if I'm lucky enough to break through to one person, I encounter fifty more with unshakable beliefs that make me cringe. As much as I want to change the way everybody thinks, I have to accept that it's futile. I'm out of my element and surrounded by a completely different thought system that has probably been the hardest thing to adjust to here. Things I take for granted as common knowledge (such as you shouldn't stereotype) can be controversial subjects here. But I'm realizing that it goes both ways. For instance, in China they laugh when I tell them evolution is a controversial subject in America.

While it may seem like I'm getting a little annoyed with living in China from this email, nothing could be further from the truth. These experiences are as much a part of the reason I came here as the good experiences. They have been great learning experiences for which I am grateful. I love it here, and as most of you probably know, I am staying another year. I've found a good niche, and my Chinese is slowly transitioning from functional to conversational. I can now sometimes last over five minutes in a conversation before falling apart and making an ass of myself!

☯

**Julie**, Tianjin
February 2006

Life in China is great. After three semesters, I am completely adjusted to everything except the constant spitting. I'll never be okay with that one! At least I have a great boyfriend who reminds me to laugh and love China the way it is. He is from the Philippines and plays bass in a house band. He makes more money doing that than he did working as a nurse in Manila and more than three times what I make teaching English. That's just not right! Obviously, I'm not staying here for the money. I met him in September after my friends were recruited at a bar to be the token *waiguoren* (foreigners) in a televised celebration of the arts. They lip-synched while his band pretended to play a John Denver song playing from a tape. The "performance" was ridiculously wonderful and hilarious, and afterward I met the most amazing man. That's why living in China is truly an unforgettable adventure. Despite the disgusting bathrooms and endless spitting, every day is filled with the most unexpected yet delightful experiences. And you never know who you're going to meet!

☯

*Even three years into his stint in China, Eric Fish's roller-coaster ride continues.*

**Eric Fish**, Nanjing
March 2010

Since my last update I've experienced a grueling blend of China highs and disillusionments that have killed my optimism about the country then yanked it right back.

The biggest disillusionment has, over the past few months, led me to do the things I've always taught my students never to do: generalize, stereotype, and become submissive. One horrible generalization I've developed is that Chinese-owned companies are corrupt slave drivers. I recently quit the English company I've been working for after my compounding list of grievances finally hit the tipping point.

One of my main worries was that since the company's business has slowed down considerably, the owner might one day soon simply disappear into the night with all the company money, leaving employees hung out to dry. This is a distressingly common scenario in China and recently happened with another famous English chain in Shanghai. One of the major drawbacks in China's economic explosion is that business has grown far faster than the government's ability (or willingness) to police it, so much of China's business world has an "eat or be eaten" jungle mentality. Even as the system is starting to be cleaned up, it's becoming worse. Like someone arriving at the buffet five minutes before closing, the corrupt are starting to grab as much as they can, as fast as they can, while they still can.

Needless to say, after I quit, I was ready for a vacation. I was lucky enough that it came right at my first full Chinese New Year in China. To celebrate, my girlfriend took me back to her small hometown called Qingzhou (Ching-Joe) in Shandong Province. I'd visited once before and met her parents, but this time her whole extended family was there, and I was treated to a few surprises. Foremost among them was her grandpa; she'd never spoken of him before. The day before I was going to meet him, she told me the unbelievable story of his past:

When he was eleven years old in 1937, the invading Japanese army came through his town and two soldiers proceeded to enter his school yard and dismember his teacher with bayonets as he and his classmates looked on. A few years later, he joined the army and fought the Japanese for the rest of World War II. Shortly after arriving back home in 1945, the Communist army came through town and recruited him to fight the Nationalists[1] until 1949. Finally, when there was peace, he settled down a few hundred miles from home to do farm work. The next year in 1950, a truck pulled up beside him as he was working and an officer told him to get in; he was going to go fight the Americans in Korea. While in Korea for three years, he spent most nights sleeping in the snow eating frozen potatoes. Then one night, an American raid wiped out everyone in his hundred-person brigade except him and one other soldier.

"Wait! What?!" I asked my girlfriend at this point in the story. "I'm going to meet this guy tomorrow?!" In school I barely remember learning about the Korean War, which is probably why it's sometimes called "The Forgotten War" in America. But it's not forgotten here. China calls it "The War to Resist American Aggression and Aid Korea." I was taught that the war ended essentially in a tie that resulted in the creation of one of the most oppressive countries in the world, North Korea. The Chinese are taught that it was a glorious victory over the militarily superior imperialist Americans and next to nothing is taught about modern North Korea. Since the war, the official portrayal of America has shown it as anything from a tolerable trading partner to an aggressive hegemon bent on murderous world domination. So I was a teeny bit nervous to meet this grandpa who hadn't seen any Americans since those that killed nearly everyone around him.

Apparently grandpa got wind of my anxiety because as soon as I walked into his home the next day he pointed at me and yelled, "Who brought this American devil?!" to which the rest of the family erupted in laughter. Good one, gramps.

For some reason I could understand his Chinese much better than the rest of the family's because of their regional dialects so I ended up chatting with him most of the day. He had a noticeable trace of senility, but was still engaging. We were a convenient match at the get-together. Neither of us really knew what was going on, we were both led around by the others like small children, and we were both the constant butt of the rest of the family's jokes. Seeing that we had made friends only intensified the jokes. While chatting, he told me more about the war: "Once in Korea the Americans bombed a whole city the size of Qingzhou, and it only took them two hours!" "Wow," I hesitantly replied, unsure if it was a compliment. Then he started speaking loudly and incoherently. "He's showing you that he can count to ten in Korean," my girlfriend informed me.

Sitting there in his comfortable heated home with his children who all had good jobs and more than enough good food to eat, I listened to stories about how he didn't sleep in a bed for ten years and spent his entire youth miraculously staying one step ahead of death. It became easier to see why it's hard to get a lot of people in China riled up about things like Internet censorship.

But I still have no qualms complaining about it. Now I'm back working at the same university I started at with plenty of time to focus on my new undertaking: freelance writing.

## CULINARY ADJUSTMENTS AND HAPPY HOLIDAZE

*One of the biggest challenges non-Chinese speakers encounter in China is feeding themselves. In the case of my husband, finding an adequate coffee supply was a top priority. As a parting gift, one of his sisters gave him a large bag of Costa Rican coffee beans. It did not occur to us until about twenty-four hours after settling in that we didn't have a coffee pot, much less a coffee grinder. The search began. We secured a coffee press without much trouble, but a coffee bean grinder was another matter. At this point, I thought he might just start eating the coffee beans straight out of the bag. The French Café down the alley served a robust, if tiny, cup of coffee at US prices. Robert might need thirty of these each day. Fortunately, we discovered Yunnan coffee and abandoned the beans.*

*Now for me, an avid tea drinker at the time, food was my all-consuming priority. Initially, I employed various survival strategies: pointing to dishes other customers were eating, pointing to meat or vegetables on display, or taking a chance on the English translation provided by some menus. Once you've mastered survival eating, new culinary adventures await.*

**Julie**, Tianjin
March 2005

Pigs Brain Wrapped in Banana Leaf, Duck Tongues and Sparrow Gizzards—all part of China's glorious culinary history. It was on every menu and seemed to be the house chicken of Xishuangbanna, so I figured I should try it. Why, why, why?

☯

**Adrian Neibauer**, Chengdu
August 2003

The other night we ate at a famous Shanghai restaurant downtown. An emperor ate there once. The food was fabulous, but the menu was even better. Many foreigners frequent the restaurant, so there were English translations of the Chinese dishes, including *squirrelly nutlets*, *ants climbing on dirty leaves*, and *fish viscera*.

☯

**Josh Leslie**, Chengdu
April 1999

One thing I haven't tried yet is *"ke lin den dui lai win si ji"* (Clinton and Lewinsky), a new chicken dish named after the president and his former mistress. The Chinese have a neat way of translating western names and places. They use characters that phonetically make the sounds, and often they have meaning as well. *Ji* means chicken, so it's a chicken dish, but it also means prostitute. Michael Jordan is *chaodan* (pronounced chow don), literally fried egg. George Bush is *bu shi* (pronounced boo shur), literally "is not," and the best one yet is Viagra, *wei ge* (pronounced way ga), which means strong big brother!!

☯

**Ian Bledsoe**, Hangzhou
March 2004

A few weeks after arriving in China, I saw a large, rickety, and rusted cart on three wheels pulled by a bicycle. In the cart is bag upon bag upon bag, piled at least ten feet high and strapped on with ropes crisscrossing the whole assembly. The bags make a stark, bright silhouette against the dusty gray horizon that hovers over this city of six million. It is stark and bright because you can see through the clear plastic of the bags into the white grains contained within—the neurological arch-enemy of so many denizens of my homeland: MSG.

MSG is an omnipresent feature of one's culinary experience in this country. MSG is used everywhere, always, no matter what. When you buy fried noodles from the portable, bike-toted roadside stand, there is always a bottle of vinegar, a bowl of intimidating looking hot sauce, and a bag of MSG. Of course, in itself this is not so impressive a cultural description. What's more interesting is a certain tendency that MSG seems to represent to me. The Chinese use MSG in their food because somewhere along their long (and, let's be honest, glorious) culinary history, someone decided that MSG was good for you. I am sure there is some proverb concerning the man who eats MSG and is healthy and morally good, and the man who does not and is a cretin, and whose pigs all die from a viral scourge. The cultural trait of note that I think this highlights is the existence of shared knowledge that guides many peoples' lives here.

☯

**Peggy Rosen**, Shanghai
September 2003

I usually have street food for breakfast. My favorite is a type of crepe made on a huge cast iron griddle over coal. The batter is spread; egg is cracked and spread over that; onion and cilantro, some other veggies, not sure what, are folded over and bean paste spread with a little hot sauce and crispy thing. It's all folded over again and chopped in half. It costs 1.8 *yuan* (approximately twenty cents). Delicious and mouth watering.

☯

**Barbara Gambini**, Shanghai
December 2000

Last Saturday I went to have dinner in one of the oldest and most reputable restaurants in Shanghai, near the Bund. I decided to taste turtle. A real delicacy, if it weren't for the fact that before cooking it, they bring it to you alive in a plastic bucket to receive your approval of the selected specimen. The very second I saw it apprehensively trying to climb up the bucket walls, and more distinctly still when I was eating it and recognized one of its paws, I had a clear vision of myself in Hell, with the turtle flogging my flesh. I am experiencing a worrying return of devotion, which is all the more worrying in that it resembles medieval superstitious faith. Do you think China may have this effect on everyone?

Be good for Christmas, and pray for my sinning soul, tarnished by the innocent blood of a helpless turtle.

**Whitney Rush**, Wanzhou
September 2009

A group of students took me to hot pot yesterday, and I think I ate every internal organ possible. I had pig brain, fish bladder (or so they told me), cow stomach, and some very slimy slices of meat that they said was pig and then just pointed to various internal organs so I'm not quite sure what that was. Some of the food almost didn't stay down, but they were putting it all in front of me so I had to try. I hope to never have brain or stomach again though.

**Mary Beth Ryan-Maher**, Kunming
September 1999

Last Friday, three of Rob's graduate students, Luke, Emily, and Natalie, came over to cook dinner and celebrate the Mid-Autumn Festival with us. The festival is a traditional family time. It is celebrated on October 15th of the lunar calendar—the full moon. On this holiday, families gather for dinner and eat moon cakes. Moon cakes are small or not so small pastries shaped like the full moon and stuffed with sugary, chewy fruit paste or ham bits. I can't quite compare them to anything I have ever eaten before, except perhaps an enlarged and ornate Fig Newton.

Emily and her "assistants" made the most scrumptious food we've eaten so far. There were about seven dishes: beer chicken, a fish soup, cabbage and vinegar, green beans, hollow vegetable with garlic, tofu and green onions, and roasted peanuts. It was a feast. Lots of ginger and lots of spicy pepper. I am growing in my tolerance for spicy foods. Rob and I learned some new ingredients, and I think it will help improve our own cooking. (We still mostly eat out!)

The students wanted to know about Western food, and we talked about some of the dishes we could prepare. They were horrified at the combination of ingredients. Natalie kept saying, "No, no, you can't do that." I don't know what we can cook for them. None of them has ever eaten pizza or spaghetti. They don't seem to like tomatoes very much. They grimaced when we mentioned putting tomato with fish or chicken. However, they also argued with each other about the food as they were cooking because they all are from different parts of China. It was a very enjoyable evening.

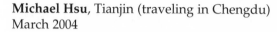

**Michael Hsu**, Tianjin (traveling in Chengdu)
March 2004

Chengdu has a lot going for it: wide streets, fantastic food, and great night-life. If you like hot and spicy food, Sichuan is the place to go to lose several layers of tongue to the effects of peppers that work like the most delicious blend of turpentine, Novocain, and hydrochloric acid you'll ever eat. Hot pot restaurants, where damp-chilled locals dip meat and vegetables, fondue-style, into cauldrons of fiery red oil, are almost always packed. In Chengdu, there actually is nightlife. There is a "scene" in the area immediately surrounding the university. It includes a Tex-Mex grill, an Italian restaurant, an Australian bar, and even a club for the real hipsters. Yes, there are a surprising number of Western restaurants, *good* Western restaurants, in Chengdu—the result, I think, of the large number of Westerners. This is the result, I think, of the high number of beautiful girls. They are another source of pride to the people of the Four Rivers (means Sichuan Province). The women have perfect porcelain skin, a result of that perpetual cloud cover and gloom.

*The "craving" for Western food cannot be underestimated. Mine kicked in the first month when I found a restaurant that featured, it said, Mexican food. I had to have it. I dragged my reluctant husband, who was perfectly content eating only Chinese food, to the restaurant. I ordered "nachos." The plate arrived: corn flakes (only to be confused with corn chips in China), a meager amount of melted cheese, some hot sauce, and a stray bean. I ate every bite.*

*At the same time, foreign teachers wish to share some typical "American" foods with their students.*

**Mary Barton**, Nanjing
June 2004

My students watched the movie *My Big Fat Greek Wedding*, which mentions Wonder Bread sandwiches. This I explained in detail, but I even went a step further. I brought all the fixins to class to make three different kinds of sandwiches: peanut butter and banana; peanut butter and jam; ham and cheese. They had a great time making and sampling the different kinds of sandwiches. The peanut butter and banana won hands down (my favorite). Only one downside, I brought only enough bread to make thirty-five sandwiches, and they wanted more!

**Whitney Rush**, Wanzhou
April 2010

I invited students over to bake cookies. They kept asking me if they could go to the market. I told them I had all the ingredients, but they were wondering if they could pick up meat or vegetables! I'm not sure they understood the whole cookie concept. Making the cookies was hilarious. They were shocked at the ingredients going in, were disgusted when I suggested they try the batter, and they kept trying to make one large cookie, as opposed to many small ones. They did all say it was delicious in the end.

*Food is a flash point. You will never know the lengths you are willing to go to obtain a turkey on Thanksgiving until you have lived in a foreign country. As good fortune would have it, my father-in-law served us a full Thanksgiving dinner in August before we flew to China. How prescient was that? Turkey is just not on the menu in China.*

*Holidays provide an opportunity to share typical US holiday customs with Chinese students and friends, but it isn't always as easy as it may seem. As Mat Brown writes, "Not one Chinese student in any of my classes has ever eaten turkey. Never eaten turkey? Try to explain what it looks like, tastes like, how to cook it, and you will definitely want to eat some."*

**Catt Stearns**, Wanzhou
November 2009

Halloween was this past Saturday. All the foreign teachers hosted the Halloween party and each of our apartments had a different theme/activity. I immediately volunteered to host the dance party and got to work making the ultimate dance party play list complete with the YMCA, the electric slide, the limbo, the Macarena, and other classic hits to make even the shyest of the shy bust a move. Overall, it was a success! My living room was packed; the students were enthusiastic; and I really think every ridiculous dance move I showed them (i.e., mashed potatoes and the sprinkler) they thought was probably really hip and happening in the United States. I can now only hope these magical moves will start to gain popularity. That night I danced for practically two hours straight because I noticed that every time I stopped dancing everyone slowed down or stopped. I danced my legs off, but it was worth every moment to give the students a little taste and open up their world to what a dance party or even just a small house party in the States is really like. Now, that is what teaching is all about.

**Ryan Noll**, Nanjing
November 2009

This is my first major holiday away from my family and home. It is weird because I know it's Thanksgiving, but it doesn't feel like it. During English

Corner this past Wednesday, the students surprised me with a gift. I graciously accepted the gift, but I had to explain to them that we don't really give gifts on Thanksgiving. That's more of a Christmas thing. I opened the gift, and it was quite funny. It was a picture frame, but on the frame part was light blue fabric and ribbons that poofed like the sleeves of a 1980s prom dress. It was great. I think I can put pictures of puppies or kittens in it. Overall, it was the thought that counted. I was sort of surprised they knew the day of Thanksgiving and considered making China more like home for me by having a tiny celebration. Afterward, we got in a big circle and said the things we are thankful for. Most of the students thanked their parents, school, teachers, and friends. Some even thanked the trees, ground, and the ability to breathe air instead of water.

I am thankful that I get to spend a year in China. China has to be one of the more interesting countries in the world. It amazes and perplexes. It can make you say something like, "This is wonderful!" And then, minutes later, it can make you say, "What the $#&@!" I am thankful that I can experience a society that is in the middle of some major changes. Most of its citizens are excited about this change. When I asked my students whether they would want to stay in China or move to the United States if they had the chance, most responded that they would stay in China. They don't want to miss the development of their country, and they all want to do their part for a better China. I don't know if this would have been the same response several years ago. It will be interesting to see what direction this enormous and changing country heads in the next few years.

I am thankful that my Chinese students listen to everything I say and are eager to do the activities. I am thankful that every time I show something from back home they are amazed and there is a collective, "Woah!" I am thankful that after I showed my students how to carve a jack-o-lantern during my Halloween lecture, one of my students received a jack-o-lantern from her friends for her birthday that fell on October 31st. She said it is a birthday she will never forget. I am thankful that during my University Life lecture some of my students had previously heard of some University of Kansas basketball players as far back as Wilt Chamberlain. When I showed Paul Peirce of the Boston Celtics, there was a round of applause. I am thankful that on my sick day some students sent texts wishing me better health.

I am thankful for the restaurant across the street that serves great *kung pao* chicken and eggplant. I am thankful for the noodle guy that cooks on the street and remembers my order. I am thankful for delightful meat on a stick, potato on a stick, mushroom on a stick, and bread on a stick. I am thankful that I can get fried dumplings on the corner past midnight. I am thankful for Shanghai Street which is lined with a Mexican restaurant, sandwich shop, Turkish restaurant, and several western bars and stores. I am thankful that it only took me two weeks to learn how to use chopsticks. Still, those noodles can be tricky.

I am thankful for all the great people that are here with me. I am thankful I have old friends only an hour bus ride away. I am thankful for all the new friends I have made. I am thankful there is at least one other foreigner in Pukou that I can talk to and watch *Blues Brothers* with on a Wednesday night. I am thankful that my colleague was able to find a real turkey for Thanksgiving dinner at her apartment—complete with stuffing! I am thankful that I found some Chinese students that actually play Ultimate Frisbee. I am thankful that I found some Chinese students actually willing to teach me Chinese. Slow and steady wins the race with that one. I am thankful for Skype that will let me talk face to face with my parents every Monday night.

I am thankful that China has so much to do and see. I am thankful that I get to properly travel and experience a different culture. I am thankful for this opportunity and the experience that was made possible by the Colorado China Council.

**Mat Brown**, Tianjin
November 2000

I am sitting here thinking about Thanksgiving, watching *The Patriot* and feeling quite American. Talking about the tradition all week has made me think about it more than I wanted to, and you have to talk about food—it's a big part of the day. Most of my upper level students know what turkey is, and that Americans eat it on this day, but not one Chinese student in any of my classes has *ever* eaten turkey. Never eaten turkey? Try to explain what it looks like, tastes like, how to cook it, and you will definitely want to eat some. I have been out on a mission in town for the week to find a turkey. Originally, I was planning to cook one for one of my classes, but this city is *mei you* (not have). I even went to the expensive Western grocery store, and they said they had a turkey, but to me it looked like a very small chicken with the label of a turkey. Pathetic. At least after some of my own research, I understand why my students have never seen or eaten turkey. For Thanksgiving here, a bunch of the Americans (both teachers and students) are going to this Western restaurant called City Slickers. (Love the name, and yes, it is from the movie.) It will be rather expensive, but the guy advertised for weeks that he was going to fly in turkeys from the United States. I hope that he is flying in someone to cook them too!

**Michael Hsu**, Tianjin
November 2003

Happy Turkey Day!
This evening, the other American teacher on the CCC program and I invited our students and some of our other friends (mostly from the MBA grad

student posse) to our apartment building's restaurant for a Thanksgiving feast. It had been a surprisingly difficult chore tracking down a turkey in this town of millions. I eventually had the manager of the apartment building make arrangements with the fancy-schmancy Sheraton Hotel in Tianjin to roast a turkey in the grand Western style. This afternoon a car was sent to the hotel to pick up the guest of honor, as if it were a visiting foreign dignitary. It certainly had a VIP price on its head. (Don't ask how much that damn bird cost.)

But, at any rate, about thirty people, at round tables of ten persons each, enjoyed the strangest "traditional" Thanksgiving meal this Pilgrim has ever seen. The turkey, which certainly looked like the roasted birds of my childhood, also had that familiar dry and solid texture to its meat, but it was not moisturized with cranberry sauce or gravy (even though I asked for "meat juice"). So, we flavored the essentially tasteless breast meat with what we could dredge up from the restaurant, mainly plates of ketchup and soy sauce. Dippin' delicious!

The sweet potatoes were not pureed and flavored with cream, butter, marshmallows, or brown sugar or anything of the sort. They came individually wrapped in tin foil. The "pumpkin pies" turned out to be little, round, Oreo-sized pumpkin "cakes" filled with red bean paste and fried to a greasy crisp. No hearty slices dolloped with Cool Whip here, folks.

At least the mashed potatoes tasted like mashed potatoes, except here in China, this dish is treated as a "cold dish," an appetizer. The sturdy mound of cold potatoes was dressed up for the festive occasion with a layer of rainbow-colored sprinkles. You know, the candy sprinkles usually seen on birthday cupcakes, sugar cookies, and vanilla cones.

These "traditional" Thanksgiving dishes were supplemented by an array of Chinese foods, including lo-mein noodle soup, braised eggplant, pepper steak, boiled peanuts, and crispy tofu. We washed it down with tea or some fiery Chinese "white liquor," a kind of liquid death that could power a riding lawnmower.

I am not sure my guests enjoyed all the strange food and bland turkey, but it was a wonderful time nonetheless. Put vibrant Chinese people around tables laden with food and you have a loud, raucous party. Guaranteed.

As I sit here writing about this East-meets-West feast, a startling thought came to me. Columbus went looking for the passage to Asia; instead, he found North America and eternally placed the unfortunate mis-label of "Indian" on the Native Americans. Thus began the slow (some say too fast) process of Europe's invasion of the New World, which included the arrival of the Puritans and the alleged First Thanksgiving of 1621. What if, what if Columbus actually made his way to Asia? What if Columbus and those Orient-seeking explorers had landed on the shores of the Asian continent instead of the North American coast? Would the subsequent colonization and settlement have taken place on the edges of Asia? Then the Pilgrims, at their Thanksgiving gathering, would not have been feasting on the turkey, pumpkins, and potatoes native to America with the Native Americans. They would most likely have been dining on noodles and tofu and tea with Native Asians. Native Asians . . . like the Chinese and their rocket-fuel liquor! Just another idea to chew on as you digest your dinner and trip on tryptophan.

**Tim Gerber**, Shanghai
November 20005

I got up early and had breakfast then met my bike guide, Melody, a local with a photographic memory of all the trails surrounding Yangshuo. I told Melody for Thanksgiving I wanted her to take me "way into the mountains" where no other tourist bikers go. I was fit from riding the past couple of days and felt up to it. Away we went, out and out and out into those gorgeous karst mountains.

We came across an unusual mountain pass full of pine trees (getting me in a holiday mood) and biked past a village. I declined having lunch there saying that I really wanted to get out into the Chinese countryside. Melody smiled and said, "Okay, *zouba* (let's go)." About two hours later, we found ourselves in stunning countryside, universes removed from civilization. No power lines, no traffic, no cars, no airplanes overhead—just peace and quiet. The only noise you could hear was the gentle sloshing of the water buffaloes the farmers used to plow their fields as the powerful beasts tromped through the surrounding streams. No other humans to be seen or heard anywhere!

The only downside was that since I had forsaken lunch hours ago, we now found ourselves literally out in the middle of nowhere (which was wonderful) and very hungry with seemingly nowhere to eat (which was not so wonderful). Melody said there was a small block of homes around the bend in the mountains, and that perhaps we could ask one of the villagers there to cook us a basic meal for a small payment. When we reached the homes, everyone appeared to be out in the fields. This was not good. Then like a miracle, Melody heard someone calling her name. It was a woman she knew from Yangshuo. The woman just happened to be visiting her mother that day who lived in this small mountain farm community. The woman proceeded to invite us into her mother's house. She took us into the kitchen area that looked very much like a cave! We sat on the stone floor as she started throwing things into prehistoric looking black pots that she had over an open fire. Curious hens peeked their heads in from the outside, and a couple of pigs snorted happily in a pen behind us (i.e., the ultimate Charlotte's Web farm experience).

I don't know what the woman put into our "Thanksgiving" late afternoon feast, but whatever it was turned out to be one of the most delicious meals I had in China. As was the Gerber family tradition, I decided to take a little hike around the mountain to walk off my Thanksgiving feast. Melody advised me to stick to the path so as not to get lost. On my own, I took a jaunt around the mountain bend. Again, no sounds except for the water buffaloes. I literally felt like I was on the moon, so removed from modern Chinese civilization. Yet, stunningly, I bumped into a woman who was headed the other way down the mountain path. Clearly, by her reaction, I was definitely the first foreigner she had ever seen out in these parts. Shortly, I headed back, and Melody said we had to get going because with our long journey back we would be fighting to get home before night and darkness fell.

Our friend suggested that we take "a shortcut" through the mountains, which turned out to be an ancient stone path built by Chinese farmers between the mountains to get quickly from the high mountain villages to the valley below. We put our bikes over our shoulders and hiked forty-five minutes down the stone stairs. When I asked Melody how old the steps were, she said "very, very old," which in American terms means about one or two hundred years, but to the Chinese means at least a thousand years. Eventually, we entered the valley and found a bike path that would take us back to Yangshuo. As dusk turned into night, we pedaled into town and my favorite Thanksgiving Day, deep in the magical mountains of China, had come to an end.

*At Christmas, I rather longed for an escape from all the tradition, but I had hundreds of Chinese students who were keen on learning Christmas carols. As much as I enjoy the mood of "Silent Night," I do not recommend it for English as a Foreign Language purposes in China. The pronunciation difficulties, not to mention translation complexity with lines like "Round yon Virgin, Mother and Child / Holy infant so tender and mild," put me into some ambiguous territory. Quaking shepherds, heavenly hosts, and redeeming grace, oh my. Happy holidaze.*

**Michael Hsu**, Tianjin
December 2003

The past few days have been surreal. On the night of the 23rd, we hosted a Christmas party for our students. Goofy games (musical chairs and one that involved a lot of barely organized chaos and balloons popping) gave way to a failed attempt to get Chinese people to dance. That gave way to karaoke, of course, and that eventually led to me straining and screaming through "Bohemian Rhapsody," complete with air guitar. Another American friend mumbled through "Ob La Di, Ob La Da," and our friend from Africa gave an emotional rendition of "Knockin' On Heaven's Door." His Korean girlfriend sang a Korean song. Our German friend brought a bunch of her students (who are learning German), and there were some strange conversations going on that mixed German, Chinese, and English. And some unidentified French showed up later.

December 2003

And what happened on Christmas Day? My colleague and I went to a Western supermarket to buy some German beer as a present for our German friend. There we were accosted by a woman wearing black eye shadow and a freaky fur coat, who it turned out, is the only English DJ/host at Tianjin TV and Radio. She also happens to be from Cincinnati, Ohio. My colleague is from Columbus, and I was born in Hamilton, Ohio. Three Ohioans standing in the liquor aisle of a tiny Western supermarket in Tianjin, China, on Christmas Day. She interviewed us about our Christmas traditions and recorded it for her radio show. Then, she bought some pickles and ranch dressing and left.

Later in the afternoon, one of my MBA friends brought a friend over to seek some English help. We ended up on the Food and Drug Administration website with me trying to help this young woman register her company's food-processing facility with the US government. Some sort of barley-beer distillery.

Right after that, one of my students, who is a literary theory teacher, and one of my colleague's students, who is a social psychology teacher, came over to wish me a Merry Christmas. The couple made a "love connection" because of our English class.

Right after that surprise visit, we went to another teacher's apartment for a Christmas dinner. He lives with a fellow Minnesotan and his girlfriend, a Taiwanese American from California's "Inland Empire," who bustled about, hustling food in and dirty plates out. She had worked all afternoon making pot roast, au gratin potatoes, salad, focaccia bread, cream of broccoli soup, sangria, chocolate cookies, and from-scratch pumpkin pie. When she finally stopped buzzing about and sat down, she spent the rest of the evening chain-smoking.

Today, I will go see some students stage a theatrical version of Dickens' *A Christmas Carol* in German.

Christmas in China, only just as strange as any other day here.

**Tim Lehmann**, Nanjing
January 2008

Greetings and Happy New Year(s) all around! It is a uniquely bizarre experience to celebrate two New Years. Really, my new year has been beginning now for more than a month. For a while, I was in a limbo between one New Year which had begun, and another, which had yet to be. Which calendar I was supposed to recognize left me in a confused funk. I approached each celebration with a sort of mild—almost indifferent—interest, as though I was observing two foreign cultures, and that my real new year was somewhere in between or maybe somewhere else. Of course, I realized quickly, and with the waning delight that a growing American has about most holidays, that nothing changes but numbers and animal symbols anyway, so what does it matter? Just the same, the collective world seems to now agree that a new year has indeed begun.

**Eva Tam**, Fuzhou
February 2007

Last night was Chinese New Year's Eve, and the foreign teachers were invited to Aiyi's house (our cook) for a dinner with her family. We had plenty to eat. There was fish, crab, different types of clams, crab cakes, rice cakes with crab, shrimp, duck, chicken, lamb, and the list goes on. There was so much food left over! When she kept bringing out the dishes, everyone said, "Stop, there's too much food. It's going to go to waste!" Aiyi, being the cheerful hostess, with a smile just replied, "Try a little of everything then." Eating Chinese food and seeing Aiyi with her family made me miss mine, but I'm lucky to have had the experience of dining with a Chinese family during the Chinese New Year.

**Cilla Bosnak Shindell**, Nanjing
February 2003

The celebration of Valentine's Day is a very, very new practice by the Chinese. I gather that only in the last few years has it become popular, and it has become wildly so. They celebrate it the same way as in the United Sates, and are very, very excited about it and the symbols of sharing one's love. They give flowers, candy, and go out to dinner. The *waiban* told us he tried to find a restaurant to take his wife to because they were just married last year, but they couldn't get into a nice one because of Valentine's Day crowding. In downtown Nanjing, the flower shops were full of amazingly beautiful flowers. You saw young couples arm in arm strolling along the busy streets. A few women carried single roses encased in plastic protectors as if the flower was a scepter. A few lucky girls promenaded with huge bouquets of flowers cradled in their arms, each flower individually wrapped, and swaddled in tissue paper tinted in the palest colors. I saw one girl with at least three-dozen yellow roses, which filled her arms, accompanied by a slightly sheepish young man. Another girl, who was simply movie star gorgeous with pale luminous skin and long jet-black hair, walked proudly, almost smugly, with an enormous bouquet in pink tissue paper. From what I understand, Chinese people traditionally avoid any overt demonstration of love, so these very visible gifts and practices mark a big change in social practices.

The next day was the Lantern Festival, which marks the end of the month-long New Year's Festival. In the evening, we took a bus to the Confucius Temple area, which seems to be the main gathering spot for public celebrations. In this area, which is characterized by smaller, narrow pedestrian-only streets, a river runs past the temple, and a viewing area is set up on the other side so that the public can see the lantern display mounted on the side of the temple. Small boats, filled with people, scuttle back and forth in front of the display, giving those lucky people a closer view. The "lanterns" are in fact illuminated sculptures. They seem to be made of hundreds of bits and pieces of brightly colored silk, stretched on bamboo frames, and lit from within. In front of the temple, there were enormous goats (this is the Year of the Goat), surrounded by a beautiful blue neon sculpture of crashing waves and circling seagulls that flickered on and off, giving movement to the waves and flight to the gulls. We crossed an arched bridge, which was lined with hundreds of fat red- and gold-colored lanterns, into the temple itself, where the really beautiful lanterns were on display. They were on a bed of blue-green waves—all in silk, all illuminated, all amazingly detailed. The entrance fee to the interior temple was twenty-five *yuan* (about three dollars), where there were three or four courtyards full of silk in every color of the rainbow, with each piece edged in gilded bamboo. Breathtaking. And to cap off the evening, we were interviewed by the local television station. It was a little confusing because the reporter, who started asking questions in English, grew excited and finished the questions in Chinese. So we smiled and tried to say nice things about the beautiful festival and wished good luck to the people of Nanjing. It was broadcast last night. Fortunately, they didn't use our words, but did show us looking at the lanterns.

## PERSONAL INTERACTIONS

*A distinct advantage of teaching in China is the opportunity to spend time with and talk to dozens of people of all ages. As a teacher, you live in close proximity to your students, and this affords a more authentic intersection with Chinese culture.*

**Christopher Angell**, Nanjing
October 2007

In the "Chinese Stereotypes of Americans" category, here are a few of the first questions I have received from students regarding life in my home country:

1. Do you have a gun? Does every person in America have a gun?
2. Is it true that in American primary schools they hand out condoms to students?

*Sophie Lewis making friends. Photo by Tim Lewis.*

3. Can you tell me what you think about the practice of running around the campus "with body uncovered?"
4. If I visit America, will I make friends if I am not white?

As I navigate the waters of international diplomacy in trying to answer these questions, I can't help but think about the image of American culture that is being projected around the world through the lens of popular media. The most popular shows amongst my students are "Prison Break," "Lost," "Sex in the City," "Friends," and "The Simpsons." My students know that the TV image of America is exaggerated, but they don't know by how much. So they are endlessly curious about what life is really like in the United States.

February 2008

Since I am a foreigner, I am something of a novelty and a source of wonder for almost everyone. My American colleagues and I have joked about never leaving China because we are "superstars" here. Just walking up and down the street in Nanjing is an experience because unlike Shanghai and Beijing, there are not many foreigners here. It is not unusual for people to stare at me as though I had just landed from Mars.

This translates into tremendous popularity among the students, who as I've said, are endlessly curious about America and the West. Interacting with them outside of class takes up most of my remaining time. I am invited to lunch or dinner, or lunch *and* dinner, at least four or five times a week, and it's almost impossible to walk around on the campus without bumping into someone who wants to chat. To be clear, this is not a burden. Just about all of my students are polite and respectful, and this makes it difficult to cut them short, even if I am in a hurry. It's really a wonderful problem to have!

**Brian E. Lewis**, Tianjin
August 2002

Things are picking up. There are three other teachers here from my program (CCC) and the teacher from last year bequeathed us a few useful items: a DVD player, kitchen equipment, speakers (now hooked up to my Walkman), and a Chinese friend. Our new Chinese friend, Qiaoyan, is twenty-eight-years old and was very close to the CCC teacher here the year before. She speaks very good English, and last evening she came over to our abode. We spent an hour practicing Chinese with her, and then about an hour and a half chatting in English. She said that the previous teacher had influenced her very much. She said that before meeting her, she had been very focused on working hard and saving as much money as possible in order to get a nice house and a better standard of living. Now, however, she feels that it is okay to spend money on things that you would like to do, such as travel. I thought that this was very interesting, and of all the ways that an American could transform a Chinese, perhaps one of the least damaging. At the same time, it also reminded me of why the government sometimes fears contact with foreigners: among friends, ideas do spread. Granted, all the teacher did to Qiaoyan was make her lazy and selfish, just like an American, but it's a short step from there to counter-revolution, I guess. Will they fight for their right to be lazy? Only time will tell.

The conversation also served to show that the Chinese are not necessarily as oppressed as we often believe. Certainly, they have nowhere near the expressive freedoms that we neglect and abuse, but I've found many Chinese here to have no fear in what they say. Perhaps that has something to do with being a foreigner, and perhaps it is easier to speak your mind to someone who is not really a part of your society and not plugged in to its subtle networks. As a foreigner, your very presence changes the things that you are trying to observe, as any cultural anthropologist can tell you. Qiaoyan was talking about how much she enjoys using the Internet. She uses it mainly to read news, mostly Chinese news sources but some English ones as well. She feels, and I agree to an extent, that the West reports only China's problems and failures, not its successes. On the other hand, she does feel that China should pay more attention to human rights issues. She loves China, and so do most Chinese. They are very nationalistic, and partly because of their painful history in regards to the West, they are very sensitive about respect. So long as China and the Chinese feel that they are not being treated respectfully, there will never be a truly stable or warm relationship between China and the West.

Flipside: Americans are very well-liked here. Bush is detested, and American foreign policy jeered, but individual Americans themselves are highly popular. Bill Clinton, amusingly, is exceptionally well thought of and his face often appears in ads of all sorts, without his knowledge, I presume. One of the foreign teachers here who teaches the history of Chinese-American relations told me the other day that if Clinton wanted, he could probably be Premier of the People's Republic. Qiaoyan says that almost all Chinese prefer to learn English from Americans and shun Australians most of all (there are a lot of Australians here; Australia and China, due to proximity, have closer ties than most countries have with China). Qiaoyan also noted that there are a great many Japanese students studying Chinese at the university. She said that they do not treat the Chinese with respect.


September 2002

Sunday we met up with Qiaoyan at her apartment. My colleague wishes to learn to cook Chinese food, and Qiaoyan had arranged for her elderly neighbors to teach us all how to cook dumplings. Dumplings are the regional specialty of the North, and particularly of Tianjin.

We presented ourselves at Qiaoyan's at three o'clock Sunday afternoon. The apartment building looked like a rotting log, and we were the flies as we mounted the stairs to the fifth floor. The interesting thing about China's stance on dirt and filth is that it is okay as long as it's all outside. By the way, everyone in China seems to live on the fifth floor. In my month here, I have never had occasion to visit any other floor anywhere else. For all I know, the elevator buttons for the other floors are some sort of decorative touch.

To continue, I was at first put off by the fierce stench and layers of soot and grit which varnished the building, and I was left to imagine what the inside could only look like. But the apartments are spotless. Frequently they are bare concrete on the inside, but they are kept clean, tidy, and efficient. After meeting her, we were led to the neighbor's apartment. I can't remember the grandmother's name, but the grandfather was Mr. Liu (pronounced Lee-oh). Neither spoke English. Liu is seventy years old and a retired mechanical engineer whose work brought him at one point to West Germany, presumably back when there was a West Germany. He was about my height (rather tall for a Chinese, though there are more than a few quite a bit taller), and appeared to always be smiling, especially when he wasn't. His wife was very friendly, near to him in age but with all her hair still black. Time had left her fairly well alone, save to remove her two front teeth in some sort of weird recompense for the un-aged hair.

With them were their two grandchildren, who were learning English from Qiaoyan: Jessica and Jeff, ages twelve and thirteen, respectively. The two elders would be our dumpling *laoshi* (teachers).

Making dumplings begins with the dough, which is made of refined rice flour and water, mixed slowly by hand and kneaded thoroughly. It is then left to stand for about an hour. During this time, the filling is prepared. First, you fill a small bowl, say, bathtub-sized, with finely minced pork. To this, you add a generous amount of soy sauce, which is stirred in evenly. To answer your question, soy sauce is never, *ever* put out on the table as a condiment, and don't ask for any. They take that seriously. Soy sauce is used as a base in many foods, kind of the way we might use salt or chicken broth. But you don't add it to food after it's been cooked because that's insulting and just plain weird. If you want to add something, use one of the three varieties of well-aged vinegar that you will see on the table. Now that's good eats.

At this point, I should describe the other ingredients for dumpling mix. There is a large bowl of bite-sized shrimp. A bowl of stalky, leafy greens called *baicai*, which is like a mix between celery and spinach, is quite oily when cooked, and generally tasty. A bowl of green onion, a bowl of garlic, and a bowl of large, soft brown mushrooms, exceedingly fresh. There are also a few pieces of ginger root. Lastly, there is a bowl of long, tubular things, very oily and slimy, slit along one side, about the same color as feces. Repeated inquiries yield nothing more than that they are some kind of animal or animal product. To me, they look like intestines, which are very popular here and are harvested from almost any animal. Pig and cow are favorites. Incidentally, the restaurant in my dorm serves duck tongues and sparrow gizzards. Guess what you're all getting for Christmas.

So, faced with these intestines, my eagerness to taste dumpling has lost something. It loses more when a dictionary consultation proves them not to be intestines, but sea cucumbers, which are very much like intestines that have somehow separated from their host and gone their own way in the world. I shall never forget my first encounter with sea cucumbers in my seventh grade biology class. Sea cucumbers are seagoing invertebrates, which are fairly long and lumpy and in general shape resemble, well, a cucumber. They have the delightful habit of spewing their intestinal and digestive tract out their mouths when threatened, then drawing them back in. I have long lived in fear of meeting one, and as it turns out, they've been invited to dinner. It occurs to me that in one of life's little ironies, when assailed by a sea cucumber, it is I who will spew my digestive tract in a defensive maneuver. Since Mr. Liu is blocking the door and holding a very large knife, I return to dumpling making. The mushrooms, onions, garlic, and sea nasties are minced and added, one at a time, to the witches' brew of pork, then topped off with a hearty dose of sesame oil, which is quite good when it isn't mingling with sea nasty.

Now, it was time to fill the dumplings. The dough was rolled out, and walnut-sized pieces torn off. These were then rolled into small circles. Using chopsticks, the pork-paste we made earlier is spread on rather thickly, and the dough then folded up into a taco shape and tightly pressed closed. There is a proper technique to this because none of the filling should ooze out the seam or otherwise peek out, and the seam must be tight as these are to be boiled. I asked rather idly if these dumplings can also be pan fried (as you usually find them in America; I asked because in many cases certain foods though outwardly similar are customarily cooked only in certain ways) which prompted them to promise me that several dozen would be pan-fried especially for me. I kept trying to persuade them that this was unnecessary, but it was no use, the damage was done and several daughters-in-law were dispatched to procure oil. I think that in traditional families, the third junior daughter-in-law was in charge of oil, but the smaller modern Chinese family has been forced to make the first daughter-in-law shoulder this burden, just one of the many tragic consequences of the One-Child system.

Mr. Liu is a master dumpling maker and passed amused judgment on our attempts. He kept holding out his fingers in such a way as to make a sixty, which was our percentage grade on the dumpling-meter. He would often show the proper way to cradle a dumpling between your fingers when pinching, fold them over softly, and then press, gruntin' loudly for emphasis. I eventually found my own way of folding in the corners and then pressing the top, which seemed to pass the inspector general's muster. It took about two hours or so to fill all the dumplings. There were a lot of dumplings. They were then boiled, except for the two bushels they fried up for my pleasure. As it turns out, I like the fried ones more, so I was happy for that after all. By the way, the boiling/frying process rendered the sea nasties completely tasteless and invisible; I suspected that without their intestines to protect them they were helpless before the heat. As a matter of fact, the dumplings were incredibly delicious and quite filling, especially when you dump red hot chili oil all over them like I did. Mr. Liu was quite impressed with my taste for the hot stuff and had a hearty laugh when I suggested to him that I would like to drink it straight from the jar.

Now, apparently the daughters-in-law also procured beer because Mr. Liu straight away began pouring me some. He toasted me, and then we drank. Now, when I say we drank, what I mean is that we drained our glasses in one go because the Chinese version of "Cheers" is *gan bei* (gahn bay) and means, more or less, empty or dry your glass, which Mr. Liu interpreted literally. Also, Chinese beer comes in two sizes: individual cans (never, ever six packs and definitely not in bottles) or in large bottles, about the size and shape of wine bottles. He and I accounted for five of these bottles with no flinching. *Gan bei, gan bei, gan bei.* In China, the person being toasted has to drink; this frequently degenerates into a game. One's skill as a drinker is measured not only by one's tolerance but the cunning with which you can maneuver your opponents into having to drink while you sit out. Now, Mr. Liu got the drop on me, but I happen to know how to toast in Chinese, so it was right back at him. At some point, my colleague nudged me and said, "I think you've bonded," and I think she was right. He was grinning at me, and I was grinning right back, happy as I'd ever been. I didn't understand his Chinese, and he didn't get some of mine, but we had a great time. He told me about his trip to Lushan, where his son was married, and showed me all the photographs of him at various peaks on the mountain and its many temples, and all sorts of things.

Then things got serious. He drew himself up very solemnly (showing no sign of intoxication) and asked me if I liked *baijiu*. Now, *baijiu* is a very potent Chinese liquor, about 52 percent alcohol, and is apparently some sort of petroleum by-product (okay, I made that part up). I had never had it, but rumors of its existence lurk in China travel stories the way dragons do in medieval legend. Old maps of China read, "Here there be *baijiu*." *Baijiu* is what Chinese use when they're trying to get a foreigner really, really drunk. So of course I told him I'd love to have some. He very excitedly broke out a new bottle and poured each of us a little of the strong smelling stuff, perfectly clear as spring water. I brought it up to my mouth, and hesitated a little. "*He man, he man* (drink slowly)," he said. You're damn right. I sipped a little. It was a little oily, very pungent, but slightly sweet. I liked it instantly. Now, here was a drink for a real man. Sign me up. "I like it," I said. "I truly like it!" My enthusiasm was plain even through my rough Chinese, and we commenced to drink about half of the bottle. Mr. Liu and I continued to play our little game of Toast/Counter-Toast, until finally he said, "This is the last drink." Then he gave me one of his cigarettes, and we had a good smoke. He invited me to come back anytime, and suggested that I might like teaching his grandchildren English. Everyone got very quiet, and Qiaoyan looked at me wide-eyed.

There's something in China called *guanxi*, "connections." When someone does something for you or vice versa, you're building *guanxi* between you. It means that you're forming closer ties, and that you can expect certain levels of help from one another. Gift giving is involved also. If a gift is large or of sufficient value, it may imply that a major request is in the batting circle. The various levels, rules, applications, and cashing out of *guanxi* is very complicated, even to the Chinese, and Americans are advised to avoid making lavish gestures or accepting them for fear of obligating their Chinese friends or themselves to requests they may be unwilling or unable to fulfill.

So when Mr. Liu asked me about teaching his grandchildren English, my friend was tense because their dumpling seminar was of a sufficient level of hospitality that we might within reason be felt to be in their debt. She took great pains to make it clear to them that we were not obligated to teach English, which is what most Chinese covet in a foreigner. I paused a moment before replying. What I said could sour the evening, smooth things over, or entrap me in an ever-deepening spiral of *guanxi*. Now, when I write the book of my travels here, I'll insert something very simple and profound into my mouth. But what I actually said was much more prosaic. I thanked him, told him that I had no objection to helping his grandchildren, who seemed quite good students, but that my obligations to my university took priority, and that I could not promise any sort of systematic help. I also pointed out that in my friend they already had a capable teacher. This answer seemed to appease him, and my student suggested that he was drunk and/or joking anyway. I didn't care. I liked him and his family, and he'd shown me great kindness. I told him I owed him a bottle of *baijiu*. "No," said grandma, "There's enough liquor in this house already."

It was time to go, and Mr. Liu offered me one more shot of *baijiu*, which I took on condition of his having one too, since he was my revered *baijiu laoshi* (teacher). We had one last drink; I finished my cigarette, put on my Yankees cap and headed for the door. On the way out, he flipped us off with both hands. On second glance, he was making the sign for one hundred, indicating our final score at his Dumpling University. The Chinese have a system of hand signals for numbers that are quite difficult to discern at first, and this one happens to involve the thumbs and both middle fingers. I thanked him heartily, shook his hand, walked down the completely unlit steps, kicked a rat, unlocked my bike, and rode off into the Chinese night.

And that's why I came to China. Dumplings are on me when I get back.

**Jeanne S. Phillips**, Fuzhou
November 1999

Officialdom still expects to get away with little advance planning and peremptory summonses. Typically, we will hear of some provincial banquet that we *must* attend for the honor of our college only a day or two ahead. Even events that some official agency wants us to attend for the publicity and seeming access to foreigners we generate are announced only a few days ahead at best. My young Chinese colleagues just laugh when they hear that the "Salon," sponsored by a sort of Chamber of Commerce and a Friendship with Foreigners group turned out to be one hundred fifty plus students and self-taught seekers of English proficiency with whom we and other gullible Westerners were expected to chat up, one of us to each table, for two hours, after a series of dull speeches.

Anyway, the lack of advance planning, which amazes me in the land of Five Year Plans, seems widespread and eradicable. I went to a wedding last Friday, having received the invitation a week ahead because the bride is a colleague and knows well our strange expectations about advance notice.

What I haven't figured out is what hierarchy and what meaning attaches to the cancellations that result from these frequent last-minute demands.

Clearly, the city and provincial government expect to trump all other commitments, and since this works, why should they plan? But no one seems to take umbrage when one calls to say someone else has bumped a date one has with the callee, seemingly regardless of who the bumper is, in contrast to the slight and annoyance most Westerners feel if a social commitment is changed in favor of another person at the last minute unless the special nature of the bumper excuses such rudeness and its message of lower importance.

I do know that businessmen are similarly relaxed about intrusions. I once visited the manager of a very successful printing firm with a thank you gift for a big favor. I brought a good friend along to interpret. Once in his office, I discovered I was interrupting a visiting Hong Kong printer who was looking into subcontracting some of his work, who in turn had interrupted the manager of a local five-star hotel who was thinking of placing an order for a lot of his paper work. We all had tea; I chatted with the Hong Kong printer and was invited to visit his plant and home next time I was in Hong Kong; my friend chatted with the hotel manager and was invited to help train the hotel staff in basic hotel English; and the printer host just beamed and poured more tea. After my initial embarrassment at interrupting serious business, I had a fine time. What a complex civilization this is!

**E. H.**, Tianjin
March 2002

My *wushu* master stopped by impromptu last night to give me some herbal medication to stick on my sprained ankle. I sprained it lightly a couple weeks ago while crossing the street in the morning to buy my breakfast. I think the thing I value the most here are the local people. Just the gesture of stopping by to see how I was feeling was beyond words.

**Christopher Angell**, Nanjing
June 2007

During a night at dinner with my student's family, the dad invited me to try some Chinese "wine," which was really grain alcohol in disguise! We both got a bit tipsy, so this helped the non-conversation to appear excellent whether we understood each other or not. Meanwhile, at the next table, a group of university students were also drinking grain alcohol, I mean, "wine," and one of them decided he wanted to join our table and talk to the foreigner. Well, this didn't sit well with the dad, my host, so while I continued talking with the mom and daughter, the "discussion" between dad and student escalated. Finally, the dad stands up and rips his shirt off!

I'm thinking, "Uh oh, here we go!" Then I notice that the dad has a coiling dragon tattoo on each breast that would make David Carradine's forearm dragons on *Kung Fu* look like cartoon characters! "Finally," I say to myself, "I'm gonna get to see some *real* martial arts right here in a restaurant! God, I *love* China!!"

Well, suffice it to say that the restaurant manager, the staff, the friends of the student, and some passersby all got involved with some pushing and shoving, but no punches were thrown. One chair was lifted above someone's head and used as a prop to demonstrate malicious intent, but it was never used. I, of course, felt very honored to be fought over, but by this time, I don't think anyone, except the mom and daughter, remembered I was even there. Of course, the night ended, as these sorts of things always seem to, with everyone apologizing and hugging each other and promising to get together again. For another scene like that? Who knows? But I am, in fact, having dinner with the family again tomorrow night.

**Brian T. Vick**, Tianjin
April 1997

My best Chinese friend here is a forty-seven-year-old steel factory worker who has been laid off due to overproduction. In my first week here, he rode by me as I was walking and shouted, "American football, can you show me?" He jumped off his bike and approached me with an outstretched hand and a magical smile. We have been getting together every week since then. He has an amazing spirit and vibrant zest for life. He is also a true Renaissance man; he can play the saxophone, trumpet, violin, harmonica, and the *erhu*, a classical Chinese stringed instrument. He knows various forms of *tai ji, gong fu,* Chinese wrestling, and he earned a law degree while he was working, and the list goes on.

His passion is American football. He has started an American football club and wants to form a league in China. I have been helping him acquire books, equipment, videos, and names of organizations that might be able to help his cause. In return, he has helped me learn *tai ji,* how to buy and play the *erhu,* and shown me how to do some Chinese cooking.

We visit each other's homes, and I think this is when we really learn about each other. He lives in a crowded and lively Chinese *danwei* (work unit/neighborhood) in a one-room home with his wife and nineteen-year-old. I never see other foreigners in this remote area, and I don't think the residents who live there do either. The weight of the stares and curiosity is heaviest here.

One of our first lessons on cultural differences involved the use of the bathroom. He was over one day and informed me that he had to go to the bathroom. We were in the kitchen, and I told him to go use the bathroom. A few minutes later I heard my Chinese name, and I went to see what the problem was. I found my friend looking at the Western toilet, looking at the sink and then at the bathtub. He held out his hands and shrugged his shoulders in confusion and said, "I just need to urinate." I told him to go in the toilet. "In the water?" he asked. "Yes, then pull the handle down," I responded. He stood there amazed, and I walked out and shut the door. I heard the toilet flush several times followed by loud bursts of laughter.

My first experience at his home was equally confusing for me. I told him I needed to use the bathroom. "Number one or number two?" he asked in Chinese. "Number one," I answered. "Okay, this way," he said as he directed me out the door. He took me outside to another small room and told me to wait. I stood and looked at all the stuff in this storage room and found nothing like the "squat" toilets I was accustomed to. The pressure in my bladder and the confusion in my brain had nearly peaked when in walked my friend with a small red bucket. "Go in here, dump it in the gutter outside, wash the bucket in this sink and put it on the floor over there," he instructed. Differences in culture are neither right nor wrong, they are just different.

Another great aspect of living in China is the foreign community. I usually play soccer, basketball, go dancing, and go to parties with people from Iran, Iraq, Africa, Russia, Korea, Japan, Slovenia, Croatia, Italy, and other countries. The fascinating aspect is that oftentimes we can only communicate in Chinese. Dancing at a disco with a friend of mine from Lesotho, Africa, a large group of Chinese formed a circle around us and stared in awe. Men dancing together is very common in China (as I have danced with more Chinese male friends than female), but I don't think they were accustomed to seeing a white man and a black man cutting some rug together while using such funky moves.

**Josh Leslie**, Chengdu
April 1999

Yesterday I attended my first wedding in China. A Chinese student and her *laowai* (foreign) groom, an Australian fellow, both of whom I met my second week here and have seen occasionally since then, invited me. The ceremony was non-existent, a courtroom-type wedding, just official stamps and paperwork. At around one o'clock, we met in a teahouse in a city park. The whole family was there, and as a result of a long-standing family feud, one half stayed on one side of the room, one half on the other. I was the photographer. I am not sure why. (Perhaps they thought a *laowai* could operate another *laowai*'s camera better or something.) We spent about five hours at the teahouse drinking tea and beer, eating sunflower seeds, chatting, and playing *mahjong*. It was a great opportunity to practice my Chinese.

Dinner was the real fun with thirty people at three tables; we had a real banquet. In China they are crazy about conserving resources, but they think nothing of ordering three or four times as much food as can be eaten. It's a great loss of face for the host to run out of food, and they don't really want to cut it close. Thus, when we sat down, they started with about ten small appetizer plates, for our table of eight. The dishes progressed from there with new and larger dishes about every two minutes for the next hour until the table was triple stacked with dishes and everyone was stuffed. No rice, it is considered a cheap filler, and don't ask for any either.

❧

**Mary Beth Ryan-Maher**, Kunming
July 2000

### Commingling: Communism and Religion

On Easter Sunday, Rob and I wandered into a Chinese Catholic Church. The church was packed, and of course, we couldn't follow the language, but thanks to the ritualistic nature of the Mass, we caught the Sign of Peace. This is the moment when US Catholics generally shake hands. Here, the custom is to bow to your neighbors.

Since the Communist Revolution, the Chinese Catholic Church is not recognized by or affiliated with Rome. The government would consider it allegiance to a foreign, imperial power. Currently, Chinese people can openly belong to a religious group; however, all of the legal churches are responsible to the central government. What about being a Christian and a Communist? Well, despite the older men with Mao hats and jackets at the Sunday Mass, it's politically a "no go." Only sixty million people in China are Communist Party Members, a small percentage of the total population.[2] And it's not easy to become a Communist! Political education begins very early, and most (maybe all) elementary school students are "Young Pioneers." On important national days, they wear their signature red kerchief around their necks. In high school, students can apply to be "League Members," and university students can apply to be full "Party Members." The application process includes writing essays on political theory, attending classes on Party history, submitting all of your academic records and several letters of introduction and recommendation from current Party Members, an interview, and even interviews with your teachers, parents, and classmates about you. To me, it sounds like much more work than applying to university or for a job in the US. So why join? It seems that Membership has its privileges. For example, certain jobs are only available to Party Members, such as positions in the Foreign Affairs Office at the university. And the most powerful person in the university is not the President, but the Party Secretary.

### Red Envelopes and Weddings

Rob and I attended the wedding of one of his graduate students held in the banquet hall of a hotel. The bride dressed in a white wedding dress (typical in the United States or Europe), and she and the groom welcomed all of the guests as we arrived. After we greeted them, and handed them a red money envelope as a gift, we were offered candy, peanuts, cigarettes, and gum. Inside, we sat at a large round table with a "lazy Susan," talked, poured drinks, ate the candy, and waited for the couple to finish greeting some two hundred guests.

When the couple came in, they went up on stage, and the hostess greeted them and invited them to say a few words. They welcomed everyone, and then the hostess asked them to tell the story of their love. Everyone laughed, and no one expected them to say anything. This would be something that they wouldn't share in public even at their wedding—a cultural impossibility. Then it was time for the hostess to tease them. She blindfolded the groom, and called up five young women. Each woman and the groom's wife would sing the same verse from a love song, and he must identify his wife by her voice. Of course, the hostess did not let the bride sing, and the groom was tricked and trapped. Everyone delighted in this. Then, dozens of dishes began arriving at our table, and it was time to eat. Various singers took the stage during the meal, and the bride changed into a traditional Chinese red silk wedding gown.

During the meal, the couple floated from table to table drinking the customary toast at each one. Another trick here is that each table gets to decide what the couple drinks, which can range from soda, juice, and beer to wine and hard liquor or a combination of it all. (I don't think the couple ate at all.) Like a US wedding, there was a photographer and videographer. Unlike a US wedding, there was no dancing, and when the meal was over everybody cleared out. (It is impolite to linger.) We went off to a teahouse for a few hours, and then the students wanted to go to the couple's house for some more good-natured teasing of the bride and groom. Interestingly, this couple had been married (on paper) for three years. However, they had not had their wedding banquet and in the eyes of their family and society in general, it's not official until after the party. Maybe it's more like an engagement period in the United States. From our experience, it seems that the couple has the party after they have their own or a new apartment. It seems a certain level of material wealth is a prerequisite.

☯

**Michael Hsu**, Tianjin
November 2003

Excerpts from Statement of Purpose for Graduate School:
China is on a roll. State media outlets breathlessly replay and review and preview every preparatory step toward the 2008 Beijing Olympics. With affable Hu Jintao at the head of government and its human rights abuses fading into the shadows, its reputation and stature continue to climb in the

global community. And, of course, it recently became only the third country to launch one of its own into orbit—on one of its own spacecraft. The
triumph of China's first man in space, Yang Liwei, is symbolic of the PRC's
sky-rocketing economic rise, but not in the ways one might suspect. China's
astronomical growth is a lot like that historic liftoff because both pack flashy
drama and grab headlines, but in the final analysis carry only a slim minority to the highest heights while leaving the vast majority on terra firma, with
moony eyes cast toward unreachable dreams.

While in Shanghai this past August for my English-teacher training, I
met "Robby," a highly educated, young Chinese professional. One day he
launched into a completely unexpected and unsolicited sociological so-
liloquy. Robby was convinced that Shanghai was full of frustrated millions.
Every day, the people see the skyscrapers rise, the neon lights flash, the department stores glow, the neighbors in their new Audi A6. The sudden and
heady rush of money has touched Shanghai too much and yet too little. Just
enough so the signs of wealth (fancy cell phone, house, and car) are easy to
see, but then not quite enough as such things are hard to have.

It is not difficult to imagine that many Shanghainese, surrounded by increasingly conspicuous symbols of prosperity and status, are suffering like
the poor Greek Tantalus, who was damned to an eternity of reaching for
delicious grapes just beyond his reach. For the Chinese people, who now
march only to the refrain "to get rich is glorious," the burst of affluence
has done little but to add more vibrant color to those juicy but unrealistic
expectations.

Countless China watchers share the view that in the Middle Kingdom,
money rules. When money rules, morality veers toward bankruptcy. In a
conversation with "Luke," one of my English students, I heard him lament
the modern saying that shows the spin of China's moral compass: "Laugh at
the poor, not at the prostitutes." In China today, it is far more shameful to
be a pauper than to sell oneself for the sake of a few *yuan*.

Luke went on to recall the years of his childhood as a happy time even
though it was a time when food and clothes were rationed by tickets and
travel from city to city was permitted only by referral forms. He said in the
old days, people would help those in need and sympathize with the impoverished but not anymore. He said in the old days, when everyone had the
same things and had so much in common, there was genuine camaraderie
among comrades. But not in the crowded Darwinian jungle of modern
China, said Luke, an MBA student, a future manager and mover-and-
shaker, a cog in the world of capital!

Indeed, as the 1.2 billion people of China join an increasingly frenzied rat
race, so many pounding feet are sure to shake the world.

☯

## CONSUMER REPORTS

*Whether you are buying train tickets, a coffee pot, or vegetables at the market, new consumer rules apply.*

**Brian E. Lewis**, Tianjin
September 2002

Monday I made a trip to Ancient Culture Street. Ancient Culture Street is a very large market in the north of the city, which specializes in items connected with China's, well, um, ancient culture. This means calligraphic scrolls, paintings, clothes, fans, jade, jewelry, statuary, seals, swords, incense, and more. This is not quite the tourist trap it seems. First, Tianjin is not really a tourist destination, so anyone who wants these kinds of things—and many Chinese retain an appreciation for their past culture—comes here. Foreigners do, too, of course, and bring the acrid stench of money with them. However, Tianjin is not the shark Shanghai is. In Shanghai's equivalent market, which really is a trap, the sellers are so aggressive that they will physically restrain you. I had a woman grab on to my arm and beg me to buy something. Tianjin is far more laid back. I walk up to a shopkeeper, explain that today I'm only looking, and they are quite happy to talk with me about their goods or anything else. If I walk by, no one calls out to me. If I come close, they come to attention, but that's about it. So it is very low key—just like Tianjin.

*Jack Lewis dons a Chinese peasant hat. Photo by Tim Lewis.*

I had a fantastic experience at this market on Monday. I had been warned repeatedly not to go without a Chinese escort or I would be famously overcharged. But I feel that it is easy to take advantage of my exceptionally warm-hearted friend, so I didn't want to ask her to go along. Besides, I think you might agree that I'm a fairly independent person, and I'll risk being ripped off if I can do it on my own. If I insulate myself from the Chinese people by always using go-betweens, my skills will never improve, and I will learn and experience less of what I came here for. So I set out on my bike early that morning with a short list of items to acquire: a seal engraved with a phrase I found in my dictionary, a statue of Guan Yu (pronounced Gwan You), who is my favorite character in the classic Chinese novel *Romance of Three Kingdoms*; a *tai ji* sword; and a painting with which to decorate my room. I also had in mind an amount I would pay for these things. I arrived, paid the old lady on the sidewalk two *mao* (*mao* are like dimes) for parking in the bicycle parking lot and went into the open-air market.

As you may or may not know, prices are not fixed in markets, so you have to haggle. And being *laowai* means prices go up, automatically. So my method was this: First, a little friendly chatter. Then, with a look of distant interest, casually ask the prices of things. If the object is large, then I start with small ones, to get a baseline. If small, then I ask about large. Gradually, I work my way up to something near in size and quality to my intended target. Then I go to it. The point of this is that if they know what you really like, it becomes pricier, so I try to smokescreen. It worked fairly well. I also compared different vendors because many of them sell the same things. For some reason, though, a few were quite adept at reading me. At least one pegged me for a Guan Yu man right away. I didn't buy from him. I managed to get a Guan Yu carved in stone about one foot high (and weighing about twenty-five pounds) for forty-five *kuai*, which is about five dollars. Score! I bought it from a young guy who spoke a little bit of English and who was very friendly. I also managed to find myself a beautiful seal carved out of a very lovely stone. These are the seals you use with red ink to stamp letters and paintings. Mine is carved to look like bamboo and is quite beautiful. Dragons and phoenixes are a little cliché, but no other seller had a bamboo one. I bought and engraved it for forty-five *kuai*.

But the real story here is not what I bought, but the experience of the buying. For years, I've wanted my own seal, so my first stop was a cart with many beautiful ones. I spoke Chinese the entire time so unless I say otherwise, assume that all conversations below were in Chinese. The owners were very friendly, and I agreed with them that their seals were very beautiful. But they were carved of jade, and the least expensive was 480 *kuai*. Now, I only make 2,500 *kuai* a month, so that's a lot. And of course, the one I was most keen on, a large square one with an elaborate lion on top, resembling an Imperial seal, was 1,000 *kuai*! I moved on. I talked with a few more people and visited a few more shops before I found my seal. I told them what I wanted on it. I had found this phrase in my dictionary, and wrote out the characters for them. It says, "Meet One's Death Like a Hero." They thought this was very funny, for reasons I couldn't quite grasp, as this part of the conversation was beyond my comprehension. But I know that Chinese often laugh not when they are amused but when they are nervous, and they can be very funny about things involving the word *si*, which means death. For example, the Chinese feel about the fourth floor the way we feel about the thirteenth, because four and death in Chinese sound nearly identical. But also, they seemed puzzled that I would want such a thing on my seal anyway, and the fact that it was about dying seemed really inauspicious. Then I told them at some length about *Guan Yu*, about my deep admiration for him: for his valor, his wisdom, his loyalty, and for his being both warrior and scholar. This broke through, and they all agreed that this was a good thing for my seal because in *Romance of the Three Kingdoms*, Guan Yu faces his death like a great hero. So they went right away to work on it. By the way, few things have been as useful to me in my time here as my intimate knowledge of *The Romance of the Three Kingdoms*.[3] All Chinese know the characters and events of this book. It is woven deep into the popular culture. I can't think of a book as widely known in America, but they know the deeds of the heroes the way we know about our Revolution or maybe more accurately the Civil War. Anyway, the owner's daughters were very friendly and helpful. One of them studies international trade at the university where I teach. With the help of their Chinese/English dictionary, we were able to talk for a while. By the way, it is embarrassing the number of Chinese here who can speak even a little English. Almost no one in America can speak even a little Chinese.

I had to wait an hour for my seal to be ready. I wasn't sure what I was going to do for an hour, so I walked around a little more. I spent the entire time talking to people. I walked past a small cart selling board games and talked to the two old women who run it about *mahjong* and Chinese chess. They were impressed that I knew how to play their chess, and I bought a nice wooden board from them, though I had to haggle hard for it. Being friendly and good-humored usually gets good results, as does being polite. I watched two elderly women shop for swords and learned from them the qualities a good sword should have. I talked with a sword dealer about the different varieties and their attributes, as well as my own wish to study *wushu* (martial arts). I talked at great length with one very friendly young woman about Chinese painting and calligraphy and got a promise of a good deal from her when I come back again. I talked to so many people, it's staggering, and they were all amazingly friendly, very interested in America and in me, why I was here, and how I liked Tianjin. The hour flew by. I was actually feeling a little high; I had never used so much Chinese in one day before. I went to the seal shop and picked up my beautiful new seal. We all admired it for a while.

On my way out, one of the shop dealers spotted my Chinese chessboard and flagged me down. He was difficult to understand, but he wanted me to play with him. We went over behind his cart and pulled out all the pieces. I told him I was very bad, but he said so was he. I finally begged off, as I had been at the market three hours and was exhausted from all the speaking, but we exchanged numbers, and I'll see him later this week for a game of chess. At the same time, I got to meet all his grandchildren who were crowding around. What an experience! Where could this happen in America? I guess I can't really describe everything that happened, but it was such an amazing experience. All I did all day long was talk to dozens of strangers who, although they were at work in a business oriented towards selling, did nothing but treat me with curiosity, warmth, humor, and patience. Even more amazing, they understood what I said, and I understood a lot of what they said. Just incredible. Real cultural contact. That's why I went by myself. And then, on my way out, I had a short chat with the bike-lot lady, and then repaid her kindness by running over her folding stool with my bike. How embarrassing! I said in Mandarin, but she just smiled and waved me on.

There are good China days and bad China days. The good far outnumber the bad, and even the bad have their good side. There are times here when I can't imagine having the strength for an entire year here, and times when I can't imagine being content with only one. Fortunately, the latter occurs far more than the former.

## ENTERTAINMENT

*I hope you like to sing!*

**Cilla Bosnak Shindell**, Nanjing
March 2003

On Saturday night, we were invited by the *waiban* here to join in with a group of visiting German students who were learning how to make the wonderful Chinese dumpling filled with meat and vegetables that I have grown to love as well as sweet and sour pork. After the cooking lesson, we were treated to a fifteen-course Chinese banquet and then traipsed across campus to hear traditional Chinese folk music played by a group of students at the university. We were seated all around the room even in the midst of the musicians. The instruments included bamboo flutes held horizontally and a few very long ones held vertically. A girl played a set of bright red drums covered in some kind of skin. There were two long, harp-type instruments set up horizontally, like a table, in front of the musicians who played them. Two wooden instruments that reminded me of banjos, but less versatile, were also part of the group. A large group of students played two-string

*Lewis family in Chinese costumes. Photo by Tim Lewis.*

*erhu* instruments, which produced a sound that was recognizably Chinese music. I was most intrigued by a young woman playing a very large hammer dulcimer. Later, she explained that the dulcimer came from Hungary, but was adopted into Chinese folk music about three hundred years ago. She had been playing since she was about eight and had earned the highest ranking of expertise on it. The music was simply wonderful. Some of the music was about the coming of spring. Other music was about the sunset over water. Another told a legend of a young woman, forbidden to marry, who watered sunflowers with her tears, and then mourned that no one would water her grave.

After the performance, all the foreigners were invited to talk with the students about their instruments and the music. I heard "Auld Lang Syne" from one corner and Beethoven's "Ode to Joy" on the two-stringed *erhu*. Afterward, I rode my bicycle home under a bright quarter moon with the fragrant smell of plum blossoms floating on the air from the school's pleasure gardens. It was one of those times that I kept chanting to myself, "I'm in China. I'm in China."

There have been other musical moments this weekend. While waiting in the school's main plaza, Julie and I met a little girl who must have been about three years old, who was uncharacteristically friendly and not at all shy like most Chinese children. She knew a little English and shouted, "How do you do?" We were charmed and delighted and started talking to her and singing children's songs to her. Well, before long we were surrounded by adorable Chinese toddlers with jet-black hair clad in bright red, pink, and turquoise-blue clothing. We were leading them in a chorus of the Hokey Pokey. It was quite a sight, these two foreigners being totally silly and putting on quite a show, not only for the kids, but for their parents.

❧

**Christopher Angell**, Nanjing
November 2007

Many good things have happened to me here in China, but one of the best has been the opportunity to channel Wilson Pickett singing "Mustang Sally" before a throng of adoring fans. At various times in my life, I have been certain that Pickett could miraculously transfer his spirit (along with the husky voice) to my body, which has also acted as a host for James Brown, Otis Redding, Stevie Wonder, Marvin Gaye, and all Four Tops, depending on what record was on the turntable.

The vehicle for this supernatural transformation was a party that I organized for the English majors here at the university. The original intention was to offer an activity that would be an opportunity for the students to practice their speaking skills outside the classroom, but it quickly evolved into a showcase for Western-style party activities. Two American teachers and a British teacher all donated their skills and audio equipment, and it was held in the Workers' Retirement Center, which featured a disco ball—older Chinese people "get down!" The kickoff was our rendition of Michael Jackson's music video for "Thriller." Since the party took place near Halloween, we decided to wear costumes for our performance, which featured Eric as Michael Jackson (or maybe Michael just masquerades as Eric?), me as a Chinese ghost, and Alex as the Werewolf of London.

The quasi-dancing and singing was followed by Lou Reed (Tim, the other teacher) playing acoustic guitar with a Chinese student and then a "limbo" contest. I brought my Caribbean Calypso music collection with me and good thing I did because the kids were completely captivated by the idea of dancing under a broomstick handle. They caught on to the technique very quickly. Meanwhile, the Chinese adults in the room were looking on and thinking, "If this is what Westerners do with their free time, conquering America will be easy!" We also featured Eric teaching how to make balloon animals, a Western culture Jeopardy game, and wheelbarrow races. A good time was had by all.

February 2008

The foreign teachers are also asked regularly by the university to participate in various activities which can be student- or faculty-related, which brings me to an interesting point about Chinese behavior. I have teased

*Sophie Lewis strikes the gong while brother Jack observes. Photo by Tim Lewis.*

my students about the Chinese "poker-face" in which the typical Chinese person will not show any emotion in a public forum, even when they are dying inside. But when there is an "official" reason to party, like a festival, a night out on the town, or eating with friends or family, there are no more enthusiastic revelers than the Chinese. The "poker-face" disappears, as do almost any inhibitions about public behavior. Chinese people love to sing, for example, and no one cares much if you are a bad singer (like me) or not. It seems that the effort and the feeling are what are most appreciated, and hence the popularity of the ubiquitous KTVs. If you've never heard of them, they are clubs with lots of private rooms, each with a large screen TV for music videos, a computer for calling up songs with subtitled lyrics, and at least two microphones with large sound systems. You rent a room and jam lots of people into it, and then take turns choosing songs and singing your heart out. Everyone seems to know the words to lots of songs, both traditional and modern, and after a few beverages, everyone's singing sounds pretty good.

*From the thrill of China as carnival to the experience of China as a "dark, smoky, smelly abyss," the teachers now enter the next stage of cultural transition having gained a new level of comfort and proficiency in China's customs and protocols. The next chapter explores some of the experiences that now seem ordinary and reflect the teachers' acceptance of the plethora of cultural differences.*

# 4

# Day-to-Day Living
*Think Chinese, Be Chinese*

I just eat, sleep, teach, learn, and live.

—Stopher Beck

*Symptoms of culture shock dissipate as expatriates establish routines, reestablish their comfort zones, and accept all or most of the incongruities of their lives in China. They find their own "China rhythm." Later in this chapter, the teachers share their experiences with China's health care system.*

☯

**Jake McTigue**, Guangzhou
October 1996

The experience of living within chaos continues to excite and frustrate so much each day—a growth that remains remarkably beautiful. Each encounter and moment provokes insurmountable emotions of frustration and joy. The opportunity to not only live, but simply see, such paradoxes would never be known if I had not taken this curious step into dark waters. Yet, as I show myself each moment, patience grows, and I soon realize that these dark waters are nothing more than a home. A home that presently exists in all of us as long as we allow ourselves to openly experience China as Tacoma, Moab, Telluride, Chicago, and other places or experiences in the past, present, and future.

☯

**Stopher Beck**, Jiaxing
October 1996

I guess I am living the cliché foreign experience here: intense periods of frustration followed by the occasional event that puts a smile back on my face. I've quit trying to figure it out. I just eat, sleep, teach, learn, and live.

☯

**Kimberley Te Winkle**, Tianjin
December 1997

The other CCC teachers and I have all adjusted to our lives here. China is a country of juxtapositions and contradictions, and we have to go along with the flow most of the time. We have been lucky to have met some incredible students, as well as foreigners. We find our emotions are always going this way and that and each day brings some new experience. We are constantly surprised, which (I think) everyone enjoys at least a little.

## CHINA RHYTHMS

**Tim Lehmann**, Nanjing
September 2007

Already the semester is zipping by under my nose. I am trying to reestablish my old meditation practice; pulling it out of the cellar and blowing the dust off it. I have heard a small intuitive voice from somewhere which says it will help me "find my Chinese rhythm," as you so put it. To an extent, I think I have always had a Chinese rhythm, but that it was forcibly accelerated against its will in the States. Being in a place which finally condones my ideal pace is a welcomed delight.

Friends are easy to make in China. Already I've discovered a fantastically generous and warm Chinese student friend who has shown me Purple Mountain and how to make copies. We both have a passion for Chinese philosophy, and through his excellent English skills, he is educating me on the finer points of Sun Tzu's *Art of War*.

What do I miss: my family, friends, Ohio autumns, good coffee, and my guitars. However, I am being compensated with new wonders every day.

**Jennie Richey**, Nanjing
March 2002

Life here remains as eventful as ever. I'm teaching English five nights a week from six thirty to nine at night, studying Chinese, learning *ta ji* twice a week from Guo Laoshi (who is seventy six but can kick my butt in any physical activity), reading Harry Potter books, studying Chinese, working on various little projects (like constructing photo albums and preparing gourmet Italian feasts for our never-had-spaghetti Chinese friends), and studying Chinese. But despite the busy schedule, I find lots of time to linger in tea shops, watch countless pirated DVDs, and go on little adventures around the city. I think this weekend we're going to pursue the small mysterious "Taco Bell" sign. If there is a Taco Bell this will be monumental for two reasons: First, Mexican food absolutely does not exist in China, except in Shanghai (believe me, we've looked). Second, the sole fast food restaurants throughout China are McDonald's, KFC, and Pizza Hut (and in abundance).

*Lewis boys on the banks of West Lake, Hangzhou. Photo by Tim Lewis.*

**Seth Cagle**, Shanghai
October 2000

I found a *wushu* (martial arts) teacher. Every other weekend I travel down to Hangzhou with a friend for lessons. There we stand in a *qigong* posture for Master Zhen. After pushing-hands with his other students and getting slammed into pillars, we get some lunch, look around, and decide whether we're going to stay the night before catching the train back to Shanghai.

Actually, I just now got back from eating at one of the Chinese English teacher's houses. Since she knew I was only going to Hangzhou over this National Day break, she invited me and some of the others over to see her house and family. This meant a huge lunch; I brought her some Dragon Well Green Tea.

**Theresa**, Tianjin
September 2007

Life in Tianjin is continuing on as normal as a life in China could be. One of my favorite pastimes, only second to going to the gym, is shopping. The stores and markets are so unusual, and it's interesting how the prices seem to have gone up a bit even from a few months ago. There was this great outdoor market a twenty-minute bike ride away from my house. It was so Chinese: busy, dirty, loud, and fantastic. I went there a couple weeks ago, and as I crossed the bridge over a main street to get to the market I saw a large expanse of emptiness in the middle of the city where the outdoor market had been just a week before. It seriously looked like a nuke went off in the middle of skyscrapers. I had to do a double-take and a triple-take to make sure I was at the right place. After investigating the situation a little bit, I found out that they had demolished the whole *huge* market in preparation for the Olympics. Apparently the city officials felt it was too grimy to be downtown for the foreigners to see, so they "nuked" it. My foreign friends and I are devastated; it was one of the coolest places to go. In all honesty, I'm not that surprised, everything here is constantly changing. I just wonder where the hundreds of people who worked at that market went.

One afternoon I was shopping with my neighbor, and we came across Christmas tree ornaments on the street. They weren't ordinary ornaments though, they were glass bulbs with live goldfish inside. There wasn't enough room for them to swim because they are put in the bulbs as babies and grow until they can't grow anymore but can just kind of turn around. The ornaments come with pellets of food you put in the top. My neighbor was *not* happy about this incredibly cruel practice and made a huge scene yelling in his terrible Chinese at the woman who was selling them. It was quite a moment. But seriously, how mean is that!? Goldfish in a little ornament!

My Chinese sometimes feels like it is progressing well, and other times I get so frustrated I don't know why I even bother. It's a love-hate relationship these days.

October 2007

Life in China continues to get better as I become more accustomed to my incredible surroundings. Here's what's been going on: I got a beautiful pink bicycle on the black market under a bridge. It was about twelve dollars and definitely stolen, but that's how things here are done. My bike's name is Penelope; she's great. I love riding her around campus, and have been venturing cautiously out into "the real world." The more I explore the city the more I like it. The weather here has been beautiful the last week or so. Blue sky and sunny! It has been such a treat, and I'm out as much as possible trying to enjoy it while it lasts.

I love to ride to the small market that's here on campus. I buy fresh daisies for my room, bananas, and Chinese "fast food." Eggplant is one of my favorite Chinese foods, cooked in a pan with lots of oil which is how they cook most everything here. I also love the dumplings. They are served in round steaming bamboo boxes, and you dip them in vinegar with a chili garlic sauce. I also love oatmeal popsicles which are like oatmeal ice cream on a stick, they are *tasty*! I cook for myself too, mostly apple cinnamon oatmeal and rice. I've been drinking a ton of tea, as well as peach and kiwi juice.

At night I go across the street to a small gym/swimming club. They have classes every night, and I've been enjoying them very much. They are all in Chinese so its extra listening practice for me. Classes include yoga, Pilates, kick-boxing, and I accidentally went to a hip-hop class and have been going ever since. I never thought I'd be taking hip-hop in China! I'm terrible, but I laugh the whole time, and an hour of laughing is good for anybody. I'm also taking Chinese ten hours a week, one-on-one classes. It's intense but it's helping a lot. It feels absolutely incredible when I can communicate something to someone that I couldn't two days before. I want to learn more!

Things that would be considered incredibly rude at home, like blatantly cutting people off on a bike or cutting in line or spitting all over the place, are fine here. Because there are so many people, the general rule of thumb whenever you go anywhere is *just go*. Don't try to be polite and let someone go first, or wait your turn, or you'll never go. *Just go* all the time. It's weird, but I'm getting used to it, and sometimes it's fun. No hesitation on the road and no hurt feelings if I cut someone off or if I get cut off.

November 2007

Ohhhh China . . .

Before Halloween I bought the only pumpkin I could find from the market, and all the Chinese people couldn't figure out what a little white girl was doing with a pumpkin half her size. In response to the hundred inquiries about my pumpkin I just rubbed my belly and said in my best Chinese, "Mmmm." I carved it with a huge happy face and displayed it on my balcony. I think I may have been the only person in Tianjin with a jack-o-lantern. I celebrated my twenty-fourth birthday on October twenty-ninth with three birthday cakes, two parties, and a night on the town frolicking on national monuments.

This month the weather has gradually been changing; it's very cold. The girls are now wearing one layer of long underwear under their jeans, and by the height of winter they'll be up to three. At night, the air smells wonderful from the scent of enormous grilled sweet potatoes that are sold on every corner. The leaves have been falling off the trees. The other day I was riding my bike and a perfectly misshapen leaf fell into my basket. It was a gift that I was grateful for. I've been riding my bike Penelope around everywhere and love feeling a part of the city life. There are moments when I'm riding along with hundreds of Chinese people in rush hour, and I just think about how lucky I am to be here.

Last weekend, a master's student asked me to go to the model UN conference in Beijing. A few days before we left, I got a call from a Chinese man inviting me (he called me "Professor") to be an honorable judge at the conference, which included my own bodyguard/babysitter named Jerry. He was responsible for making sure I attended all the meetings and conferences of the weekend on time and was well dressed on Friday night for the opening ceremony where I found myself in the VIP room of one of the nicest hotels in Beijing rubbing shoulders with UN delegates from all over the world, former ambassadors, and a number of famous Chinese people I didn't know.

On Saturday, I was a judge for the competition and spent the whole day working with Ambassador Li Daoyu, former ambassador to the United States. I enjoyed his company so much and tried to soak in every word. I was introduced to some of the smartest kids I have ever met and listened to them debate and discuss world issues for hours. They were incredible, and I had an opportunity to tell them so as I was asked to give a speech Saturday night to the whole delegation. I tried to refuse by saying no, I didn't want to give a speech, but in true Chinese fashion they told me I would anyway. Standing in front of all the students and UN delegates and former ambassadors was nerve-racking, but with some spiritual assistance I managed to pull through.


May 2008

It's springtime in Tianjin. The cherry blossoms are blooming. Walking around this beautiful campus with fragrant, pink petals blowing everywhere felt like it was right out of some cheesy romance movie. I feel like I'm living in a totally different city now that everything is green, and it's a pretty vivid green, so much so that part of me wonders if it is fake, because it's no lie when they say everything in China is fake.

In preparation for the Olympics the city has gone *nutzo*. All along the main streets they are painting the fronts of buildings and planting beautiful green gardens with cute little fake white picket fences. The Olympic torch will pass right in front of my university, which has been totally transformed. Most of my students doubt it will last, but I am staying optimistic.

The fashion here grabs my attention every time the seasons change. Spring is my favorite thus far. The girls' outfits are absolutely fantastic: bright pink puffy skirts with high striped socks and long sweaters with little Japanese dolls hanging all over them and large rimmed red glasses with a panda backpack and high pigtails. These are the college students! I love it and have been indulging myself in the ridiculousness of the season. I refuse, however, to wear beige skin-colored socks with sandals even though everyone else does.

**Larry Davis**, Hangzhou
April 2000

I think we are now official residents of Hangzhou. We have a library card to the Zhejiang Library, a yearly pass to all the parks and temples, and a monthly bus pass. I've started picking up the local newspaper at the bus stop or supermarket. I wanted to know what entertainment was going on in town. A friend helps us read it. It has been interesting; it reads like our local hometown newspaper. We are finding out about the problems as well as the local happenings. Some Chinese teachers think the crime rate in Hangzhou is on the rise as they are always reading about it in the newspaper.

*And while life in general tends to settle down, some teachers relish life in the spotlight. Unlike in the United States where foreign students and teachers receive very little attention, foreigners in China are often treated as demigods!*

**Eric Fish**, Nanjing
October 2008

There's no way to say this without sounding cocky so I'm just going to go ahead and say it: Some of the other teachers and I are becoming pseudo-celebrities on campus, and it's swelling our heads to the size of hot-air balloons. A few weeks ago I did my "Thriller" performance at the party we hosted, and since then, we've been getting all kinds of "gigs." Deep down inside I know that they only keep inviting us to perform for the novelty of having foreigners make asses of themselves, but at a shallower level I like to think that China is finally recognizing my superstar talent after the US scene chewed me up and spit me out.

## HEALTH ISSUES

*Ni shenti hao ma? How's your health? This Chinese greeting is familiar to foreigners living in China. And when the answer is bu hao or not good, the question is who will come to your aid? What kind of care will you get? In the course of a year, one is bound to get sick, maybe even injured or hospitalized. Teachers who lived in China in 2003 experienced the SARS (severe acute respiratory syndrome) epidemic, and in 2004, the outbreak of bird flu. The tales shared here are varied and surprising glimpses of coping with health care crises of varying extremes.*

*Medical care is different in China. Some long-term visitors embrace it, and others are more skeptical.*

**Jack Early**, Qingdao
November 1996

One thing that struck me about China was the administration and dispensing of medicine. Many of my students told me they were sick or their classmates were sick and that they must go for shots. I was concerned and often saw people walking around campus and the city with IVs that they themselves or a friend were carrying. I spoke to our Chinese friends, and a Chinese doctor friend who said it was very common for people to get IVs. It seems that the IV is a common solution for people who need penicillin as they believe that only an IV will solve a sickness and that the hospitals also can charge more. We asked about the spread of hepatitis and AIDS, and they just shrug and say, "That's China." Needless to say, all of our medications and diagnoses will be with a Western-based clinic.

**Jennie Richey**, Nanjing
September 2001

Yesterday I finally decided to go see a doctor after struggling with bouts of diarrhea a couple times a week for the past six weeks. I looked into the SOS International Clinic in Nanjing, but it would have cost me US $260 for one visit or US $1,000 for a year's membership. I'd be willing to pay this if I thought I was dying, but I'm not, so I attempted to go to the local hospital. After getting the runaround there, we stumbled upon a little clinic called Global Doctor. For US $145 I purchased a year-long membership, which includes unlimited office visits, six home visits (if I can't get out of bed), 24-hour emergency hotline and medical services, medicine at cost price, and more. The nursing staff was very friendly, the Chinese doctor spoke perfect English, and the facilities were very clean. I was totally impressed. They also have clinics in Beijing, Chengdu, and other Asian countries where my membership is also valid. I thought it was great considering the lines at the hospital were worse than the train station, and nobody we talked to spoke English or understood my boyfriend's fairly decent Chinese, and nobody seemed to know if there was an English-speaking doctor at the hospital.

**Alex Weymann**, Shanghai
January 2001

I have been on crutches now for three weeks. [*Alex was hit by a taxi while crossing the street.*] They've become my new best friends. I've even named them: Leo and Reggie. I'm somewhat mobile. Everything just takes a lot more time and patience than I've ever had to dedicate toward even the simplest tasks. And I've learned a lot about vanity. There's no room for it when you're tall and foreign and crutching around China.

I still have three weeks of crutching. These days, it doesn't hurt too much, but it is really stiff, and I'm very nervous about a full recovery. It seems impossible now that it could be as good as new anytime soon. But hopefully, it will be satisfactory in eleven days, because I'm on my way to Thailand! I'm so excited to get into the warm weather and swim or maybe just float in the ocean.

❦

**E. H.**, Tianjin
February 2002

Aside from a semi-adventurous and pleasant Lantern Festival, with fire-works everywhere, this is to tell you about some practical problems I've been having. When I went to Taiwan, my aunt, a doctor, did a check-up due to the frequent colds I've been having since December. They weren't colds; they were allergies! She then did blood tests, and the allergies came out to be mites, those little microscopic insects crawling in sheets and curtains. She immediately informed my mom and asked what my environment was like. My mom told her about my place, an older guesthouse, with a rug, old curtains and sheets. That was what was triggering it. Mites were probably everywhere; she gave me some medicine, but warned me that regardless of the medicine, if I stayed in such a place for so long, there was a thirty percent chance it could trigger asthma.

She told me I'd have to wash my sheets and curtains with hot, hot water. Another aunt bought me a mite-free comforter; I bought a similar pillow and covered my mattress with a shower curtain. Now the problem is the rug. It's everywhere, and it looks like the unmovable kind. I asked about another place I could move in to without such a nasty, old rug. No place.

At first, the guesthouse staff was willing to wash the rug and on top of it, install a temporary plastic tile looking like hardwood. That was cool until they wanted me to pay for the installation of the tile. The problem with washing the rug is that after a few weeks, the mites would come back, and I'd have to wash it again. I'm really not up to paying for an expensive instal-lation, especially since I'll only be here for only a few more months. When I went to ask the *waiban* about what could be done, she suggested tossing the rug completely and putting a roll-on rubber like tile on the floor, much less expensive. She talked to the folks harshly, and they said they'd get back to her. But the hotel guesthouse doesn't seem willing. Yesterday, they told me they couldn't wash the rug, and all of a sudden today they told me they'll wash it Friday. They seem awfully keen on moving fast. This is an allergy problem, not a fetish for luxury. Why are they being penny-pinchers?

❦

**Jessica Davis Pluess**, Tianjin
April 2003

After one of the longest weeks of my life, I've decided to return to America as soon as possible. I have resisted leaving, believing that I could survive wearing a mask, hibernating in my room, and washing my hands twenty times a day. It wasn't until my mom called crying and pleading with me to come home that I started packing. The situation in Beijing and Tianjin is getting more and more serious. Five hours after the other teachers left things spun out of control. Within twenty-four hours, ten cases of SARS were reported in Tianjin including two deaths and two cases at the university. Classes dropped from thirty students to five students; all classes of over one hundred students were cancelled indefinitely. Foreign students have been fleeing the campus like a mass exodus; the markets are sold out of rice, salt, and other essentials; my tutors are afraid to leave their homes; and the *fuwuyuan* (housekeepers) distributed masks and thermometers to all the teachers today. I really don't want to leave, but I'm afraid with my history of respiratory diseases, China is not a safe place for me right now. The *waiban* and my department have been very understanding about the circumstances.

**Ellen Axtmann**, Lijiang
November 2005

Bird flu is the hot topic. We now have badges we are supposed to wear to come and go from campus, and our *waiban* has requested we not "go off to the countryside" on our weekends. Apparently, there is a reported outbreak of bird flu between Dali and Kunming. Needless to say, there has been nothing on the news.

**Eva Tam**, Fuzhou
February 2007

Before I left home, my dentist informed me that I had a cavity and that she didn't have time to see me again before I left for China. She said I should see her in one year, and that I should brush my teeth well until then. Okay, not a problem, I thought, until I noticed that my tooth had turned a grayish color. So I needed to see a dentist.

Another teacher here told me that when he got his cavity fixed in China the dentist dropped one of the tools he was using and just rinsed it off and continued to work on him. Not only was sanitation an issue for him, but the dentist also didn't use an X-ray. The dentist tapped on his teeth until he found the one that hurt—that one had the cavity. Then he proceeded to drill the cavity out and stuff some medicine or other substance into the tooth to fill the hole. He was told to come back in a few days. My friend thought, "Hey, ok, this is normal, the dentist is just filling in the hole." But then when he came back a few days later, the dentist removed the stuff he had placed in his tooth and started stuffing more stuff into his tooth. Finally, he asked what the dentist was doing. And he was told "Kill tooth." The dentist was putting poison or something to kill the root. My friend freaked out, and now he still has problems with that tooth.

After I heard that story, I got a little apprehensive. I started asking around about dentists and even considered flying home to see a dentist. I talked to my contact at the Foreign Affairs Office, and she told me that it was normal to do that. I guess that's how a root canal is done in China. She recommended a hospital that she has taken others foreigner teachers to for dental work. I considered it, and then asked other people. I wanted to know my options. I even told the cook about my problem, and she was sweet and recommended another dentist that she's been to who has had training in Japan.

Finally, I decided to go with a dentist that one of my foreign friends has actually visited. I was so scared that one of the other foreign teachers agreed to accompany me. When we arrived at the hospital, it smelled of chemicals and medicine. It was very sterile with lots of steel everywhere. There was steel along part of the walls from the bottom of the windows to the floor. I was told that since it is a Chinese dentist there might be people crowding around and watching what the dentist does to me. To my relief, people didn't crowd around me. It was only the dentist and me. My friend made sure to let the dentist know that I did not want my tooth pulled or my tooth "killed." The dentist told me what I had wasn't a cavity but a deep canal so she began to pick at the tooth and drill at it, then she put in some kind of filling, I think, and topped it off with a sealant. She showed me what she used and said that it was imported from the United States. Besides not knowing what she was putting into my mouth (there were lots of unlabeled clear glass bottles with brown or black liquids inside), the whole experience wasn't too bad, but when I get home, I'm definitely getting my tooth checked out. The total cost of the procedure ended up being sixty-two *renminbi* or less than ten US dollars.

**Whitney Rush**, Wanzhou
March 2010

After five days, I am happily freed from the confines of Wanzhou's hospital! Last Thursday, I had a high fever and felt like absolute shit. The fever kept going up near 104. I got a shot from the student clinic, but it didn't bring the fever down. On Sunday night, my *waibans* decided a fever for that long was not good and to the hospital we go. Note that I look practically homeless and am wearing five mismatched tops/sweaters, a large hat, and brown capris that are too short to reach my boots, but thankfully, my green ski socks cover up the in-between calf area. People just gathered and stared.

The emergency room doctor thought it was just a high fever, so he hooked me up to an IV for three hours, and I watched people smoke in the ward. After the IV though, my fever was higher than when I came in, so they realized it was something more serious and admitted me. I shared a sparse white room with a very elderly man whose sweet wife was sleeping on the cot on the floor. No dividing curtains, no private bathrooms, just a big white room with two beds. I was given three buckets—one to spit in, one to wash my feet, and one to wash my face. All night, doctors gave me more IVs and checked my temp. I felt awful and could not swallow.

The next day, the head doctor and head nurse come in. They were sweet and explained that they knew this hospital was not like the ones in America, but that they hoped I would like it. My *waiban*, who also acted as my translator, stayed for the night and day just in case I needed something translated. Then Mama Alice made some phone calls, and the US Consulate from Chengdu called the hospital to check on my status. Shortly after that, the president of the hospital heard about me and offered me their VIP room. This room was swank! We're talking two plasma TVs, a living room, my own bathroom, gorgeous window views, and so I essentially stayed in a place as nice as a hotel for the next four days, with an IV in me the whole time. There are no monitors or anything, so you have to watch your own IV. Of course, I fell asleep at night, and the IV emptied out which caused my blood to go *out* of the IV instead of the meds going in, and that really hurt. It was frustrating to not be able to communicate with the nurses and doctors, but I usually had a translator. There certainly were some very sad, lonely nights, but it was quite the learning experience. In the end, apparently it was acute tonsillitis and/or strep throat.

I was beyond impressed with the health care—more efficient, prompt, and caring than anything I've witnessed in North America. Granted, the hospital was in dire need of resources (like digital thermometers and hospital gowns), but the doctors and nurses were incredible! And they kept me there until I was completely good to go. Always weird to get special treatment just because I'm an American, but at some point, you just have to roll with it. Friends and students were always stopping by which was nice, and now I have a bouquet and a large blow-up fish as room decorations. And I now realize the value of hospital gowns. Because of the IV, I couldn't take a single layer of clothes off for almost two days until they switched IVs. Even when I was getting a chest x-ray, I had my five layers of tops piled up at my elbow while I hugged this large box.

**Elene Johnston Kapp**, Shanghai
September 2009

Having spent the day in two different Chinese hospitals, I have to say I am amazed. I got the CT scan done and left with the films and the report in less than two hours. That cost less than forty-five dollars. I met with a doctor at the Jiading Hospital in less than five minutes after I got there. They have a separate area for foreign patients, and I was the only one there. The doctor spent at least thirty minutes with me and wrote a report for me to give to the Clinic. That cost was seven dollars. Both hospitals were very clean and everyone seemed to go out of their way for me.

**John McGee**, Guangzhou
November 2000

Speaking of food though, or should I say beer, I had a wonderful experience the other day. We went to dinner with our downstairs neighbors. He is a teacher from England who is married to a woman from northern China; he has been in China for about six years now. (They are a whole story in themselves but I'll have to save that for another day.) We ordered some sort of Mongolian hot pot–type dish. We ordered beer too, but I told my friend that I could not drink the local beer (made from unfiltered Pearl River water, I believe) as it gives me noteworthy diarrhea, and I didn't really want to lose any more weight. So we ordered another brand of Chinese beer.

Well, the next day I developed a case of what we veterinarians call "garbage gut" in dogs. After a dog gets into something like a compost pile, it will develop a lot of vomiting and diarrhea in six to twelve hours. They often develop various neurological signs as well (i.e., anything from muscle tremors to full-blown seizures). I don't know if I just fished something out of the gurgling abyss before it was fully cooked or if it was the beer, but I was not a happy camper the next morning.

As I was paying homage at the porcelain throne, I either passed out or had some sort of seizure. Bev (my wife) thinks it was a seizure. She found me on the bathroom floor, and she said the lights were on, but nobody was home. I remember slowly waking up and wondering where the hell I was. In fact, I remember yelling just that, "Where the hell am I?" I have my arm around a purple toilet, and I'm staring at a purple bathtub. There are lime green curtains on the window, and all of the pipes are exposed and have packing tape on them. I'm sitting on a brick (used to weigh down the drain in the floor so the rats can't push their way in), and my other arm is resting on a big pink duck (Sarah's potty training seat). I'm telling you at this point I have no clue where I am. I start to hear some familiar voices (Sarah is asking why Baba fell down) and things begin coming into focus. I finally realize where I'm at and ain't that a huge relief: I'm in China puking my guts out and shaking like Katherine Hepburn.

Anyway, enough for now, I survived, and I'm on TV in a few minutes, so I have to go turn on the *dian shi* (TV).

*Resilience, a sense of humor, and trust factor into the recovery process for all of these major and minor health crises.*

# 5

# Travel

*From Shanghai Skyscrapers to the
Bamboo Houses of Xishuangbanna*

I like the easy lifestyle of the wanderer: some exotic food grabbed on a street market, the chance encounters that add up like beads on a string to form a fanciful ornament.

—Hélène North, Shanghai

*Travel can be anxiety provoking, no matter where you live or how far you're going. This chapter will familiarize you with travel in China on trains, buses, and planes. In the accounts here, the teachers go it alone, travel with another foreign teacher, travel with a Chinese friend, or join a group as* "proper Chinese tourists." *Peak travel times in China are the first week in October (October first is National Day, the birthday of the People's Republic of China) and Spring Festival or Lunar New Year, which typically falls in late January or February.*

**Hélène North**, Shanghai
October 2007

My expeditions require five major ingredients: sleeping bag, backpack, pocket knife, money pouch, and camera. Like a shaman, I lay out my most precious belongings and check that they are roadworthy. Unfortunately, the ritualistic approach to my trips is but a flimsy security blanket that hardly covers the lack of serious preparation that would involve linear and logical thinking. The logistical support usually gets thrown into the backpack haphazardly and arbitrarily. I am supposed to read the travel literature "on the way there" and come up with a daily plan. In reality, I rely on a great deal of improvisation. I put my faith in my magic carpet and shamanic amulets. Carrying all of my useful possessions on my back instills sufficient reassurance in me. But then, the life of the traveler is remarkably simple. Robert Frost said it well as he was contemplating the woods filling up with snow; we all need to choose between taking the trail into the unknown deep and dark forest or staying close to the village with its lights and friends and too many things to do and the burden of responsibilities to fulfill. I like the easy lifestyle of the wanderer: some exotic food grabbed on a street market, the chance encounters that add up like beads on a string to form a fanciful ornament; walking aimlessly, absorbing the sights and sounds and smells, and finally sleeping it off in some unfamiliar bed. Start again the next day, add more beads and trinkets, and take home an intangible treasure to credit to the memory bank.

I have just returned from a magic outing; I had not planned much but the outcome could not have been better. I explored the colorful *hutongs*[1] and stately sites of Beijing, and I walked the Great Wall, *Chángchéng*. Well, not all of it, of course, only a tiny portion of it, and it was bloody scary!

I joined a two-day tour of a nonrestored section of the wall. I did not mind walking on a ledge that was only a couple of feet wide at times, nor did I mind the bushwhacking or looking for a trail below the wall when it had crumbled down to an impassable pile of rubble. The wall follows the lay of the land, which means the line of the ridge; if the ridge suddenly drops into a sheer cliff, so does the wall! With time, the steps have eroded and the smooth surface has disintegrated into superimposed layers of loose rock. Going down a steep section is similar to attempting to descend a nearly vertical scree slope without displacing a single rock. You miss, and there is no telling where you end up dismembered, hopefully not on the Mongol side of the mountain! It was exhilarating!

I knew I wanted to see the Great Wall, but I had not anticipated the questions. The Great Wall shakes your confidence: How can one justify the building of a three-thousand-mile-long fortress, some of it perched on a precipitous ridge? How does one justify it in terms of labor, cost, human lives, and resources, unless it is part of a vast experiment meant to test the solidity of the imperial system? The sheer monumental size of the Wall is dumbfounding, incomprehensible, overwhelming. You look ahead, you look behind, and sure enough, the snake-like ribbon hugs the ridge as far as you can see. Like the ocean seen from the beach, it has the potential to go on forever. Where is the end of forever? The wall stretches forever; that becomes a certainty once you are up there. But the typical modern trekker cannot possibly relate to the Chinese of ancient times exposed to the threatening Huns or Mongols; did the wall provide reassurance to the local populations? As for life on the wall, that too is locked in the eternally silent stones. What must it have been like to be a guard assigned to one of the watchtowers? Did the guards worry about the food supply not arriving on time because of the snow, or was the lack of hygiene an issue—lice, flees, smelly companions? Or maybe the boredom of being literally in the middle of nowhere with a very limited choice of pastimes was the real psychological hardship. Would they play cards and bet money? Would they fear for their lives? Would they get into fierce arguments with other guards?

**Brian E. Lewis**, Tianjin
October 2002

### Chinese Train Gods

My journey last week was in no small part a pilgrimage to the places and remains of the people who drew me here, and who continue to pull me forward in my studies of Chinese thought. I was a pilgrim, and in many ways, my trip was a measure of my progress—both in how far I've come, and in how far I have yet to go.

The tale begins around the outset of the National Day holiday. With one full week to play with, how could I be content merely to stay in Tianjin? Plainly, I had to get out. So I prepared an itinerary. I would go a little south to Shandong Province, site of some of the more important cultural achieve-ments of the Classical era. In the city of Tai'an, I would climb Mount Tai, most important and hallowed of the five sacred Daoist Mountains. Everyone of eminence in China has climbed it: the First Emperor, Confucius, even Chairman Mao. Forty minutes from Tai'an is the town of Qufu (pronounced choo foo), birthplace of Confucius, and site of his chief temple, his home, and his tomb. These are among the most important and famous cultural sites in all of China. I was quite ready to find myself among them.

I was also quite prepared to venture alone, but I was really pleased to get an email from one of the American teachers I had met in Shanghai. He had been one of the few to actually appreciate the Confucian temple we had visited in Shanghai, and I knew that he'd appreciate the particular nature of this trip. He was one of the two teachers to stay in Shanghai, much farther south than our destination, and a long train ride awaited him—some fifteen hours, on the average. After a few days of trying to nail down the logistics through emails, we went out to buy our tickets. Unfortunately, he was less successful in this than I, and a few misunderstandings at the ticket office left him holding the wrong ticket for the wrong train at the wrong time. Uncharacteristically, he almost decided to abandon the quest, but with a few words of encouragement, he was able to get on a train after all. The arrangement was for me to get into Tai'an on Wednesday afternoon, and then meet him Thursday morning.

As for me, getting a train ticket proved somewhat easier, though what to do with it once I had it was still something of a problem. I went to the station a few days ahead of time with my oft-mentioned friend Qiaoyan. Planning trips in China requires the hand of Providence because in almost no cases can you buy a train ticket more than five days in advance, and when you do go, you'll almost always find that the train you want to take is sold out. Such was the case with me. I accompanied Qiaoyan on several trips to the ticket window, before she decided that I was dragging her down, where-upon I was told to stand by the wall like a good boy and wait patiently. She then went continually, doggedly, to several different windows, trying to find some train somewhere going to Tai'an. Eventually she was rewarded: a space on a train (no seat, just a space) for an eight-hour ride to Tai'an. It's no exaggeration to say that minus her help, I might not have gone. As it was, I'd have to stand, but I was indeed going to Tai'an.

Chinese train stations, by the way, are not for the faint of heart. My initial title for this email had been "Madness and Civilization," and it remains a fitting epithet for the experience of travel here: organized, bureaucratized, madness, and brutality, compounded by the Mother of All Holidays. The train stations are packed, stuffed, crammed with people, so full that the station threatens to vomit any moment. The ticket "lines" are metal corrals punctuated with "chicken chute" gaps that lead to the raised window be-hind which sit the Arbiters of Fate, dispensing with uninterested, mechani-cal voices the utterances that begin or end a prospective journey: *you* or *mei you* (have, don't have). You don't want to hear *"mei you"* coming from the lips of these oracles, because unless you think fast, you are immediately pushed out and away by the next hapless supplicant.

The Chinese have perhaps a pathological fear of orderly lines. Very seldom do they line up, and the greater the need for a good line, the less likely there is to be one. Here, they bite, kick, shove, and claw in order to get to the window. While actually trying to get the ticket, you will probably have fists clenching money thrust past your head and into the booth, if you are not actually pushed aside. The bodies of the fallen litter the floor of the train station, pictures of human misery as they cradle their heads in their arms and stare blankly at the train schedule, mocking from its place high on the wall. Going to buy a train ticket is a little like answering the riddle of the Sphinx: if you don't know exactly what you're going to say, and if it isn't exactly right, you will be eaten.

Qiaoyan saved me. For an encore, she took me around the station and showed me where to go and how to read the arrivals board, which is pretty simple once you've had it explained to you. Later, I had her give me a thorough lesson in all the phrases necessary for purchasing train tickets and getting hotel rooms, as I would be completely responsible for these myself. The commonly accepted tactic among Chinese travelers is this: upon arriving at their destination train station, they immediately get back in the ticket line and purchase their return ticket. This way, they can be more certain of actually being able to find a ticket home. My appointed task was to do this for Nick and myself, so I needed to be ready.

Wednesday morning, I arrived at eight thirty and reported to my gate. The other passengers were mildly surprised to see a foreigner consigning himself to the Chinese Train Gods. Train travel and stations in general resemble air travel and airport more than the train service we're accustomed to in America. Trains run numbered routes that always leave and arrive at the same times and travel the same stops. These times are probably not convenient. The stations are big multi-story places with gates and waiting areas instead of open platforms. They're lined with the same over-priced food and souvenirs as any airport and have the same filthy bathrooms. The line at the gate, however, begins to form anywhere from ten minutes to thirty minutes before the train actually pulls in. This time, the line forms just a few minutes before the train arrives. Two different trains are loading from my gate, and I stand in the wrong one. The result of this is that I get stopped at the turnstile by a uniformed woman, who yells something at me in a really brassy voice and pulls me out to wait by her. Many Chinese have the strange belief that everyone speaks Chinese and that my inability to follow directions stems either from stupidity or insolence. These character flaws can, of course, be corrected by yelling even louder Chinese. This is the approach that the train employees take, and it is often shared by the people who work in the particular Internet cafe I sit in now.

Anyway, because I was in the wrong line, I'm now ahead of all the other people on my train, which irks them a little bit. The only good thing about it for them is that I look really confused and humiliated. Eventually, the doors open, and a mad rush begins. I can compare it only to the way cattle behave when the doors to the slaughterhouse open: driven forward by equal parts fear, confusion, and fury, they propel themselves along at full speed towards their own doom. I allow myself to be swept up in the tide and carried along, expending little of my own energy. Upon reaching the platform, I face a choice: the train on the left or the train on the right? Neither one has any discernible marking. All around me, mothers are clutching their children; conductors are barking, shrieking, and whistling; there is screaming and shouting. I catch a glimpse of a girl I saw in line earlier, whose train number I can see on her ticket; it's the same as mine, so I hurry after her to one of the train cars. They only open one door on each car. At each, there is a half-moon of frantic people. Some of them are actually climbing through the windows (I'm not making this up) in order to avoid the mess. If you try to wait for an opening, you'll be left standing when the train takes off. So I shoulder my pack, repeat to myself, "Think Chinese, be Chinese," and start knocking people out of my way. Very soon I've cleared enough space to grasp onto the handrail, which all but assures my position, and I pull myself up and squeeze past some guy yelling out to his girlfriend. I'm on board. Nothing was broken. I think I'm on the right train. The car I'm in is completely full, or mostly full: the seats are filled with dazed, sodden-looking passengers, between sleep and wakefulness. One of them near me, a middle-aged woman who looks like a jumped-up peasant, sits up suddenly; she looks at me with a mixture of contempt and carnality. The businessman next to her invites me in very rough English to please have a seat, which I do. I'm grateful for not having to stand eight hours on a crowded train; so grateful that I don't even mind the woman next to me as she contemplates mating and then devouring my head.

At this point, I should probably say something about the word "peasant." It's a word used a lot here and not by foreigners. You're more likely to hear it from natives. A few of the larger cities in China, like Beijing, Shanghai, and to a lesser degree Tianjin, could pass for American cities, but in the countryside, conditions have changed far less drastically. There still exists a class of people who are more or less peasants. They are discernible from other Chinese by their manner of speech, their appearance, and their manner of dress. One of the signs of China's rapid modernization is an eroding of the "comradeship" of the early Communist days. Peasant is not usually a bad word, and it is most often used neutrally (it must be remembered that Marxist terminology is still strong here), but said by certain people it carries with it a certain sneer, as the increasing gap between living standards in city and country permit. This is not a good trend, as in China it is usually the educated and the affluent who pay when it's time for a crackdown, so I often think they might do well to sneer less.

In any case, the two women seated near me are obviously of a different class than the two businessmen seated near the window, and though they are playing a very noisy and animated game of cards, I find myself wondering just what they have in common. The women look and talk like peasants, but their clothes are a little too nice. The men are obviously educated and not laborers, so I wonder how they all hooked up. Their card game has no rules, as far as I can tell, and is played by slapping the cards on the table as loudly as possible. It is accompanied by much laughter, winking, nodding, and thigh slapping, and the occasional furtive glance at the foreigner. It has an undertone of menace to it, and it reminds me of nothing more than the Mad Tea Party in *Alice in Wonderland*. Had one of the men revealed a drunken dormouse in his tea thermos, I'd not have been surprised one bit. I ask them if this train is going south to Tai'an, and what I understand of their answer reassures me enough to relax.

Over the next few hours, I encounter a problem I had not thought of: I can never tell where we are. Most of the stations we pass have no signage, and the ones which do have signage bear completely unfamiliar place names. Eventually I give up on that, and just try to keep my eye out for a giant mountain. People hawking useless crap are everywhere in China, and trains are no exception. An hour into the journey, a man in an Army uniform comes in. He starts to talk loudly, and I assume he's making some kind of announcement. In fact, he's selling small disk shaped tops. When you pull the plastic ripcord the top spins, and it can be balanced on your finger, in your palm, on top of another top (so please, buy two). As if that were not enough, it also plays "Happy Birthday" through a series of high-pitched electronic beeps. Everyone in the car is fascinated by this: young, old, rich, poor, peasant, city slicker. It's as if they're watching magic happen. The Army guy goes to every seat in the car and gives his spiel each time. It takes him about a half hour to move through to the next car. During that time, I hear "Happy Birthday" countless times, in various combinations. My sanity is quickly reaching its breaking point. Even after he leaves, the trip is punctuated by the occasional festive burst of "Happy Birthday."

In the meantime, food sellers burst into the cabin every ten minutes. The choices are quite interesting. I particularly like the Bag O' Duck. This is a foil bag featuring a cartoon duck giving an enthusiastic thumb-feather up. Inside is half of a roast duck, still moist and flavorful. Apparently, the preparation process is something like this: 1. Take one duck. 2. Cut it in half. 3. Put each half in a bag. 4. Rip open the bag and eat it. The duck really is just half of a duck, and as you eat it, thick clouds of rich, gleaming fat bulge out from the skin and hit the floor. There they mix with the accumulated peels, oils, saliva, and snot of previous travelers.

My particular favorite moment involved a young boy, maybe seven years old, who amused himself by taking big mouthfuls of cola and then spraying the man opposite him. When the man protested, the boy laughed, and then began to punch the man repeatedly in the shoulder. The man moved to a different seat. He should be glad he did. Later, I observed the boy with a big Sprite bottle, maybe forty ounces, with the top cut off, but a little bit in the bottom. The boy stood in the aisle, holding the bottle, and was turned a little away from me. I thought he was holding the bottle a little strangely, when I observed a small, struggling stream of urine trying to land in it. It overshot at first, brushing an old man's pant leg and piddling to the floor of the car. The boy adjusted once, twice, and on the third time managed to get it in the bottle. By that time, of course, the floor was nice and slick. Now, you may think that remarkable, but really it isn't. What is remarkable is that no one else seemed to find it remarkable, including the old man who got wet. He gave the kid a piece of candy.

After about four or five hours, we pull into a large station, obviously a city of some kind. I look around, but I don't see a mountain. I'm confused because the station does have a sign; it says Tai Shan. Tai Shan is the name of the mountain I'm to climb, and I recognize the characters. Also, I'm aware that the train station in Tai'an is not called Tai'an train station but Tai Shan Train Station. But we're here too early, and there's no mountain. I can't quite make up my mind whether or not to get off. I turn to one of the businessmen, and I ask him in Chinese: "Excuse me, but is this Tai'an?" "Tai'an, yes." Alright, guess I'd better get off. I gather my things and head for the door. Glancing out the window, I see a Chinese character on a building nearby. It says *Nan* (south). Jinan is the capital of the province, and just north of Tai'an. Could this be the Jinan station? But why would it say Tai Shan and not Jinan on the sign? I go back to my seat, and this time I say, "Excuse me, but is this Jinan?" "Jinan, yes." Well, he's very helpful. Since I haven't seen even a small hill to this point, I decide to risk staying on the train and to avoid asking this guy any more questions. One and a half hours later my patience is rewarded when we pull into the Tai'an station. Once again, I'm confused, as I still can't see this mountain. But I saw the characters for Tai'an all over the place, and I'm really sick of being on the train, so I decide to get off. I figure the mountain must not be visible from here. I get off, go out of the station, and realize why I can't see the mountain: the pollution is so thick I can't even see the other side of the station parking lot. Off, far, far in the distance, a vague looming shape can be seen, which I figure is Tai Shan. It doesn't augur well for our trip.

It hardly matters now, however, as my priorities for the moment are getting two train tickets and then finding a room for the night. So I go back up the steps and into the station. As soon as I walk in, I hear "Brian!" which startles me a little. My friend from Shanghai walks up to me, and I'm glad to see him. Miraculously, his train was a good half-day faster than had been reported. We arrived within minutes of each other. In a crowded train station, it's pretty easy to spot another foreigner.

We catch up for a few minutes. Then we try to decipher the schedule board. After picking our trains, I prepare some written slips to hand the Ticket Harpies, and I coach Nick on what to say if it goes wrong. We get in line, and of course, they don't have tickets for any of the trains we want. Fortunately, Nick is a strapping young man, and he's able to block the "line" long enough to buy us some time. Thinking as quickly as I can, I suggest a few other trains to her, and eventually I secure our tickets. (This will prove to be one of the only times during the next few days when my Chinese was both useful and successful.) Flush with success, we take a cab to the bus station, and buy tickets to Qufu. I'm happy because it's only a little after four, so it looks like we can make it to Qufu before sundown. I really wanted to avoid having to walk around an unfamiliar town at night trying to find a place to stay, and I also thought that if we arrived early enough we might be able to see some of the sights. Needless to say, things didn't work out that way.

First, there was some confusion over just which bus we were supposed to get on. Then, there was confusion over when it would leave. We were told it would leave soon. But then we learned the unwritten rule of bus travel: the bus doesn't leave until every seat is filled. We sat there for almost an hour, but that wouldn't be the longest we would wait for a bus. Finally, after five, we got rolling. It would be dark when we reached Qufu. Still, things were going well overall. I was enjoying bantering with Nick, and I had the great sights still ahead of me. All I needed now was a place to stay.

October 2002

**Pilgrim's Progress**

A brief description of the typical bus: first, one should not imagine anything as large or as grand as a Greyhound bus or even your typical school bus. Almost all the buses I've seen used for inter-city transport are smaller, like an airport shuttle. They cram the seats as closely together as possible to fit more people. The inside is usually very dark, both because of the faux-wood grain paneling and the accumulation of scum, smoke, and grease on the windows. Buses have little in the way of shocks. In one case, on my way back to Tai'an, the metal flooring had peeled up and unattached itself; it curled up behind my legs like a scroll. Like most things here, there is little consistency from one bus to another. Some are in relatively good repair; others look one pothole away from the scrap yard. Bus drivers, like all Chinese drivers, are characterized by their utter scorn for the sanctity of life, including their own.

Our little chariot deposited us in Qufu after dark. On the way into town, we wondered why the air seemed to be getting worse, not better, as we left

Tai'an behind us. Tai'an is a city of about five million or so, so bad air was to be expected. Qufu, however, is much smaller and in the middle of an agricultural district. Surely the air must be at least a little better in the countryside, right? As our bus carried us through the sunset and into the night, the air only grew fouler, choked with some kind of acrid smoke. It smelled like a giant campfire. After darkness had completely surrounded us, we noticed the fires, at first only one or two, but then steadily increasing both in number and in proximity, until by the time we were in Qufu, we had seen raging fires right beside the road. These were controlled burns, apparently, but of what, we couldn't tell. Nick theorized that they were burning the remainders of the harvest, which seems reasonable enough. But everyone in Shandong Province seemed to be doing it. All throughout the land, fires burned, sometimes singly, sometimes in groups, sometimes fiercely, sometimes gently. The air hung with smoke, and reflected an eerie, Halloween-like glow for miles and miles.

The bus dropped us off in what was ostensibly the bus station. The station looked more or less closed, though it was only around seven. The area was completely dark and deserted. We had been deposited in a dirt-paved courtyard, which was filled with some shifty-looking individuals whose faces could not be made out in the dark. As we approached, they made straight for us, and although crime is rare in China, I still felt a little trepidation. Fortunately, all they wanted was to sell us food and drink or maybe a taxi ride. They were quite insistent, so we really had to push through them until we emerged into the street. I whipped out a sketchy map of Qufu I had torn from my travel guide and tried to figure out just where the hell we were. There were two less expensive hotels near the bus depot, but I really wanted to try for the Qufu Post Hotel on the main drag, and literally right across from the Confucian Mansions. The prices listed were reasonable, anyway.

Now, nothing causes a scene quite like looking at a map, and in a very short time we were surrounded by a school of pedicabs, circling and wheeling around us like sharks. We determined to walk the short distance into town center, though we had only an uncertain idea of where it lay, so we waved them off. One was very insistent, however. We took off walking, and he followed along behind us. Every once in a while, he'd call out his offer to take us into town.

About this time, a young woman approached us. She was wheeling a small suitcase behind her and had been walking in the same general direction as us for a while. I had noticed that she kept looking at us like she wanted to say something. Now, she pulled up near us and started to speak in shaking English. She told us her name (which, alas, I have now forgotten), and asked us where we were going. She knew the hotel, and said she'd lead us there. Nick shot me a skeptical glance as we began to walk with her; I could tell he didn't quite believe in her altruism. I nodded it off, though. Nick lives in Shanghai, I in Tianjin, and the two are quite different experiences, I think.

I'd probably be skeptical too, but in my travels around and in Tianjin, this kind of friendliness was normal. In my time here, I've been helped out and entertained by dozens of strangers whose names I never knew. We followed her with the pedicab driver in tow, scowling. Our guide's English was limited and heavily accented, and she was obviously nervous, but we had a nice enough conversation with her. She was in her early twenties, not long out of school. She had recently moved to Qufu to teach middle school. If I recall, she was principally a math teacher. She seemed to prefer talking to Nick more than me (like most people), which was fine, because it left me the space to think my own thoughts as we approached the heart of the town.

Strangely, the town center was darker than any of the outlying areas. As we approached, there were more and more trees, fewer and fewer people, narrower and narrower streets. Finally, we reached the old town wall, my first great sight of the voyage: a high, thick wall, made of stone, captained by a tall gate tower, itself crowned by an ornate wooden pavilion. The great copper-sheathed doors of the gate itself had been removed long before, but as we entered the cool tunnel way, their old joints could be seen and the deep wells in the walls where the cross-beams could be fitted. The wall seemed wonderfully preserved and mostly intact; it led into a small court-yard with another gate beyond. When we passed through it, we were in a small traffic circle. We bore right, down a deserted alley lined with small, shuttered shops. There was almost no light. On our left, another ancient wall lined the street, marking the boundary of the great Confucian Temple. Ahead, in the distance, I saw a squat tower and another gate connected to the temple wall by a short spur of crenellation. The arc of its arch was punctuated by a single orange streetlamp; the streets were still smoky from the fires, and the whole scene was given a quiet, tense atmosphere, almost noir. It took little effort to imagine myself in Qufu's streets two thousand years ago, going home past the great temple, the streets deserted. Just short of this bell tower (for such it was) we turned right, and emerged on the main street of modern Qufu, and there was the Qufu Post Hotel. We haggled for a room. We were both tired and filthy from the train, so we sprang for a room with a bath and shower. Our guide helped out a little bit, and then we thanked her and said good-bye.

The room was adequate. Generously sized, it featured beds that were a little softer than the boards I slept on in Tianjin and a bathroom that looked usable. The real problem was the smell, like someone's basement: mildew, water, and smoke. We didn't stay long before deciding to venture out for something to eat. Just a little bit away from the old bell tower and right across from a loud, tacky hotel, we found a restaurant. The menu was in Chinese, of course, but Nick is quite good at ordering food. He saw something with mushrooms and chicken in it, so we agreed to it. He also ordered three other dishes. Nick eats a lot. He has a lot of muscle mass to support. I eat very little. I'm small. Our chicken and mushroom dish turned out to be a thick brown stew whose principal element was boiled chicken feet. I contented myself with the oily vegetables and a bottle of beer. This touched off a continuing controversy for our journey: my gastronomic skittishness vs. Nick's culinary swashbuckling. He ate the feet with great relish and gently admonished me for being so picky. Guilty as charged, I'm afraid. I'm not afraid of eating strange types of food, like dog or snake or something, I just draw the line at certain parts. Really, I'm only interested in their flesh. I don't really savor their organs, joints, feet, eyes, or ears.

The next morning we set out for the Confucian Temple. The entrance is in the little courtyard we had walked through the night before, just past the second portal of the old city wall. The temple is surrounded by a high wall, and the front gate is framed by an old, sprawling tree. Although we were arriving only a few minutes after its opening, the temple entrance was already seeded with a hungry crop of Chinese tourists arranged in neat little clumps. They wore red or yellow hats to identify themselves and were led by megaphone-toting tour guides. Such groups are sadly unavoidable at major sights in China. We bought our tickets and hurried in.

A little background: Confucius was, in his lifetime (c. 551–479 BC) steadily ignored by the people whom he most wanted to influence, the rulers of the various feudal states. He did attract a stable core of disciples, however, to whom he passed along his ideas concerning the intertwining of good government and personal virtue, which required self-cultivation and proper education. He died more or less in obscurity. As the years went on, his ideas became more and more influential, until by the time of the Han Dynasty (c. 206 BC–220 AD) they became part of the official state ideology. Confucius began to be treated with great respect, and his heirs became important symbols of China's heritage. Eventually, a temple was erected to pay him homage, not just in Qufu, but in many cities in China. The "temples" were not really religious buildings as such, but places to pay respect to the Master's memory. Many Confucian temples were the locations of the civil service exams that selected officials for government office, as well as serving as centers of learning and for the storage of academic records. But it was not until the Song Dynasty (960–1279 AD) that the "deification" of Confucius began in earnest, and he began his transformation from a reverenced teacher to a quasi-religious figure. During the Song, Ming, and Qing dynasties the temple was successively enlarged and glorified, and it became increasingly common to offer homage to the Master.

The temple in Qufu is the largest Confucian temple in China, and its scale is difficult to take in. Chinese temples make a different use of space than the churches in the Western tradition. The buildings themselves, often called "halls" or "pavilions," are often smallish, and house little more than a statue or gilded image of the entity in question. They are quite compact, and in crowded areas, a temple may consist of one great hall, a couple of small side buildings, and a tiny paved courtyard surrounded by a wall. Grander temples have more halls, arranged linearly like gates, but with vast open areas planted with trees and punctuated by decorative rocks or by monoliths bearing ancient inscriptions. The Qufu temple's colossal main gate gives way to a long, wide avenue planted with undulating, swirling cyprus trees, some tall and straight, many curving and turning, all extremely old. These were the objects of my friend's fascination throughout our journey. He seemed to feel a simultaneous attraction and repulsion. It seemed to have something to do with the role of human hands in shaping these trees into their sometimes gruesome shapes; some of them were severely deformed, and almost pleaded to be allowed to die. I think he has as many pictures of trees as I do of venerated temples.

The complex stretches on and on with all manner of things to see, past one hall and gate onto another. It is a little like an archaeology lesson: the newest halls and pavilions are closer to the main gate, and the farther into the complex you go, the older the buildings get. Of course, in China, wood was the usual building material, not stone. So although the land you are walking has been inhabited for thousands of years, and the foundation you stand upon has held places of worship for centuries, the buildings themselves are often the refurbishings of later generations. Even the main hall, the site of the oldest temple, was rebuilt in the Ming Dynasty, and although that still makes it about six hundred years old, it's far short of the antiquity of the Confucian mystique itself.

The complex itself is beautiful and fascinating. The vast sea of people surging within it, however, is enough to kill any joy and prevent any savoring of the past. It wasn't long before we were overtaken by the determined march of tour groups, all converging on the main hall like divisions of an army led onward by their generals shouting orders through pink plastic megaphones. Quiet was impossible to achieve. Contemplation was a joke. The irony is that Chinese tourists are sensitive enough to their past to come see the Great Sights, but not enough to treat them with respect. They let their children crawl on fragile arches and doors. They lean against weathered stone columns, and rub off what little is left of their color. Worse, they throw their trash where they will. I saw people tossing empty Coke bottles into the main hall of the temple where they had accumulated into a debris field of considerable size. Compared to the great care with which most countries treat their treasures, it's a disgrace.

When I got to the Apricot Pavilion, the small platform which marks the spot where Confucius taught his students, it was swarmed with children climbing about, men smoking cigarettes, and people eating boiled eggs. It couldn't be seen for all the people clinging too it like wasps on their nest. The main hall itself was worse. It's quite famous for its carved dragon columns, stone pillars on the porch, exquisitely carved and highly detailed; not even the palace of the emperors can boast of such an honor. Now, the columns are partially covered in chicken wire, small children, and chewed gum. As for getting a glimpse of the great image of Confucius in the main hall, be prepared for some serious moshing. We managed to shoulder our way to the front, but with dozens of people literally pushing, shoving, and pounding on your back, it was more or less impossible to get a photograph or even a clear idea of what I was seeing.

**Michael Hsu**, Tianjin
October 2003

West Street in Yangshuo, Guangxi Province, is a place of legend. It is a pedestrian street lined with souvenir shops, Western restaurants, and cheap hotels and hostels. It ends near the banks of the Li River and is flanked by green karst peaks. Weary backpackers of a Western persuasion come to this street to stuff themselves with delicious pizza and banana pancakes, pound good cups of coffee, quaff bottles of Li Springs beer, sip fresh-squeezed orange juice, watch free DVDs, surf the Internet, and stock up on cheap Chinese knick-knacks. The countless cafés lure the Westerners to their umbrella-protected tables where they plop into seats and eat and drink all night. Chinese tourists come to the street to gawk at the Westerners, all fat and happy at their tables. You see, West Street is a zoo of foreigners.

The café culture of people watching is undeniably Parisian, but at night the cobblestone road is filled with revelers, and the place vibrates with the strange desperate magic of Bourbon Street. After spending our days trekking about, another CCC teacher from my university and I spent our evenings and nights sitting at a table outside, watching the streams of people: rowdy packs of German tourists; young women traveling solo; modern girls from Shanghai; hunched old women bent like commas selling oranges and apples and peanuts out of wicker baskets; other old women snatching up empty Coke cans and Li Springs beer bottles from café tables eager to collect meager deposits; flute vendors blowing mournful tunes into the night air; and one particularly resourceful fellow playing his music through an amp, the lilting sound cutting through the clatter of plates and mirthful roar. We met a blond-haired, blue-eyed family of Christian missionaries. We met a group of co-workers traveling together at the expense of their Japanese boss, a smiling guy who said he golfed twice a week. We met some young people from Guangzhou, one of them nicknamed Ducky. We met a young man who was a chef at an Italian restaurant. We met Sally, a Yangshuo girl who had returned home after two years away in England, where she was living with her English husband. We befriended the hard-drinking, muscle-bound owner of a local bar, who spent many evenings grinding with female customers, challenging the manhood of male customers, and pounding tequila shots with any and all. We befriended the owner of the art gallery, and I bought a beautiful ink painting of a Yangshuo hamlet from him. He poured us a traditional Chinese tea, and by the end of the night, he was drinking beer with us and sharing stories of his childhood and bitter memories of the Cultural Revolution.

At two in the morning, West Street was covered with piles of bottles and paper and beer-soaked tables and empty chairs and the glow of red lanterns on balconies and naked light bulbs above the barbecue skewer stands.

In the mornings, we ate fruit and wheat bread on the balcony of the second floor of Café Under the Moon. From there we enjoyed the view up and down the street, and in the calm of the morning, we could see the old women begin to sell their fruit.

## March 2004

Yes, the Chinese have already handed out department-store gift certificates to their female comrades to celebrate International Women's Day, boycotted cruddy cafeteria food and reported egregiously shoddy products to hotlines to observe Consumer Advocacy Day, and watched with blood boiling as the so-called "Taiwanese" held their so-called "election" for the so-called "President" of its so-called "country." All this has passed and still, still I had neglected to write to all of you.

For my winter break trip, my colleague and I took a taxi from the university to the Tianjin train station, took the train to Beijing train station, took a shuttle bus to Beijing West train station, boarded the train and then sat there for the thirty-one-hour trip to Chengdu.

The post-apocalyptic landscape of industrial north China gave way to the general darkness in historic central China, which gave way to the skinny passes and narrow tunnels amid precipitous mountains and sweeping somber valleys of Gansu Province, which gave way to the hills and terraced rice fields of green and gray Sichuan. Sichuan means "Four Rivers" in Chinese and means "*kung-pao* chicken" to Americans with an affinity for Sichuan cuisine.

For the long train ride, we had eaten nothing but instant ramen and dried tofu; we slept on bunks stacked three-high and as wide as ironing boards and about as soft; we had been subjected to the very best of Chinese muzak and PSAs about the dangers of smoking. But we were none the worse for the wear as we arrived in Chengdu, the capital of Sichuan. We hopped in one of the green Citroen taxis that blanket the city, sporting images of the pandas that are the area's claim to fame. We made our way to Sichuan University, where two friends we met during the training in Shanghai greeted us and took us to their small apartment.

The next couple days consisted of a lot of shivering and playing ping-pong. The most prominent things in the young couple's home are a ping-pong table and the Perkins-sized Chinese flag tacked to the wall above it. The weather in Chengdu is much warmer than in northern cities like Tianjin, but none of the homes have heat and the air is considerably damper. The sun never came out during our stay in the city. Instead, there seemed to be constant drizzle, mist, or fog. Think Seattle with a head cold and a constant nose drip.

We saw the requisite cultural and historical sights in the city, but the big adventure was a short trip to Jiuzhaigou National Park, China's "Yellowstone." Rather than risk broken necks and shortened lives on the eleven-hour bus ride through the mountains in the winter, we took the thirty-minute flight. We came down right between the most forbidding peaks I've ever seen. We were not far from Tibet—the "rooftop of the world"—and there, on the northern border of Sichuan, we were traipsing along the eaves.

The Jiuzhaigou airport, which opened just last fall, is new, modern, and in the middle of the province of nowhere. We had to get in a shuttle, which whisked us across a blazing and wind-blasted plateau, back and forth through countless switchbacks, up and down hillsides, and into the town of Jiuzhaigou, "Valley of the Nine Stockades." The town was deserted save for a few Tibetan men hunched in the last rays of warm light through the mountains' slats and a Tibetan girl who stood staring silently down the empty road. I can still picture her waiting at the bend. The main drag was lined with deserted resort after deserted resort and shuttered souvenir shop after shuttered souvenir shop. We went to the cheaper of the two hotels that somehow still stayed open during the off-season. There we were, in the middle of the province of nowhere, at a hotel that only ran the heat at night and had an eerie ambience not unlike the one in Jack Nicholson's "The Shining," cold and marble and utterly empty. It was just another one of those moments in China when I ask myself, "Where am I? Who are these people? And what if I die here, right here, just like this?" Oh, and the only restaurant that seemed to be open, the one in the hotel, served tea laced with corn and food tainted with the unmistakable stench of charcoal. We ate with our gloves and bravest faces on.

There wasn't a lot to do in the city, and I wasn't about to explore the hotel's so-called "swimming pool." The shuttle driver, in the absence of anybody else, served as a de facto tour provider and arranged for our group, six damn Yankees and a Cantonese couple that looked as lost as we were, to have tea at a Tibetan home. This sounded like a good deal, but what we got was a few hours in a room that seemed like a converted garage, listening to a Tibetan boy belt out some songs on a Laserdisc karaoke machine that skipped a lot. We were treated to cold honey wine and thick, eggy tea and some Tibetan treats that looked suspiciously like the fecal matter deposited by some shaggy mammal. One member of the group declared these few hours as "the worst experience of his life." We took his unhappiness in stride as he is a gloomy old hippy from Maine who lived alone for a while in a cabin. He was reading Jorge Luis Borges at the airport and writing in his journal with stunning cursive penmanship.

The highlight of our few days in Jiuzhaigou was, of course, the park itself. We hopped on a shuttle that took us to all of the sights within the sprawling park. We were in a group with middle-aged fellows and their young wives/lovers. The oldest fellow, some rich Taiwanese businessman, bragged how his companion was Miss China 1995. (Or was it 1996?) The young women kept posing like pouty models by the Kodak-stamped signs that marked each scenic spot. Fortunately, their antics didn't spoil the views.

The park is famous for its string of lakes that are of an intense blue color that is so bright and so unreal that you would swear the water was lifted from a cartoon (the Smurfs come to mind). I have had to assure people who see the pictures I took of the lakes that, indeed, the water really was *that color*.

The place also happens to feature Nuorilang, the widest waterfall in China, which, in winter, is half-frozen into crystalline stalactites and weird growths of ice that puff like cold cauliflower. We saw freezing streams, wide and shallow, rushing around bare shrubs that stood out like potted plants in the water. We saw hairy cows and cattle graze on grass lightly touched by shreds of mid-morning fog. We saw Tibetan stockades (for which Nine Stockade Valley is named) and candy-colored prayer flags. We saw prayer wheels turned by torrents of brook water that ran below shambling shacks.

And, most happily of all, we felt like we were able to breathe. Fresh air, not sifted through the nostrils of a thousand emphysemic neighbors. They say that Jiuzhaigou is most beautiful during the late summer and early fall when all the colors of the trees add to the sensory riot (God was in a good mood when he painted this place). But the park is also packed with visitors during those months, and I would gladly walk there in the dead of winter, if it meant hearing some quiet in my soul. On the last day in Jiuzhaigou, we hiked around the park on paths that were supposed to be closed during the winter months. We were all alone.

The morning we were to take the shuttle bus back to the airport our shuttle driver/tour provider said there was a chance the only flight out would be canceled. But nonetheless, we set off as the snow began to fall. It was light in the valley of the stockades but got heavier at higher elevations, and the wind was swirling through the gorges, which plunged deeply just off the side of the narrow mountain road. The road was patched with ice and odd straw mats haphazardly flopped about to provide traction. Out the window, the scene was bleak and beautiful and suddenly, the shuttle fishtailed wildly.

The driver struggled to regain control and then said something inane like, "Whoa it's slippery" or something. One of the passengers yelled at him to go more slowly. And so we did. We crept through the switchbacks, and I remembered that the driver said he was from Guangzhou, a southern province that never sees the water freeze. And again I thought, "What if I die right here in these mountains, in an environment so far in distance and detail from the lands of my youth?" It was a long and silent ride until we emerged onto the high, wind-blasted plateau and found the sun to be blazing away, and the airport not too far off. Our flight back to Chengdu was far less eventful.

We had to go see the pandas, of course. There is a panda research base just outside of Chengdu, and we spent several wonderful hours wandering amid fenced bamboo groves. I have never seen and likely will never see so many pandas of all ages and sizes in one place. We spent many minutes watching the antics of two young panda fellows who were twins, first chomping on bamboo, then wrestling each other, then chasing each other about the enclosure, then calling timeout to drink from a stone basin. They drank facing each other, tête-à-tête, and as they bent to drink their fuzzy foreheads touched. It was an image that belongs in poster-form on the wall of a ten-year-old girl's room.

Another highlight was that I got to stand next to a panda! A sign advertising this unique opportunity said that for one hundred *yuan* (that's about US $12, a ton of money for a Chinese person), I would get the chance to pet a panda and, at the same time, make a beneficent contribution to the invaluable preservation and worthy protection of a beautiful, rare, adorable and, uh, lovely animal. I have a feeling the chain-smoking worker just pocketed the one hundred *yuan*. He called the panda over and enticed it with an apple, and I stood behind the creature and had a bunch of photos taken with it. The panda, quite happily munching on its apple, smelled like a wet dog, and its fur, which always seems so cuddly in photos, was actually quite bristly.

After that, we returned to the packed train stations and to slurping ramen.

Our next stop was Xi'an, one of the ancient capitals of the Chinese empire. To me, the only thing better than an ancient city is a *walled* ancient city. The first thing we did in Xi'an was walk along the Ming Dynasty–era walls surrounding the old part of town. From these high walls, I watched the sun go down over the smoke, tenements, and traffic. The light was orange and cold coming through the flags waving from the ramparts. Screechy, scratchy sounds of Beijing opera floated through the treetops below us from hidden parks and green spaces.

It was almost closing time on the top of the wall, and we were alone against the wintry wind again. When we at last took the steps back to street level, we walked a long way searching in vain for a taxi during rush hour. We eventually found one on a street lined with potholes and flower shops and occupied taxis. We lodged at the YMCA hotel, and, yes, it was fun to stay there. (Sorry, I couldn't resist.)

Xi'an suffers from a lack of nightlife, and our one foray into a bar, a "country Western bar," yielded us a few minutes at a table in an empty room overlooking the crowded street. But the old capital is not without considerable charm. The area around the Bell Tower is heavily populated by the Hui Muslim minority. We lost ourselves one morning on the side streets and alleys of the Muslim district, our senses inundated. There were old men with stringy beards and skullcaps and middle-aged men with weird earmuff-looking things that have straps tucking under their chins. Animal skulls. Great steaming cauldrons of steam and stuff and animal heads and piles of spice. Countless grill fires over which lamb and squid were roasted on skewers. Long lines of shuffling, shoving mobs in front of the most popular butcher shops (only mutton, of course). We left the neighborhood through a gate in the old city wall as pushcart vendors, Audis, and hordes of people on foot and bike tried to squeeze simultaneously through the tunnel. It was a great thrill for my imagination: here, here was the historic beginning to the Great Silk Road. From Xi'an, on the western edge of the old Chinese realm, one could strike out to the west, to the deserts and the nomads and the world beyond fiction or legend. How many grand adventures and last voyages began with the sights and sounds of such trampled markets?

The greatest attraction in Xi'an, however, is undoubtedly the Terracotta Army, which you may remember from your middle school geography text-books. We took the public bus to the outskirts of the city, and along the way we stopped at the Tomb of Qin Shi Huang, the First Emperor of China and the megalomaniac who the Terracotta Army is protecting in the underworld. I can't say I recommend going to the tomb site. There is a big mound of earth with steps you can climb in order to get to the top, and a collection of plac-ards and captions in unintelligible "English" and a bunch of hawkers selling "real" antiques wrapped in newspaper.

But seeing the terracotta warriors was indeed a memorable experience. Gazing at this field army of countless clay soldiers is almost indescribable. What is most remarkable is how unbelievably lifelike the faces are (the ar-tisans supposedly modeled their work after the faces of real soldiers, their friends, or even themselves). It is a strange feeling staring into these faces knowing that they are indeed "real." I feel the distance of more than two thousand years separating my eyes from his evaporate. Suddenly, I am as much in his world as he is in mine.

We had a tour guide who could speak English. She was amusing, espe-cially after she found out that I was a) an American, b) a teacher, c) a teacher at a distinguished university, and d) a teacher of professors and graduate students at the university. She reacted the way about ninety-eight percent of Chinese have reacted to my revelation of these facts—a mix of incredulity and hearty guffawing. When I tell tour guides, taxi drivers, new students or shopkeepers, it's always the same reaction: incredulity and hearty guffaw-ing. Yes, I am blessed with a guileless countenance and a baby face.

At one point during our tour of the complex (there are three excava-tion pits of terracotta warriors), we stopped by the souvenir shop. Behind a table of books sat an old man who, apparently, was the famous farmer who stumbled upon the terracotta warriors as he was digging a well back in the 1970s. If you bought one of his books he would sign it. Business was not good and the farmer, now a wrinkled old man, was smoking a cigar and looking bored. At this point, I sauntered to the WC and pulled up to a urinal. Next thing I know, there was the old farmer—a quasi-celebrity and quasi-legendary folk hero all across China—at the urinal next to me, puffing away at a fat stogie and taking a piss. I'll always remember that magical moment, and unfortunately for you, dear reader, maybe only I am amused by my retelling of it.

☯

**Josh Leslie**, Chengdu
May 1999

This weekend (May first) was a holiday weekend, International Workers Day, and I had five days off and a chance to take a short trip in Sichuan Province. Of course, first I had to explain to my students that "International Workers Day" didn't mean everyone and no they don't have this holiday in America, only in Communist countries, all five or six of them left. Incidentally, I had a very funny conversation with a student yesterday. We were discussing how China and America were learning to get along so maybe they would become great friends. And China was becoming more important in the world's economic and political scene (something very important to most Chinese). Thus, many Americans were now studying Chinese, right? Just like all Chinese students are learning English, many American students want to learn Chinese? I had to delicately explain that most Americans didn't know where Shanghai was, much less study Chinese.

Anyway, with my five days ahead of me, I decided to get out of the city for a while. One of my students invited me to go to Emei and Leshan, a pair of cities about four hours south of Chengdu by bus. Emei is famous for its holy mountain, Mt. Emei, one of the four holiest mountains in China, and a place where many Buddhists make pilgrimages. This was our first destination. Of course, the bus ride down was the usual chaos and hard negotiation. China is a place where no one plans ahead. The idea of reservations is kind of a strange concept. If you want to fly somewhere, you drive to the airport with your bags and buy a ticket. Same with the bus, there seems to *always* be a bus leaving wherever you are going, and it is usually full. So we hopped on and the journey was fairly uneventful. We were supposed to change busses near the town of Emei to head to the base of the mountain, but that bus wouldn't accept me, no *laowai* allowed (supposedly they weren't "insured"), and thus we had to continue on into town and take a minivan over to the mountain.

The no planning concept also applies to packing. For our five-day trip, I brought a medium-size backpack with a raincoat, thermals, an extra shirt, flashlight, and fleece. My student brought just an extra shirt and change of underwear. The no preparation concept only works in an environment where everyone is on the same page. Thus, at Mt. Emei, if it rains, umbrella sellers will begin appearing everywhere. If it gets cold, rent a coat, only ten *yuan*; don't have enough water, you can buy drinks and snacks about every ten minutes up the mountain (although the higher up you go, the more expensive they become).

Of course, the minivan driver had her own plans for us, and took us to a nearby hotel, which we did not want. In front of the hotel were a variety of people hawking various services, hotels and restaurants, and they quickly descended upon us. One was the proprietor of a hotel about a third of the way up the mountain. She offered to take us there, and we, having no better idea, agreed. It is fairly common for hotel workers to scout for customers at the bottom of the mountain and then hike with them for hours at a time until they reach the hotel. At around four in the afternoon, we set out, first spending about thirty minutes viewing the largest monastery, *Bao Guo Si*, at the bottom. We caught a portion of some religious rituals with many people praying and chanting, all quite fascinating, and had our pictures taken by a combination tour guide, photographer, hotel operator, and religious icon, the type of which are so common at Chinese tourist haunts.

After viewing the monastery, we began climbing in earnest a never-ending series of stone steps, laid into the mountain by god knows how many peasants over how many years. China is a country that is not afraid to use their large, peasant workforce for the most painstaking and time-consuming tasks. Human labor is the most common kind. In Chengdu, the traffic problem is compounded by an endless train of old men trailing around carts of building materials and coal. Our party was now four strong: me, my student, the hotel hawker, and a "carrier." You can, in fact, choose to be carried up the mountain, but it is worth more description here. For ten *yuan* per kilometer, you can lie in a wicker hammock-like structure and be hauled all the way up, as long as you can pay. Of course, the carriers are aggressive salesmen. They will walk with you for great lengths, as long as an hour or two, asking you every five minutes or so if you are ready to be carried. As you huff up those endless steps, they effortlessly walk past you, puffing a cigarette, "You want to be carried?" Of course, we just as often say, no, no, no, no, but they can sense when they have a potential customer. And they did in us. My student began feeling quite ill and soon needed some assistance. We were trying to cover fifteen kilometers before dark, and we weren't going to make it. Of course, there was only one guy with us, and he didn't have the hammock, so after her decision had been made, he shouted down the mountain to an informal communications link of farmers, vendors, and fellow carriers. Within five minutes, another fellow appeared with the hammock, and we were off.

**Tim Lehmann**, Nanjing
February 2008

Although I longed to go around the southern border of China during the Spring Festival holiday, my own Mandarin ability had me doubting. Luckily, a couple weeks before the students began their official holiday my Chinese friend (self-named Tom) invited me to travel with him and his friends to Shaanxi Province and then to his home in Sichuan.

First, we took a half-day train journey to a city west of Xi'an called Baoji. There I stayed with a Chinese family in their countryside home. The home was nestled in a snow-covered Chinese hamlet (for lack of a better word). Everyone knew everyone, and my travel companion who grew up there called everyone "uncle, aunt, or brother." Everyone was a member of the family, regardless of blood-ties. My friend's father was a local brick maker. His method was extraordinarily simple and seemingly primitive using a series of clay heated-chambers fired by coal to form the bricks. He managed it all quite successfully, and put two boys through college; so what struggle I might have assumed to accompany this lifestyle seemed entirely nonexistent. I received a lovely dose of humility while staying with this family. I ate their spectacular Shaanxi dishes of sour noodles and pretzel-tasting bread. I slept in the corn-husk-and-chicken-manure-heated *kang* beds. I tried clumsily to sharpen my squatting toilet skills and overcome the lack of doored privacy. I slowly, but resolutely, mastered the acrobatic act of stomaching *baijiu* and food together. I simply learned a much, well, simpler life. All the while, I was touched by such immense generosity and hospitality. I knew no way of fully expressing my gratitude, but I gave them a candle that was hand-dipped in America.

From Baoji, we took a bus to Xi'an where we were put up in a surprisingly elegant hotel by my friend's uncle. (The web of social connections in China will never be untangled by me. I can only hope to tread carefully and benefit from its reach.) During the days, we did the tourist spots, including a bizarre tour bus trip which I had originally assumed would directly take us to the famed Terracotta Warriors, but proceeded in the following order of progressively maddening destinations: 1. A museum of artifacts recovered near the Terracotta Warriors including "relics" of the Buddha himself (tiny pearl-sized pieces of skull supposedly); 2. A ski lift up a snow-covered mountain which contained Daoist pavilions and a cave where Chiang Kai-shek once hid in naught but his jammies; 3. A most random and frustrating stop at a nondescript building where we were treated to a live cutlery infomercial: "I'm tellin' ya, that cleaver went right through the phonebook!"; 4. A lovely jade gift-shop housing an enormous sailboat made entirely from jade. Our group yielded no buyers; 5. A meager and expensive lunch of too-dry rice and one bone-ridden dish to share between six people; then 6. A "Ripley's Believe It or Not"-esque "Eight Wonders of the Ancient World" wax and fiberglass "museum" where we saw laughable re-creations of the Gardens of Babylon, the Colossus of Rhodes, and more obscure and mythical landmarks. All contained "constructed" and "destroyed" dates. I began to wonder whether this tour would take us to the Warriors at all; 7. Yet another "museum" where the kingdom and tomb of the first emperor was re-created in miniature. When I leaned over the railings eager to see how they imitated the rivers of mercury, I saw only a strip of white Christmas lights; 8. The tomb itself, still buried beneath a small hill awaiting advancements in archaeological technology to unearth it. This would seem remarkable to be near but only in an abstract sense. The hill itself was covered with snow and young trees, leaving all to the imagination. 9. To the Warriors? No, not yet. As dusk was arriving, we went instead to a snack emporium of sorts where long snaking aisles of dried apricots and unshelled walnuts were sold at unreasonable prices. I sampled a strange granola and had nearly given up hope. 10. Finally, the bus made the fateful turn, and we arrived at the gate of the Terracotta Warrior museum.

The sun was on its way down, and we were advised to "hurry up." We walked quickly through one gallery of Buddhist paintings and to a large hanger-like building where the warriors were standing. A quick half-circuit, ten-minute perusal was all we were afforded. I took what pictures I could, hating the fact that I spent more time that day watching a man hit a metal pipe with a big dent-resistant knife than appreciating one of the most remarkable assemblages of ancient Chinese culture. When we left, night was falling, and we were gently led to the exit. I glared at our tour guide.

At last, Tom and I took a bus to his home city of Luzhou in the southeast corner of Sichuan. His "suburb" was a mostly pleasant, but dusty town, where "socialist messages" (so named by Tom) still played from speakers set up on street corner poles. The town was largely centered around two chemical factories and a segment of the Yangtze that ran nearby. I spent nearly two weeks in this place and ate many a meal with Tom's family. We would play basketball and go on random and unannounced (to me at least) excursions to mountains and fishing holes. The fireworks and *baijiu* toasts came and went with the New Year, and I made Luzhou and Tom's family my own home for a time.

**Julie**, Tianjin
March 2005

My beloved friend from childhood made my year by visiting for three and a half weeks. A blonde and curly-haired duo, we earned more than our fair share of stares, and now appear in countless strangers' photo albums. After showing her around my home base of Tianjin, we hopped on a night train to Harbin to check out its famous Ice Lantern Festival. Harbin, one of the northernmost and coldest cities in China, is an amazing winter wonderland with cobblestone streets and Russian-influenced architecture.

Unfortunately, Courtney was ready to go back to the States before we even made it to our hotel. First, there was the train ride. We had the pleasure of sharing our compartment with a family that appeared perfectly presentable and friendly, but alas, looks can be deceiving. They ate nonstop and threw wrappers, seeds, peels all over the beds and floor. The uncle and the father were chain smokers, and the uncle constantly spit everywhere. I thought Courtney was going to kill me.

In the morning, they were shoveling food in their faces and coughing everywhere with no effort to cover their mouths. Experienced with this type of thing, I hung a blanket from the middle bunk and pulled it around us. So, we hid in our little fort until the train arrived, and they probably thought that we were weirdos. Then, as we exited the station in Harbin, a man turned his head and blew a gigantic snot rocket all over Courtney's legs. Being the sensitive friend that I am, all I did was laugh. Welcome to China!

Despite all that, we really enjoyed the next few days frolicking around the icy city despite a handful of attempts to scam, pickpocket, and overcharge us. We decided against taking another train and flew back to Beijing, where I gave Courtney a tour of my favorite places. We took a day trip to the Great Wall at a tiny town called Guimeiguan, three hours from Beijing on a tiny dirt road. Isolated and authentic, it was incredible! The unrestored wall snaked along the mountain ridge for miles and miles without a single other person to be seen. Parts were crumbling and parts were still perfectly intact thousands of years later. What an amazing feat of engineering! The only bad part about our day was that it was negative fifteen degrees Celsius, and the wind was howling. The driver said it was the single coldest day since he began going there more than three years ago.

After enduring the most biting cold of our lives, off to gloriously warm weather we went. We flew from Beijing to Jinghong, the capital of Xishuangbanna Autonomous Region (along the border with Laos and Myanmar). The region is hilly jungle forest scattered with temples, stupas, and minority village communities. There are over thirty different ethnic groups in this region of China. It has got to be one of the most fascinating places on earth. It was about eighty degrees and a completely humid jungle. We were smelly, sweaty pigs the entire week, and life was wonderful. We hiked, biked, and even rafted down the Mekong from village to village. Menghun, a tiny farming village near the border with Myanmar, is perhaps my favorite place in China thus far. We visited the Sunday market, when swirls of hill tribe people and villagers from all around trek to Menghun to buy, sell, and trade every kind of good imaginable. The women sport their finest leggings, headdresses, and jewelry that is distinct for each group. Xishuangbanna was definitely my favorite part of the holiday, although we did encounter some rather interesting and unappealing accommodations along the way. One "hotel" had no toilet paper or soap in the bathroom, as they apparently spent all their money supplying guests with condoms. We felt quite classy and were afraid to sleep under the sheets.

We spent our final week in northern Yunnan Province and had a jolly good time. We were in the charming town of Dali during Spring Festival, a huge celebration for the Lunar New Year. Old women wearing traditional local clothing sold cookies and trinkets on the street. They would often whisper in our ears, "Come my shop. You smoke ganja." They can't speak a single other word of English but have taught themselves how to invite *wai-guoren* (foreigners) over for some weed. Gotta love globalization! We passed on the ganja and instead rode horses, went cormorant fishing, wandered around old towns, and did mucho sightseeing along the way.

Overall, the people in Yunnan Province were very nice, but the service people really did not want to help foreigners. At one point, I was practically in tears trying to arrange bus tickets from Lijiang to Kunming. We went to the bus station and four or five travel agents, who were really busy since it was a national holiday, told me they couldn't help me or that they had no tickets. Then I would listen to them book similar tickets for the next Chinese person "in line." Don't even get me started about "waiting in line" in China. At least one travel agent was honest enough to flat out tell me that they don't book for foreigners. Finally we ended up stumbling upon a five-star hotel and bought tickets through their business center. Didn't even charge us a commission and were extremely helpful. They did, however, tell us to go to the wrong bus station so we almost missed our bus. The bus itself was an adventure. It was a ten and a half hour "sleeper" bus, although I doubt anyone really slept much. We were in the back row of beds with three other Chinese girls about our age. At least we were not immediately next to anyone disgusting because the beds were so narrow and short that we had no choice but to cuddle all night with each other and the strangers beside us. We were right over the wheels so it was a bumpy ten hours. The entire bus smelled like feet and smoke. Taking the night bus is quite the experience; Courtney was not impressed. Once in Kunming, we indulged for one night at a posh hotel.

☯

**Ellen Axtmann,** Lijiang
January 2006

We were very happy to leave Xishuangbanna in the dust. The hiking was generally unpleasant (although we only did a two-day hike, much of it along a road that was being hacked into the forest—really lovely walking as you might imagine—heavy equipment, mud, huge rocks) then some gratuitous walking through "jungle" (small enclaves of forest between large tracks of clear-cut land where tea bushes and rubber trees were being planted). We stayed in a "village home"—read, on the floor of an impoverished hovel in a tiny village that was paved in trash and human refuse as there are no latrines, even for individual houses and no systematic way of disposing of garbage. We are hoping not to get any serious illnesses. The whole experience had some anthropological interest. We participated in

*Sophie Lewis hitches a ride in a basket courtesy of a kind lady in Guilin. Photo by Tim Lewis.*

a wild, drunken Jinou New Year's celebration with a bunch of tiny Jinou (mostly women) who were completely trashed and smoking huge home-rolled cigarettes and beating on drums and cymbals and forcing *baijiu* down our throats.

We are filthy and worn out, as all this was followed by a night in Jinghong adjacent to a wild New Years' backyard firecracker exposé. We are looking forward to a more peaceful time up north. It was quite beautiful flying out of Kunming and into Lijiang last night with all the fireworks going off.

February 2006

We had a great four-day hike from Bao Shan Stone Village to Lugu Hu, Yunnan. It was incredible. We stayed in the homes of various minorities such as Mosu, Naxi, and Pumi, walked in hot sun and falling snow. We crossed the Yangtze in a wooden "ferry" (more like a large canoe!) with our daughter Bei's horse; she rode, we walked.

July 2006

Xinjiang is pretty wild. We really liked Urumqi. (It was billed as "just another Chinese concrete city," but it feels like another country there.) Turpan was hotter than hell but interesting, and now we are in Kashgar, and that *must* be another country. It feels so much like the Middle East to me with

*Ellen Axtmann and daughter, Bei Driese, on camel at Karakul Lake, Xinjiang. Photo by Ken Driese.*

women covered head to toe, men with shaved heads and Muslim hats, delicious *nan* bread (!), and lots of mutton and mutton parts. The big Sunday Market is tomorrow; it's one of our primary destinations. We had somehow forgotten how hard it is to travel with Bei, especially when the weather is hot. Five-year-olds are just not that interested in sightseeing and certainly not in walking very far. Our treks in Yunnan were more successful as we were able to hire a mule to carry Bei. It is harder to do that in a city.

**Mary Beth Ryan-Maher**, Kunming
March 2000

Next we traveled north to Dali and Lijiang. Both towns are known for their beautiful mountain locations, traditional Chinese architecture, and the surviving ethnic cultures. Dali is nestled between an enormous lake and large mountains. Lijiang is a UNESCO World Heritage Site. Its Old Town, made up of traditional Naxi homes, small lanes. and canals, is well-preserved and protected even as multi-story tile buildings of "new" Lijiang surge all around it.

In Lijiang, we went to a performance of ancient Naxi music. The emcee explained that he had spent twenty-one years in a labor camp in Kunming as part of his re-education under Mao, and now he is completely dedicated to reviving Naxi music. Many of the instruments, he said, only survived because people buried them or hid them in walls because they were forbidden as "bourgeois" during the Cultural Revolution (1966–1976). Most of the

*Bei Driese with Naxi men. Photo by Ken Driese.*

musicians were between seventy and one hundred years old with only a few middle-aged men, and now, they have even permitted women. This is not to say that the Naxi culture is male dominated. Actually, the Naxi have a matriarchal system. According to our emcee, since the women make the decisions and do most of the work, the men have time to study music. Another highlight of Lijiang was a gondola ride up the Jade Dragon Snow Mountain. We were at 4,600 meters (15,000 feet). Glacier peaks everywhere.

The university's Foreign Affairs Office organized and subsidized a tour for the foreign teachers to Hainan Island. Rob and I and only one other teacher took advantage of this generous offer. Typical of tours, I suppose, it was go-go-go fashion. Breakfast at eight o'clock; drive to this site or that, lunch at noon, one and a half hours on the beach—no more. Fortunately, the van driver and our tour guide were a couple of real characters, so despite the fact that letting us hang out at the beach was torture for them, we got along quite well. The van driver, think bouncer, wasn't the best driver, and several times we were sure we were going to be involved in vehicular manslaughter. Between answering cell phone calls, this big, burly fellow from China's most northern province wanted to be sure Rob and Martin (the other teacher) were aware of Hainan's illicit sex industry. (All of this had to be translated by our young, demure Foreign Affairs officer, who also spent a great deal of her time on her cell phone with her boyfriend who was back in Kunming.) Needless to say, our driver was a little disappointed that Rob was married to me (and I was there), and that Martin was a steadfast

Buddhist. So he contented himself with ordering plenty of beer and *baijiu* at meals. I'm actually not sure if his driving was better or worse in the afternoon after he had consumed two bottles of beer with lunch.

"Wesley," as our tour guide liked to call himself, was physically the exact opposite of our van driver. A lanky, rag doll of a guy with big glasses who smoked incessantly, Wesley was a great talker, and only a moderate drinker. His favorite topic was the "Big Mouths" (politicians and rich folks) who come to Hainan for holiday. He also liked to talk about growing up in the countryside referring to himself as a "Water Buffalo Boy." In terms of Hainan Island itself, the beaches and the countryside are beautiful. Resorts are flourishing. It's a popular package tour spot for Chinese tourists, but it doesn't really cater to budget travelers, so we were lucky to go there courtesy of the university.

☯

**Ian Bledsoe**, Hangzhou
March 2004

### The Old Women of China

This image you can't see. You can't see it because it's too short, and you're crammed into a bus tighter than you knew was possible, one arm desperately clinging to the railing above you as the bus driver whips from lane to lane like he's driving a motorcycle. All you really see are heads and arms and backs in all directions, pressed against you with considerable and frequently uncomfortable pressure. What you don't see is a disturbance considerably closer to the floor of the bus where you feel a forceful parting of the human sea. As the waves come closer to you, you might, if you're lucky, catch a glimpse of a streak of grey hair traveling four feet above the ground, but you would only manage to see this for half a second before you felt arm after arm punching you off to the side as their owners charge toward the bus door to exit.

Yes, these are the old women of China. They are very, very short, and are usually wearing bundled corduroy jackets and dark-colored pants. Their hair is never long, and their voices are sometimes startlingly low. And they're tough. They are tougher probably than anyone you or I have ever met in the States, and there's good reason for this. They've learned ways of surviving that must have been necessary to live a life beginning before the Chinese Communist Party came into power through the entire Cultural Revolution to the present. I am not kidding when I say you wouldn't want to get in their way—they will push you out of it. This is never done in a mean-spirited way, mind you; usually they're gabbing with their friends in loud and exuberant tones and laughing heartily. The image, though, of a gentle grandmotherly type from the west always seems so startling to me in contrast.

*Lady with pipe in Liming, Yunnan.*
*Photo by Ken Driese.*

### Young Monk in an Internet Café

Another image comes from the other end of the age spectrum and also the other end of China. It is in a smoky Internet café beneath a Thai restaurant. Intense sun shines in through the open doors and lands on the arm of the boy sitting next to me. He is ten years of age. He is wearing bright orange monastic robes, has a cigarette dangling from his mouth, and is blowing people up on the computer screen. He has a religious intensity on his face and never moves his arms from the computer to attend to the cigarette. Occasionally, he will smile briefly after some digital martial triumph.

He is not Han Chinese. Instead, he is Dai (essentially Thai people who for one reason or another have ended up on the Chinese side of the border). While traveling over my Spring Festival break in January, I had the pleasure of observing this scene of nicotine-enhanced holy violence in Jinghong, a city in a jungle region of China called Xishuangbanna, which borders Myanmar on one side and Laos on the other. The language of the Dai is closer to Thai than Mandarin, but still has certain Chinese qualities to it. Their religion is Thai Buddhism, and all Dai boys are (apparently) required to spend a number of years in early adolescence in apprenticeship to local monasteries.

### The Pool Table and Unending Karaoke

Hop on a bus, endure six hours of dust, twists, bumps, and disconcerting grinds, and you will find yourself admiring the green mesh of jungle on all sides. If you follow the right trail in the right direction for a few hours, you will arrive at a place called Yiwu just in time to see the sun set over the next image: a pool table resting on a cracked sidewalk with pieces of cardboard folded up beneath two of its uneven legs to create a barely flat surface. Locals cluster around the edges of it watching whatever game happens to be played at the moment. Some lean against the decrepit building; some squat and watch. A teenage couple looks on disinterestedly from their motorcycle before spinning up gravel and jetting back down the one street this village has to offer. A few squatting men breathe in smoke from bronze-colored, traditional water bongs. The table, along with the entire village, seems to shake with every insipid Chinese pop beat that is emitted from the three karaoke bars that line the street. With only perhaps two hundred people in the entire village, that's one karaoke bar for every sixty-six people. Sometimes you can't help wondering if this ratio is consistent throughout all of Asia given the cultural stir it's caused. You may wonder this over and over until three o'clock in the morning when the last drunken note is slurred; the final sharp ring of feedback silenced; and you can finally go to sleep.

### Bamboo Stilt Houses and TVs

In the morning, after eating a bowl of noodles and pork in spicy broth, you make your way down a narrow dirt road that winds through the jungle in a northerly direction. You will probably be able to convince someone on a passing tractor to give you a ride for a while, and you can rest your feet as you sit next to the Yi women in their beautiful, color-drenched dresses, hauling buckets and machetes to the bamboo harvest site down the road. After getting off the tractor and walking for a couple more hours, you will start to get hungry and would like to get out of the sun. You'll stop at the next village, this one much simpler than the relatively modernized village you set out from only a few hours ago. The huts are all made of wood and some are set up on bamboo stilts. Their roofs are all grass-thatched, and animals wander about freely—cats, chickens, and pigs, and don't forget the pair of water buffalo that will suddenly charge at you as you leave, though that's another story (thank god for that tree).

You will make enquiries at the first hut you see. In your broken and very limited Chinese you will ask the man, surrounded by four or five children, if there is a guesthouse or a restaurant anywhere in the village. When he answers in the negative, you will be quite pleased when he himself offers to cook you up something for lunch and will follow him inside the hut. There you will see a sparse interior, the walls consisting of only single wood slats. You'll notice that the walls are all blackened from the smoke of the fire they keep burning on a pile of ashes in the middle of the kitchen floor. He'll ask you to sit on a stool next to the fire as he cuts up pieces of pork and pickled vegetables he keeps in a cabinet. One of the children will bring in a bucket of water from outside and pour it into a basin in the kitchen. The meat will sizzle spiritedly in the pan, and you will try your best to make confused conversation with the man as he walks over to a wicker basket and scoops out rice kept moist inside.

After eating, you'll thank him profusely, and after a final conversational attempt you'll be led out of the house. As you pass by the living room, you'll be startled to see a large television, VCD player, and stereo in an adjoining room. Despite a lack of running water or a refrigerator, the digital age will appear to have encroached upon this area as much as in the world surrounding it.

How many other images do I have to share? Too many, of course. I could talk about the old, blind man who plays his rosin-covered *erhu* at the bus stop sitting cross-legged on top of newspapers. Or I could describe the Naxi women in mountain fields only a hundred miles from the Tibetan border stooped over row upon row of cabbage and cauliflower throwing greens into baskets on their backs. And I could certainly mention the stone guesthouses perched precariously above a thousand foot drop that is lined with granite and sandstone and descends straight down until it meets the roiling whites and greens of the Yangtze. But this is long enough already. It never seems like enough when you're trying to tell someone what it's like somewhere very different.

*Travelers to the same regions often recount very different experiences. Julie describes Xishuangbanna as "definitely my favorite part of the holiday," while Ellen Axtmann writes, "We were very happy to leave Xishuangbanna in the dust." In the next two accounts of travels through the Three Gorges—one with a tour group— each has its own challenges and rewards. The Three Gorges is the scenic region along the Yangtze River that is now home to the world's largest hydroelectric dam.*

**Catt Stearns**, Wanzhou
December 2009

The next day, we departed on our weekend trip up the Yangtze River on a cruise to check out the famed Three Gorges, one of China's most scenic tourist destinations. We packed our bags with books, magazines, and cards thinking we would have ample time to relax and enjoy the sites from the comfort of our little cruise ship rooms complete with picture windows. We were wrong. Come Saturday morning we were thrust into the Chinese way of traveling: *massive tour groups!*

We were forced to start the day at seven after the temple tour the night before ended at eleven thirty. We awoke when the speakers in our room, which could not be turned off or down to an acceptable level, started blabbering announcements in Chinese accompanied by the instrumental version of "Colors of the Wind" from Pocahontas. Later in the morning, we docked and were then put on dragon boats that took us to some scenic spot that the Chinese deemed "not scenic or exciting enough" so they added a tightrope across the river with a man riding a bicycle on it and another one hanging from the bike, along with a horrible dance/opera show where it was apparent that the performers hated their lives, and some buoyed bridge contraption that made you wonder if they took into account the safety level of this thing with one hundred plus grown Chinese trampling across it. Just another morning in China.

In the afternoon, we were shuffled around like proper Chinese tourists on big buses and visited the Three Gorges Dam viewpoint, the Three Gorges Dam museum, the park dedicated to the Three Gorges Dam, and some random temple where you could once again see the Three Gorges Dam, but just from the other side. I'm not really sure if you know this, but this Three Gorges Dam is kind of a big deal in China.

The fun doesn't stop there. On Sunday morning, we were up before the sun at six in order to "hike" to the top of a peak called Empress. It was a brutal trip up some of the steepest stairs of my life, but well worth it, and in the afternoon we were able to finally have the leisurely time we were hoping for as we admired the downright beautiful scenery from the deck of the boat.

❧

**Patrick Tartar**, Lijiang
January 2008

Twelve days ago we arrived in Central China (Changsha, Hunan) and found ourselves in the middle of the worst winter weather China has had in forty years. It's been about ten degrees most days, with snow pouring from the sky. In Wuhan, Hubei, we were without power (meaning heat) and water for over twenty-four hours. We haven't let this weather stop us. We just have to wear all of our clothes every day! Three socks, two jackets, etc. Our plan has been to take a cruise down the Yangtze River from Wuhan to Chongqing, a six-day journey.

On the morning of the cruise, our agent actually did arrive at our hotel in the middle of incredible snow. We paid her, and she gave us a handwritten address to the dock, one hour out of town. We caught a taxi to the dock, but when we were about ten or fifteen kilometers away, the police closed the road due to treacherous conditions. The cabbie shrugged his shoulders and kicked us out of the car. There we were, way out of town, in the snow flurries, with all our baggage, and no idea how far to the dock. Heather was about to cry, and we pleaded for help from the cops. They miraculously told us to hop in their car, equipped with chains, and drove us the remaining way to the boat. Without that police escort I really don't think we would've made the cruise. It was an ulcer-inducing effort all the way until the end.

When we finally managed to get on the cruise, it was heaven. We had the most basic room, but it was heated to the max. The bed was the softest I've slept on in China, and we even had our own deck! We also had CNN and HBO, the best gifts of all. I stayed up until almost two each night watching election coverage and movies. The cruise company was American, so the food was Western, and we spent four nights eating buffet servings of pasta, cheeseburgers, French fries, bagels, pizza, salad, and bottomless Italian coffee. It's incredible how these little things can just turn your life around when you've gone for this long without. The river, I'll never forget. I spent three whole days watching it flow by. Huge boats stocked with coal, cities that were halfway flooded, water level signs all over showing where the final level would be, crazy cities built for relocation, gorges that were so steep and dramatic that it's hard to describe. Trip of a lifetime. It was incredible to see all of that before the flooding and construction was finished.

We took a small boat up the lesser three gorges, up the Daning River from Wushan, and the water level was at sixty meters, when before it was only knee deep at best! We floated over countless cities, a football field below. We saw pictures of the cities before the dam, now so far underneath us. Because we were going upstream, we had the chance to go up the five-stage locks through the dam. I think that was the coolest part of the whole cruise. About eight enormous ships entered the first bay of the locks with massive cement walls on each side and approached these one hundred and fifty foot gates that reminded me of *The Neverending Story*. Our boat was in front, so we got the best view.

The bay would flood with water and the ships would begin to rise. We'd watch the water slowly climb up the depth scale painted on the wall. Eventually the water level in our bay would reach about halfway up the gates (we were previously thirty feet below), and they would begin to open with the loudest creaks and groans you've ever heard. When they were open, all the boats would toot their horns and sail into the next stage. The gates behind would close, and the water would rise once again. After four such stages, we were through. All I could think about was what an insane amount of construction and engineering took place to make this possible. We were one of eight giant boats that looked like little toys against the scale of the dam and its locks.

Our boat had a staff of one hundred and fifteen, but due to the winter weather, there were only fifteen passengers on board, including seven Aussies. We had both the river and the boat to ourselves. It was downright magical. *Chun Jie Hao!* Happy Spring Festival!

*And after the teaching and the traveling, it is time to think about returning to the United States. But first, let's consider China with children. Ellen Axtmann has already set the stage, "Five-year-olds are just not that interested in sightseeing."*

# 6

# Families Coping
*Babies, Rabies, Scabies and Flu, No Problem*

Hello Alice. No rabies or flu, but definitely scabies.

—John McGee

*In this chapter, seven families go to teach and to learn and to plunge into Chinese culture. Five families have adopted Chinese daughters. Ann's two children were adopted from Guatemala; her husband, Gustavo, is Chilean. Jack Early's wife, Doris, is Taiwanese; their daughters are American-born Chinese. The full range of multi-cultural families is represented. Parenting techniques and children's behaviors are all subject to cross-cultural scrutiny.*

*These intrepid parents enroll their children in Chinese kindergarten, regular Chinese school, the Chengdu Waldorf School, and try homeschooling as well. Kindergarten in China is equivalent to day care or preschool in the United States and includes children ages two to five; regular school starts at age six.*

*Bouts of skepticism, trials and doubts, rewards and challenges punctuate each family's year in China, and there are unique epiphanies along the way as well. The 2008 Olympics and the Mianyang earthquake in Sichuan Province also shape these personal narratives, which for families, as well as for single teachers, is very much about establishing a routine and finding normalcy on the other side of the world.*

*Many of the families are serious travelers; highlights and lowlights are included.*

☯

**Jack Early**, Qingdao
November 1995

The first and most important reason for going to China is to expose my two daughters to their Asian heritage.

Another important reason is for my wife to have the opportunity to reconnect with her family in China. She would like to have the old photographs of aunts and uncles embellished with their personalities and meet firsthand the cousins she has read about. While maybe we could visit these locations on a tour, we would not assimilate the long years of separation and accumulated experiences an extended stay will offer.

The last reason to go to Asia is because it's there. My wife and I have always been adventurous. We have often been described as "What time and where" people. I can think of no better way to teach our children to be motivated than to get up and go.

November 1995

Both the girls are in school and are secure and well treated. Jackie (Ting Xin Ru) had trouble at first in that the Chinese kindergarten is more like a nursery school. The children are put to bed (in cribs) after brunch and told not to move from eleven in the morning until two in the afternoon. Xin Ru couldn't do that so after about two weeks she started to misbehave (she hung around with the cleaning lady) and refused to go back to class. We had a meeting with our dean, and he understood immediately. We have since taken her out of school for lunch with the rest of us, and she adjusted perfectly, and in fact is learning Chinese faster than all of us. In her school, no one speaks any English so she has no choice.

Frances's school is about a fifteen-minute walk or a five-minute bike ride away. When you think of China with all the people going to work in the traffic and bikes, think of Frances (Ting Kang Mei) and her dad weaving in and out of traffic every morning. This past Friday, Kang Mei and I were riding along, and we passed a guy riding a bike with the carcass of a cow tied to the back on the way to the market.

The apartment is definitely survivable. It is small by our standards, but luxurious by Chinese standards. We have two bedrooms and a sitting room where we eat at a small card table. The kitchen is more like a galley with a two-burner gas stove that uses a propane tank, a small fridge, and a tiled sink with an outside-type faucet. The best way to describe the apartments is that it is US tenement-style circa 1938. It is basically a coldwater flat. We have a small electric hot water heater hanging from the wall in the bathroom for our showers.

What do we miss? A dishwasher. It takes an hour to an hour and a half to do the dishes at the end of the day. If we want any hot water to clean with, we must boil it on the stove. We never once thought about washing clothes and boy, has that turned out to be a troublesome procedure. We have a portable washing machine that you move halfway into the bathroom with electric cords draped over everything, and we wrap a grounding wire around a pipe (no one can use the bathroom). The machine has two drums; one fills for washing, and you must control the draining and filling the water manually. By turning a dial, the clothes can be turned back and forth in the soapy water. When the clothes are done you load them into a drum that spins. Usually the water is everywhere as the drainage hose just empties into a drain in the floor. We use a brick to hold down the drain hose, but it usually snakes around the drain leaving the bathroom soaked. (I know you just said, "God, he better watch it with water all over the floor and wires all over the place!") The first time I came home Doris was in two inches of water with the ground wire in the water, and she said, "I took off my runner sandals because there was so much water." Our neighbor and friend came over and explained that every week in China someone dies in the bathroom washing the clothes! What to do with our clothes? They're still not dry. Hang them up in the bedroom, of course.

❧

**Bev McGee**, Guangzhou
September 2000

I will pass along some cultural differences that I think all of you will find interesting, especially those of you with adopted Chinese children. Please note: although all of this is true, I mean it in good humor.

Sarah (age two) is in a Chinese kindergarten, and one of her teachers speaks a little English, so I get lessons (aka, nice reprimands) from her each day. First of all, I don't dress Sarah correctly. According to the Teacher, her clothes are too thin, and she needs more layers. We have to bring a dry washcloth to school and at least one change of clothes. They use the wash-cloth to wipe off the sweat, and they change her clothes when they are wet with sweat. (Now, why does she need more layers??) Next, we have to bring a blanket to school for naptime. I brought in a thin blanket (my first mistake) along with a thin mat for her bed because it is so hot here. Well, as you can imagine, the blanket is too thin. The Teacher brought in a thick towel from her home. Now I am supposed to bring in a thick mat and a thick blanket because the air is getting "cool." Let me remind you that we are on approxi-mately the same latitude as Cuba. If there is any "cool" air on the way, it will be a very welcome change. I guess that means it will go from being *extremely* hot and humid to just *very* hot and humid.

Sarah has one t-shirt that is a little loose around the neck, and sometimes you can see her shoulder. I was told to repair it so her shoulders don't get cold. I did find a thick blanket this weekend, but I did not take it in today because it is so hot. The Teacher told me she will go home at lunch and get another towel until I have a chance to bring in the thick blanket. I might have to have someone send over a snowsuit by the time this "cool" air comes. Well, the list goes on. Sarah does not eat as much as the other toddlers. She does not take a three-hour nap like the other toddlers. She also won't drink the herbal tea. In summary, she is just being an independent two-year-old, and they don't seem to be used to that. It must change by the time they are five years old. We have not had any of these requests from Katie's teachers.

October 2000

I am happy to report that we finally had a cool breeze here in Guangzhou. The temperature dropped down to the low seventies over the weekend, and it was so refreshing. We could finally go outside without melting from the heat and humidity. (Katie always uses the word "melting" to describe how she feels when she goes outside.) As you probably guessed, the natives of Guangzhou were cold.

One Chinese teacher told me, "We don't have autumn here. It goes straight from summer to cold winter." (No, that wasn't a typo. I said low seventies.) I tried to respectfully reply that we are used to cold weather. One of my students talked earlier in the week about going to the zoo this weekend. She called on Saturday to say it was too cold to go to the zoo. Small children are now being dressed in heavy sweaters and coats. Babies are now wrapped in heavy blankets and wearing heavy clothing. We are still in our short-sleeved shirts. I did dress the kids in long-sleeved shirts over the weekend in order to avoid a friendly scolding from strangers about the way they were dressed. I don't have to understand Chinese in order to know when I am being scolded.

Unfortunately, I think our cool breeze is over. It was already hot at seven thirty this morning when I took the kids to school.

Katie's teacher told an interpreter (one of my students went with me to pick up the kids one day) that Katie is very sweet to the other kids in her class. However, she is shy about speaking Chinese and is still adjusting to the language barrier. Katie likes singing the Chinese songs and participating in the activities.

Sarah got into trouble at school last week. Teacher Wu was very upset because Sarah hit a classmate. Teacher Wu just couldn't understand why Sarah would hit another child. We asked Sarah about it when we got home. She said that Mei Chin took her toy away. So, Sarah hit Mei Chin and took the toy back. She even showed us how she hit Mei Chin. She said, "I hit Mei Chin like that and took the toy back." We videotaped the whole explanation. (I find it hard to believe that Sarah is the only two-year-old hitting other kids at school.) Sarah doesn't need to speak Chinese at school. She relies on her nonverbal communication skills.

**John McGee**, Guangzhou
November 2000

Although we got tricked/trapped/suckered into jointly teaching a class of eight-year-olds on Saturday mornings, it pays another thousand *renminbi* a month so we are set for money. We hope to save enough to do a lot of traveling over the New Year's break. The Saturday morning class consists of the children of many of the university big-wigs so we didn't think it would be beneficial to turn it down. Our first meeting with the parents was set up under misleading circumstances. The *waiban's* assistant told us that there was a group of children of university staff members that routinely met as a playgroup and that they would like Katie to join as these kids were also studying English. We thought it would be a great idea. The kids could improve their English by hanging out with us, and Katie could make a few friends, and pick up a little Chinese as well. When we meet the parents, they show up with all of the course materials and other paraphernalia that the kids have been using to learn English. It turns out that they are looking for a replacement English teacher as the previous one had returned to England or America or wherever he had come from. We couldn't really say no at this point. All in all our dealings with this assistant have been good. I will, however, be a little more careful in the future. The *waiban* is also quite helpful, but he does not really seem to have much English. The net result is that he always tells us everything will be okay, and that he will take care of it, but he usually says this before we have finished telling him what we need.

The building staff is great. When we first moved in they saw Bev carrying loads of laundry down to the washroom, and they just carried a washing machine up to our room. We asked if we could get a small refrigerator, and they went out and bought a brand-new full-sized one. They treat the kids well and are always friendly. The waitresses at the restaurant next door have also been great. They play with the kids whenever possible, and they never get upset with Sarah for chucking rice and tofu across the room onto other patron's tables.

January 2001

Our downstairs neighbors got into quite a row with the building staff here yesterday. It was over something that in principle we probably also should have been upset about, but Bev and I weren't really bothered in the least. The staff had come through our apartments to do an inventory of furniture and appliances, and they put little ID stickers on all of the university property. The problem arose because they did it while we were gone, and our neighbors were upset that their apartment was entered when they were not home. Under other circumstances, I may have been bothered, but I felt the whole thing was really quite innocent. Our neighbors are in a different position, so I can understand why they were a little upset.

Let me briefly introduce you to them. The husband is from England and has been teaching in China for six years now. His wife is Chinese, and they met when he was teaching in Northern China. She accuses him of being an alcoholic and of frequenting brothels. He admits to too much beer and also reports that he suffers from depression, but has decided he doesn't want to take medicine anymore. He says that his wife suffers from schizophrenia, but she is also off of medication because she is pregnant. I am not a psychologist, but I believe that they both do in fact suffer from the mental illnesses that they lay claim to. She is definitely not all there and does go through regular bouts of paranoia. And he does drink excessively and hole up in his room for hours and days on end sometimes. They have been divorced once already because she thought that he was going to kill her with an ax. Isn't it great to have a good babysitter so close by? Anyway, they are in the process of applying for a visa for her so they can have the baby in England. They plan to stay there and bring up the child in England. If all goes well, they will be leaving sometime in January. Keep your fingers crossed.

January 2001

I'm almost certain the bus I was riding across town on today ran over someone. The driver actually came to a complete stop after slamming on the brakes, got out and ran to the front of the bus. There was quite a bit of yelling and screaming in that language. We call it Cantonese. I only know a few words of it (the more universal tongue or "standard Chinese" is Mandarin), but there's no mistaking it when you hear it. To obtain the proper intonation the men reach down into their pockets and squeeze their nuts at the end of each sentence. I haven't yet been able to determine what the women do. Anyway, those passengers who didn't immediately jump ship took turns running to the front of the bus to see what happened. Each one then got back on the bus and gave a report to those people who presumably missed crucial parts of the previous account. It was such big news that the men gave their reports with both hands in their pockets the whole time. I watched the women as closely as I could, but I'll be damned if I can figure out how they did it. Being the old China hand that I am, I did not run to the front of the bus. I wasn't about to lose my seat. At last, something was pulled to the side of the road and off we went. At the next stop, the driver came back and gave a pen and paper to a man and asked him to write something. I think he was the man who gave the most entertaining account, and they wanted to make sure he got a prize.

February 2001

Alice, we have returned from travels to Kunming, Dali, and Lijiang. We are recovering from two and a half weeks of twenty-four-hour kids and hotel rooms. However, since we've returned, we've been plagued by a skin disease (mites, lice, poison ivy, allergies, who knows?). We are treating for all of them. We have had our stroller stolen (although it was locked up right in front of the store security guard). Now I go over to the store on a regular basis and just stare at the security guard. I guess I'd just as soon get back to traveling. We are in fact going to head off again real soon towards Hangzhou, which is where Katie is from. We have made arrangements to visit her orphanage, and we will also be meeting up with a couple from Boulder who have a daughter from the same orphanage.

We enjoyed Kunming and the surrounding area very much. It was nice to be away from the smog and congestion of Guangzhou. I found a small park that also seemed to serve as the local hangout for retired minorities. Every afternoon they would gather there and play their instruments and perform little skits for each other. Many of them, especially those who would act, would dress in their traditional costumes. It was pretty much just for their amusement, and Bev and I were the only white folk that I ever saw there. The combination of the kids and us, as you can imagine, caused quite a stir. One day when I was there I got roped into a dance with a woman who I am guessing was about sixty-five. Since most Chinese people are much older than they look I guessed she was probably closer to seventy-five. The dance seemed to be some sort of courtship or "pre-sexual" type thing so you can imagine how absurd we looked: "I'll show you my wrinkles if you show me yours."

*Bev, Katie, and Sarah McGee stranded, Lijiang.*
*Photo by John McGee.*

I also found a guide who took us out one afternoon to a nearby village of Yi people. Everyone was very hospitable, and we even spent a little time watching the new TV and satellite hookup at one house. Still no running water, but they've got MTV. Bev and Sarah got "lost" one day when they took a taxi to nowhere. (They thought they were going to the horticultural expo but ended up at some forest preserve filled with barking dogs and who knows what else.) They walked and walked until they found a bus that was heading back into town. At least Bev still had the stroller at that time.

From there it was on to Dali and a new set of germs. I managed to eat something that didn't agree with me. (I think it was the yak bacon that I chewed for about fifteen minutes without making any progress. I finally decided to just swallow it, and I think that it is still lodged somewhere between my pylorus and my appendix. Next time I will just spit it out and forget what my mother told me about wasting food.) As it turned out, about all I saw in Dali was my hotel room. I recovered before we arrived in Lijiang so I had a more pleasant stay there. Although by that point in the trip, I was about ready to sell the kids and use the money to buy one of those "around the world" airline tickets. We really enjoyed the Old Town portion of Lijiang and ended up spending most of our time there. Guides were not very receptive to customized tours, and we really did not want to do all-day tours with the kids.

We did take a taxi out to a group of smaller villages one day and were stranded once again. I thought we had learned from Bev's Kunming incident so I asked the hotel staff if there was a lot of taxi traffic to the area I wanted to visit. I asked multiple times and each time was assured that yes, plenty of taxis go out there. The guidebook also listed these villages and a temple in one of them so I figured it was a safe bet. The only safe bet was that we would end up walking again. We knew as soon as the taxi dropped us off we were in trouble, but we went ahead and got out anyway. We eventually found the temple, but I believe we were the only visitors that week. It was a very small temple that served as a hangout for a few local card players. We were greeted at the entrance by a beggar/mentally disturbed man. I could not communicate to him in my broken Mandarin, and it seemed that all he was really interested in was groping Bev. I told him that if I couldn't, he sure as hell wasn't going to get to. As I was telling him in a couple of languages to buzz off, an old lady working in a nearby field gestured to us that he wasn't quite right. We might have been able to work something out if he had a taxi though. After we sat in the town square for about an hour without seeing any motorized vehicles, we decided to start walking. For some reason, we did not have Sarah's stroller, but we managed to get her to walk some by having her chase the pigs down the road.

February 2001

Hello Alice. No rabies or flu, but definitely scabies. I am trying to get a Western medication to treat Sarah. (The rest of us seem to have successfully cleared ourselves of the little critters.) The medication is called Acticin (generic permethrin). I tried calling SOS to see if I could get something from their pharmacy, but they wouldn't even give me the time of day since I only have the evacuation coverage. The medicine from the local clinic has not been effective. Do you have any suggestions about who to contact? We're just itching for any information you might have.

**Bev McGee**, Guangzhou
February 2001

Both girls are doing fine in school. The school system in China is mostly driven by test scores. Even in Katie's kindergarten, they do not use manipulatives in the classroom. The classes are taught entirely in Chinese. Without the use of manipulatives, Katie does not have anything to link the language to so it has been a little difficult for her. Katie learns primarily by watching her classmates. Katie is a bright girl and is now starting to understand a lot of Chinese. Math seems to be especially easy for her.

An English teacher comes to Katie's classroom once a week for about an hour to teach the kids English. (Katie said the English teacher does not know very much English.) Katie's kindergarten teacher tells us (with the help of an interpreter) that Katie is a very smart and pleasant child, and she plays well with the other kids. The teachers all love Katie (future ambassador). Katie has one main teacher and one assistant teacher, and an aide is there during lunch and rest time. There are forty kids in the class. (And to think, I was concerned about the one teacher to twenty-five kids ratio in Boulder.)

Katie and Sarah come home every day singing songs in Chinese. Sarah sings in Chinese more often than she sings in English. It is a lot of fun listening to her sing. Sarah also counts in Chinese more often than she counts in English. Sarah talks to us in English but talks to her teacher in Chinese. We still get reports that Sarah (future captain of the debate team or professional boxer) is too independent and she wants to do everything herself. This is, of course, nothing unusual for an American child, but it is very unusual in Chinese culture. At least she hasn't beat up any of her classmates recently.

**John McGee**, Guangzhou
March 2001

The *waibans* here have always done everything they can to meet our needs. One of our colleagues here has worked for five different universities in China. He said ours is the best *waiban* he has ever worked with.

Our accommodations are typical Chinese style teacher's housing. The apartment meets our needs. The kitchen consists of a Coleman-style camping stove, water, and a drain in the floor (no pipes). We do have air conditioners; I couldn't live in Guangzhou without them. We don't have heat. The coldest spell was right after Spring Festival when it got down into the forties. The temperature was the same inside the apartment as it was outside the apartment. During that cold spell, we also had several days and nights of non-stop rain. I had a very hard time keeping the kids warm enough, especially at night. That was also when we were infected with scabies. This was definitely the low point of the trip. The weather is warming up now, so the apartment is much more comfortable.

We could write several more pages on both the good and the bad here. As you know, in China something can be really great on the one hand and really frustrating on the other hand.

June 2001

Things are winding down here. Or are they winding up?

The last couple of months have flown by, and I am just now ready to admit that I won't get everything done that I wanted to. My Chinese still gets me into more trouble than it gets me out of. I am not an expert at *tai ji*, calligraphy, or table tennis. I did not learn to play the *erhu*, and I did not write my journal (I did think of a great title though). I did learn more about gastrointestinal disease than I had anticipated, and let me tell you, clutching a lamppost as you send all the contractile neurological signals you can muster down below only gives the kids more to talk about. Respiratory diseases were well represented as well. I'm fortunate that I've had over fifteen years of experience diagnosing all of those bizarre animal illnesses. [*John is a veterinarian.*] Now when some alien material bursts forth from my nose at the dinner table I can impress my Chinese friends with intelligent comments such as, "Jesus H. Christ. What crawled down into my bronchi (notice the medical term) and died this time?" The Chinese, being the ultimate hosts that they are, don't miss a beat. They throw a bowl over it and wonder aloud what the "H" in his name stands for.

It's been a memorable year to say the least. Who could forget living in such close quarters with his spouse and daughters? No dark room to retreat to. No bathroom door that one could lock. Chasing lizards and cockroaches around with broom handles (I was the one who had the broom, not the cockroaches). Listening to the kids fight in Chinese. Sarah, by the way, can now say "piss off" in three languages. And who could forget the daily practice with the "charades" dialect of sign language, constant scrutiny and judgment, constant noise, pollution, and a never-ending population. But every day was new. I got some killer photos, and I now know about one hundred Chinese students who will bring tears to my eyes whenever I think of them.

*John McGee and track team members. Photo by John McGee.*

☯

**Ellen Axtmann**, Lijiang
August 2005

We are investigating kindergartens for Bei. It is sort of unnerving after Montessori. Here there are more than forty children to a class, snacks of rice gruel, and open latrines. I guess it is all part of the adventure. Bei seems game, although we have yet to enroll her. We looked at one yesterday and will try to arrange to see another tomorrow when Ken is done with his classes. I think the woman who is helping us with this process thinks we are rather peculiar for needing to do so much investigating.

☯

**Ken Driese**, Lijiang
September 2005

Don't worry, Division of Family Services watchdogs, neither Bei nor her parents have succumbed to reefer madness. Yes, *Cannabis* grows wild in Yunnan Province although few, except foreign English teachers, seem to pay much attention to it. In Liming, we saw lots of cute and wizened old women happily puffing away on their pipes, and in the markets of Lijiang, pipes and hookahs are not rare. Smoking tobacco through enormous bongs is a common sight on the streets and may explain some of the paraphernalia.

*Ellen Axtmann and her daughter, Bei Driese, accept apples from a Liming lady. Photo by Ken Driese.*

October 2005

Part of our motivation for coming to China this year was, of course, that China is our daughter Bei's home country. The Chinese are immensely curious about Bei, and they are surprisingly confused when they see her with us—two white parents. There is little shyness in China about staring, and people stand on the street looking back and forth from Bei to Ellen to me in confusion. If it is just one of us with Bei, they may ask if the absent parent is Chinese. The relief of understanding a mystery leaps onto their faces when we tell them that Bei is adopted (*Ta shi shou yang de*), and the reaction is always a thumbs-up or an expression of how lucky Bei is, to which we reply that we are the lucky ones.

During our train ride from Shanghai to Kunming, we passed directly through Bei's hometown just after dawn on a dreary Sunday morning. Feng Cheng is a small, nondescript, typical southeastern Chinese city with concrete apartment buildings and stores surrounded by rice paddies and, in this part of the Jiangxi Province, coal mines. Evenly spaced trees line the highway that follows the railroad tracks, and a few trucks and bicycles moved along it in the early morning. I snapped some blurry photos through the train window to save for Bei, who was still sleeping.

In one field I saw a man with a little girl about Bei's age, and as we passed, he hoisted her onto his shoulders for the walk back into town. I couldn't help but think about how easily Bei could have been that girl living an utterly different life in China, instead of sleeping through the dawn in a soft sleeper train bed with two American parents. And I couldn't help but imagine that somewhere in that town, maybe even within sight of the rail line, Bei's birth mother was busy making breakfast, unaware that the one-day-old girl she had left at the school gate in 2001 was passing through town and dreaming four-year-old dreams in English.

It is not just foreigners who adopt children in China, and it has been interesting to learn that adoption here is viewed quite differently than it is in the United States. One of the most surprising things that we have discovered, initially through conversations with a Chinese friend in Shanghai, is that in China adoption is often a huge secret kept from the adoptive child for as long as possible. In fact, it isn't a stretch to imagine adopted people living their entire lives here without ever knowing that they were adopted. And remarkably, according to our friend, who has an adopted cousin, everyone else in the family and in the family's social circle, *except* the adopted child, knows the truth.

Of course, our philosophy in the United States about sharing the adoption story (domestic or foreign) is quite the opposite—we start talking about adoption and birth parents from the earliest opportunity so that it *isn't* a big surprise for the child. Our thinking is that if the child is aware of adoption from the beginning, they integrate this identity as they grow up with their adoptive parents, and they avoid dealing with an unanticipated sea change in the context of their lives upon discovery of their history. And of course there is an implicit understanding by us that adoption is not shameful or something to be hidden away.

So why do the Chinese take the opposite approach—hiding this enormous truth, a huge elephant in the closet?? I can speculate based on a few conversations, some reading, and the results of an assignment that I gave my second-year writing students here in Lijiang. An obvious hypothesis is that there is a sense of shame in China about adoption—aren't big secrets often related to a need to hide something shameful? But if this were the case, why would everyone, *except* the child, be let in on the secret? This suggests that perhaps the parents are not themselves ashamed, but feel that the child's very history might be shameful for the child. To them, keeping the truth a secret may be designed to protect the child.

One could imagine that protecting the child from shame by keeping the secret may have something to do with trying to save "face" for the adopted child. The concept of face in China is more important than it is for us in the States (though we have it), and perhaps there is a belief here that an adopted child would experience a loss of face upon finding out about her history. This does not seem a huge stretch, and according to Hu and Grove in *Encountering the Chinese—A Guide for Americans* (1999), "face" is important in China because of the nature of society here. In contrast to the relatively transient social relationships in the States and some other western countries, the Chinese are strongly tied to their families and social groups for their entire lives. As a result, it is critical to maintain these relationships, which means maintaining a stable self-image or "face." In a sense, losing face means losing status in your entire social support group, almost like being exiled.

But does this really apply to the dilemma of whether to tell a child about adoption or to keep it a secret? It seems to me that if a child's identity includes early knowledge of adoption, then there is no issue of "face" since there would be no catastrophic change of self-image (loss of face) for the child within the child's family and social group upon revelation of her story. So maybe this concept doesn't explain the issue after all.

An explanation offered by our friend for the secrecy in *her* family was that the parents feared that if a child knew she was adopted, she might love her parents less. This viewpoint is supported by at least some of the students in my classes who, aside from representing the relatively rare slice of the Chinese population that goes to college, come from all over China and offer a geographic cross-section of Chinese thinking among their generation.

Many students shared the opinion that to tell a young child the truth about adoption would break the child's spirit and taint her view of the world. All children should see their world as a beautiful and happy place with no lurking shadows to darken their days. To these students the illusion of a perfect world for a child is the most important thing. This central philosophy of a sacred happy childhood was repeated in paper after paper as well as in class discussions. When a child is young, their ability to cope is low and adoption truth could be catastrophic.

This, of course, implies that the truth about adoption, while fundamentally devastating, can perhaps be swallowed when a person grows to maturity with the strength built upon the foundation of an idyllic childhood. The majority of students felt that eventually, an adoptee should be told the truth. When pressed, they surmised that "eventually" meant when they were fully mature adults.

As Westerners steeped in individualism, we have confidence in the strength of our children and in their ability to grow strong in the shelter of our love with full knowledge of their adoption histories. Life books, adoption stories, heritage camps, and early musings about birth mothers are part of our roadmap. And of course for us, this system feels like the right path. But as I glimpsed the little girl and her father, walking home between rice paddies outside of Feng Cheng in southeastern China, how could I ever know what her life might be like? For me and Ellen and Bei, the train left Feng Cheng on its way west to a different life.

**Ellen Axtmann**, Lijiang
March 2006

Our rental house in Old Town is great. Our commute is thirty to forty-five minutes to school depending on whether we bike (less time) or walk and catch a bus. The rent is fifteen hundred dollars for six months paid six months in advance.[1] The house has a huge kitchen (although we had to buy a stovetop burner and gas bottle), a bath with a sort of hopeless shower (very hot solar water, however), and four bedrooms along with a large living area and dining area, which we seldom use because the courtyard is so lovely, and we have a huge veranda that surrounds the courtyard. The upstairs is unfinished (used for grain storage originally). The neighborhood is all traditional Naxi; and it is considered a separate village, although you wouldn't know it walking from Old Town. Our neighbors have been incredibly welcoming and warm. I like living here and walking through the cobblestone streets to catch the bus. We found a woman to take Bei to and from school and also to stay with Bei in the afternoons two times a week; she speaks fairly good English and has promised to help Bei with Chinese.

**Ann**, Kunming
September 2007

Alice, we need your sage advice. There now seems to be a problem with enrolling the kids in kindergarten. The *waiban* contacted the kindergarten people earlier in the week, and she said "no problem." Now, today, she said there will be a problem because the kids are foreign and don't know Chinese; the teachers don't know English; and the school is "full." The class size is around fifty kids with two or three teachers. She said that we should consider a private kindergarten, but she wasn't sure about where it's located or the cost. I told her that we want the kids in the university kindergarten because it's convenient, and the kids will meet others who live in this vast faculty housing. I said we weren't concerned about the language difference or class size.

We hope to go see the kindergarten in action on Tuesday. I don't know how hard to push the issue. The main reason we are in China is to expose the kids to Chinese, and this will only happen if they are in school. We were not planning on homeschooling them. I feel that the *waiban* really doesn't want to deal with the school and doesn't want to be our advocate on this issue.

September 2007

The problem is now "*no problema.*" The kids will begin kindergarten at the university on Friday. Somehow their enrollment opened up, and foreign kids are now not a problem. When I met our *waiban* today to go to the other university's kindergarten, she said we had an appointment at our university's kindergarten. We met with the director and assistant director, asked and answered questions, toured the building, and got information on costs. With all the (crazy) fees included, it'll cost just about six hundred dollars per child for the year. It was a bit more than I budgeted, but I figured the per-day cost, and it's about three dollars per child per day. I am so relieved. The kids need structure for their days and kids to interact with. They will go full days, but will come home for two hours while the other kids nap. Such an advantage when one is less than a ten-minute walk away. Thanks for your support.

October 2007

We've been keeping busy. The kids love school, and I'm enjoying teaching. Gustavo has been a great help in keeping the flat running smoothly. No soccer for the poor guy; everything is centered around basketball. He also called a couple of people who were looking for a Spanish teacher, but nothing panned out. But for now it's okay because he's the one that gets the kids to school in the morning.

I'm finding that Kunming is not that much cheaper than Shanghai. Food prices have gone up around twenty percent and that's what we spend the majority of our money on. And that's been my biggest source of frustration—trying to stretch 3,000 *yuan* monthly to feed the four of us.

November 2007

**100 Days**

We ❣ at the one hundred day mark here in China and so far, so good! It's past the midpoint of the first semester too.

The Chinese love foreign kids! Everywhere we go, people smile and say "Hello," teenagers want their picture on their cell phones, ladies will put them on their lap on the bus, and grandpas are constantly giving candy.

We've received a few puzzled looks if we mention that the kids are adopted. Although thousands of Chinese children (mostly girls) are adopted internationally and domestically every year, adoption is not well known to the average citizen. Most people are very accepting; however, ever since knowing that our kids are adopted, one parent from the kids' school no longer speaks to us. Many of the blogs that I read are written by Caucasian parents in China with their adopted Chinese child(ren). They are *constantly* questioned and stared at. Today, while shopping, Carlos and I were waiting for Gustavo and Elena to come back from picking up an item. A grandmother stopped, looked at me, and looked at Carlos, touched her face and said something that included the word *Baba* or father. She was asking me if Carlos's father had the darker skin. Then she kept repeating and pointing to us about our difference in skin tones, shaking her head as if to say "Impossible!" I do often wonder when the four of us are out and about if people assume I'm the stepmother, since the kids and Gustavo share the "Latino look."

Now that we have a routine, know our way around some, and the *sheer overwhelmingness* has subsided, Gustavo and I have decided to become more serious about learning Chinese. This week we will start a language exchange with one of the university students—thirty minutes of English for her and thirty minutes of Chinese for us. We are getting frustrated not knowing much more than from our days in Shanghai. Gustavo has been studying and trying more than me. His learning style is very different than mine. He likes the integrated approach with words and sentences; he wants to hear, say, see, and write it. In language learning and teaching, there is a method called the Natural Approach, where one component is a "silent period." This is akin to a baby learning a language. A baby will take in a language silently for months, and then suddenly begin to speak. This is how I operate. I like to hear the language for a while, then pick out sounds and words, and put more and more together to form my own speech. I've also become much more curious and aware of the written characters and am now ready for it to make sense. The kids are progressing nicely in Chinese. Elena will tell me a word, I'll repeat it (usually incorrectly), and she'll say, "No, no, like *this*. Listen!" and repeat it. She gets the tones naturally and knows I'm repeating it wrong, but can't say, "Mom, use the second tone, not the fourth tone!" This evening, the kids were "playing school." The two of them talked in a "pretend Chinese" for well over a half-hour. To them, that's how school is—in Chinese.

### November 2007

Today, when telling me about her day, Elena announced, "I'm not Guatemalan, not 'Merican, not Chilena. I'm a Chinese girl!" I asked her what makes her Chinese. She replied, "I *love* eating with chopsticks." I thought, "Oh my, what have we done? Should we be thrilled that she's embracing the Chinese culture and feels like she's a part of it? Should we be worried that we're setting her up to have a major identity crisis?"

Later, Carlos was looking at his English book practicing today's lesson. His teacher is a young Chinese woman and English is her second language. Carlos was saying, "Where is she goING?" She is going to her grand-MOTHer's house." He was putting the emphasis on the wrong syllable in a sentence, which many Chinese English speakers do.

So there you have it. We have one child who thinks she's *culturally* Chinese, and one that may end up *sounding* Chinese!

### December 2007

To celebrate the New Year and to commemorate the upcoming Beijing 2008 Olympics, the kindergarten held its own version in the field house on campus Saturday morning. Opening ceremonies, including the national anthem, required speeches from dignitaries and the parade of athletes walking the outdoor track. Carlos and his Papi "took the gold" in the wheelbarrow event.

### February 2008

*All my fears about living in China have never materialized!* This is what was keeping me up nights about a year ago (in no particular order).

*Bugs, bugs, and more bugs:* After learning that we'd be in Kunming, close to Vietnam (which conjured up images of jungles), I imagined sharing our humble home with the creep-y and crawl-y variety. We've only seen *one* bug in the apartment, and much to our relief, we have screens on all the windows.

*Filth, filth, and more filth:* China, in general, is fairly clean. Public areas are not as clean as we would like, but it's not *too* bad. People regularly use public wastebaskets and streets, stores, and the like are constantly being swept out. There are *armies* of sweepers everywhere, unlike the US, where a machine does the job. I have found (though Gustavo will vehemently disagree) that the public spaces in China are much cleaner than those in Latin America.

*The kids wouldn't adjust:* And just who loves school, life in general, and speaks and understands Mandarin? Now, *that* was a waste of a worry!

*I'd hate my job:* The job is wonderful! I have great students, a fantastic schedule, and complete autonomy. My only "complaint" is that it isn't that much of a challenge. Gustavo is now teaching English to five people, involved in soccer, and loves exploring the mysteries of the Chinese language, customs, and culture.

*Living on campus would be suffocating:* Living on campus has been the *best* thing about being in Kunming. It's quiet, pretty, private, and a ten-minute walking commute. The apartment is decent; we enjoy having the dining halls available for meals; and the kids' school is on campus. We love being part of the university community.

*The language barrier will do us in:* Learning Mandarin is certainly a challenge, but we're making progress. Looking back to August, it's amazing what we now can *say and read*! People bend over backwards to help us understand. Also, several students, colleagues, and neighbors have come to our "linguistic rescue."

July 2008

**Full Circle**

Looking at a globe today, we traced the route to Kunming from Michigan. So many miles! It's hard to believe that only one year ago, Kunming was only a small dot on a map. Now, it's a place that represents many memories of good times, friends, and places that are dear. A year ago, we were in the process of stepping into the unknown—a bit nervous, a little scared, but fully excited about the possibilities. And we're glad we took the plunge.

The adjustment to coming home certainly has been much easier than adjusting to life in China. We're in full swing: playdates, grocery shopping, and doctor appointments. The biggest adjustments? Where is everybody?! The stores and streets seem so empty. Traffic is orderly, and everyone obeys the traffic laws! And the very best, we can now read everything!

Two things I miss most about living in China are walking and good, cheap food. In China, one walks everywhere, every day, up and down, and in and out. And I love to walk, but I need a specific destination. And there are no more meals waiting at the university dining halls and no more dumpling dives.

Thanks to everyone who joined us throughout this journey. It's much appreciated. I tried to show our everyday, nothing fancy life. A goal of ours was to live a simple life on a Chinese teacher's salary. We purposefully didn't mega-travel and limited our "Western needs." A main goal was to give the kids a language immersion experience by attending a Chinese school. We are so thankful that Carlos and Elena had a wonderful, fun-filled school year of making friends while becoming quite proficient in Mandarin. That, in itself, was worth any "discomfort" experienced.

*Minus the toddler fisticuffs incident, the stories from families with preschool-aged children suggest a relatively smooth transition for the kids. As Ann said, her fears that her two young children wouldn't adjust was "a waste of a worry." For families with older children, adapting to life abroad is not as easy, but not insurmountable. For older children, fitting in to Chinese school is more difficult as the emails from JB and the Lewis family will disclose.*

**JB**, Chengdu
August 2007

Our apartment was a bit of a shock. The first jolt was that there were only two bedrooms. There was a baby bed and an oversized twin in the small bedroom. Not only was it a baby bed, but a well-used baby bed. Needless to say, Charlotte (age eight) was not impressed. The girls shared the small bed the first night, but we have now switched. Bryan and I are sharing the small bed, and the girls are sharing the larger bed and the larger bedroom. The walls had been painted, thankfully, but the trim around the doors and the doors themselves have not seen fresh paint in quite some time. I have scrubbed the door into the kitchen three times and there are still black smudges around the handle. The wood around the doorframe in the bathroom is full of termite holes. We have completely scrubbed the walls in the kitchen and bathroom, mopped every horizontal surface, and washed as much linen at a time as we can. The view from the kitchen leaves something to be desired unless you enjoy looking at another tenant's cast-offs: an old mop, pottery, and a broken toilet seat. Those are some of the negatives.

The positives are we can easily walk to the school. The staff seems great. The program director is a gem, and we had a lovely luncheon yesterday after our scheduling meeting. Our tentative schedules are perfect so we are keeping our fingers crossed that they don't change.

We miss the convenience of the campus in Shanghai [*where they participated in the CCC's Summer Institute in August*] and have yet to discover a vendor's row where we can purchase breakfast, but we have found the Trust Mart, IKEA, and Carrefour. As I type, Bryan is assembling a freestanding closet for us so we can hang up our clothes. Most of our free time has been spent trying to put a household together. Today we bought a rice cooker, and I am looking forward to making brown rice. We will purchase a wok next.

We have been out to the Waldorf School. The setting is lovely. It was a resort at one time. The original building is very "traditional Chinese," and it overlooks a small lake. There is a huge garden and lots of area to play

outside. There is a resident goat, chicken, duck, and dog. They have a ways
to go to have the site ready for school to begin next week, but we will go out
this Saturday for registration, and we will see if classes will really begin on
Monday or not.

## October 2007

The girls really do like school. They go off willingly each morning and
come back happy in the evenings. There are two other girls (who are also
both adopted Chinese) that ride a private van to school with Esme (age
eleven) and Charlotte (age eight).

We have found two dance schools that we are going to try out this weekend. The girls have definite ideas about which school they want to attend,
but we are going to try a lesson at each school before making our final decision. Let's just say it does not appear that Chengdu is a mecca for aspiring
ballerinas.

## November 2007

Esme is doing better with the school situation. I think when you were here
we had all hit the bottom of the barrel. We still have some rough moments,
but she feels better in class with her sister and her sister's teacher. It was her
choice, and she feels good about how it is going so far. Having the Lijiang
trip to look forward to helped her a lot too, and now we will start planning
for Spring Festival. Her class back at home is a very special group of children, and she has had the same teacher and gone to the same school where
everyone knows her and loves her since second grade. This experience at
the Chengdu Waldorf School, especially as she is on the cusp of puberty, has
been a major challenge for her. She will be a stronger person because of it.

As far as the apartment goes, we did get a "new" mattress. In was newer
than the one we got rid of and not quite as mildewed, but unfortunately it
is still mildewed. When Bryan helped the building maintenance man carry
it to our apartment he thought he detected some offensive smell, but the
maintenance man said he didn't. As I said, it wasn't as bad, but since getting
it here the smell has permeated the mattress pad. In fact we had everything
airing while we were in Lijiang, and it didn't seem to do any good. Short of
a brand-new mattress, we will be dealing with mildew. The area outside of
our window looks just the same. Nothing has been cleaned up.

## May 2008

Esme is very excited to be nearly finished with school; it has been her biggest challenge. The Chinese children of her age group have not embraced
her. It is too bad, and one of the saddest aspects of this whole trip. I think

had she been white and blond, she would have had a different experience. But instead, she is dark-skinned and Chinese. She is a good traveler and is looking forward to traveling after school is out. Given the choice of traveling or going home to see her friends, I am not sure which she would choose.

I am growing a little nostalgic. I will not miss my living conditions, but there are things about China I will miss. For all of us it has been a positive year; for Esme more challenging but even for her, I know she will look back on many things fondly (fortunately she is a positive person). I will miss the students. I will miss fresh green tea, and the natural beauty of China and much more. Who knows? We may be back one day.

May 2008 [*This email was written after the earthquake in the Mianyang area of Sichuan, northwest of Chengdu. The 7.9 magnitude earthquake on May 12 killed over seventy thousand people, including many schoolchildren.*]

It was very intense here for a while. Esme in particular in her tender preteen state was very, very frightened. I was afraid I was going to have to take the girls and leave Chengdu. But the aftershocks are less frequent, and she is turning her attention toward other things now. We got involved in helping get relief goods to the orphanages in the earthquake zone, which helped us all take our minds off of our own small problems and fears.

Many of my students come from towns in the earthquake area. Classes are suddenly smaller as students head off to volunteer or go search for families. We have had many things to talk about over the past few weeks when we have had class. My classes this quarter have been great. I love teaching for this program. I will miss teaching here. The *waibans* have been so great, so accommodating. We will miss them.

June 2008

Living through a natural disaster in China has provided an aspect to the experience that we hadn't counted on, but not all of it was negative. We got the chance to help some of the orphanages and to witness the incredible spirit of our students, of Sichuan, and of China.

Bryan and I have had a wonderful time teaching. This term in particular has been a lot of fun. The girls have had a mixed experience. They attend a Waldorf school, but it is not quite like the Waldorf school back home. It has been a challenge for them, but they will be stronger for it. Their Chinese is much better than ours, and they are proud to be able to translate for us when need be. Ballet lessons have also been an experience. Their teacher really loves them and appreciates their talent. Their teacher will be one of the people we will miss the most.

In some ways the adults in this family wish we were here for another year. The girls really miss their friends, grandparents, and school. As Alice said,

I think once they look back on the unique freedom and growth they experienced this year, they will end up missing China more than they think they will. I already know I will.

*Tim and Sue Lewis took their three children to China: Peter, age nine, Jack, age seven, and Sophie, age two. Sophie was adopted from China. Tim and Sue also decided to live off campus to be closer to their children's schools. No one bothered to mention that the entire apartment building was under massive remodel.*

**Timothy Lewis**, Hangzhou
August 2007

Alice! We're doing great; the major problem is the construction (like building demolition) that goes on outside our window twenty-four hours a day! But we're putting our earplugs in and trying to make do. I'm sure it won't be forever. I got cell service, and I was able to order water service in Chinese! We'll have Internet service on September first they tell me, and then it will be home sweet home.

We also bought four bicycles so we go cruising down the road just like the Chinese, and we get a lot of stares, especially with Sophie on the back of my bike! We've gone native!

*Sue, Sophie, and Peter Lewis ride a tandem bike in Xian. Photo by Tim Lewis.*

September 2007

School is going great for Sophie and the boys. It is quite difficult for them due to the language challenge but I told them they had three goals: Do their best. Don't stress out. And learn one new word a day. Already they are saying simple sentences in Chinese and ordering food in restaurants. They are making friends in school. Kids are giving them origami or buying them soft drinks. Sophie is in kindergarten and loves it. I don't think she cares that everyone is speaking Chinese as long as there are the other kids to play with.

Neither one of us starts teaching for another week. Sue and I have more time to explore Hangzhou. There are so many beautiful spots here!

Sue went to orientation and is all set with her schedule. I will go there this week to check it out myself although I haven't been officially invited yet. I'm not in the Foreign Language School, but in the School of Graduate Studies, so I think I'm on my own a bit. I will call and invite myself.

September 2007

The boys are still in Chinese school and making friends. However, the language is very difficult for them. They are being troopers and powering through it. They are miserable doing all of the Chinese, but the Chinese kids make it bearable. Sophie is loving every minute of her preschool. We all get a lot of attention wherever we go.

☯

**Sue Lewis**, Hangzhou
November 2007

It takes time to make friends, but we have met such kind and thoughtful people. We are planning a trip with a couple of the students to the water town Tixiang. I am looking forward to it and am grateful they are willing to buy the bus tickets, book the hotel, and be our guides. Hopefully, our kids will behave enough that they will want to go again with us.

The one thing that is discouraging is the language. It is not coming as easily for me as I was hoping. I actually have to study, and I have never been a great student. I am not that motivated, except by guilt!

December 2007

Yesterday I went to school, the market, and then my Chinese class and had the feeling of being home.

The boys are now home Mondays and Fridays for the month of December to give them a bit of a rest. I will bring in a tutor; we have been learning about life by watching some good movies and talking. *Gandhi* was a good movie and showed what a good lawyer can do to make the world right!

❧

**Timothy Lewis**, Hangzhou
December 2007

They said the water would be off for three days, but in reality it was off for only twenty-four hours. We were schlepping buckets up the stairs from across the street! They were replacing a water main under the road. I think if it would have been three days we probably would have retreated to a hotel.

They also drilled four-inch diameter holes in each of the rooms for air conditioning; we have filled the holes with plastic bags until they get around to hooking up the air conditioning units. When they drilled they made a huge mess inside of mud and dirt; Sophie's bed was under one of the holes! Ugh! But, we looked at each other and said, "That's China!" Inconvenient to be sure, but everyone else in the building is dealing with it, so we are too.

It would be nice to know when they are doing things like drilling holes in our walls so we can move stuff away from the construction. I'm so happy my computer and camera weren't sitting next to the wall that day!

Anyway, these are just the inconveniences, and the construction appears to be finishing up, though I would guess they have at least another month to go.

❧

**Sue Lewis**, Hangzhou
January 2008

Some cheery good news! I hired a local student to teach the boys. She goes to the school by our house that has the grass field with the goats. She said we can use it anytime and took me there. She also took me shopping for art supplies to start Chinese painting. (Of course, it always saves me money to have a local ask the price). She doesn't speak a lot of English but wants to learn more to be a better teacher. My Chinese studies will suffer, but she and I get along well and she wants to spend time with me so we are going shopping today for gifts to send home to my girlfriends and their kids. We only have 173 days left, and Tim and I both feel that we are just starting to do the things we want: Chinese tutor, art teacher, friends, and don't have much time left.

January 2008

I think that I will have a hard time going home for the Spring Festival holiday. One of my US mom support groups sent a little story about how

*Peter Lewis shops for Chinese calligraphy brushes. Photo by Tim Lewis.*

hard it was for the mom to put the kid on the school bus all by himself. That seems like small potatoes after putting your kids in Chinese school and having them fend for themselves with no language or friends. The kids are also excited that our friends are picking us up in their van for dinner. No bikes, walking, or trying to catch a cab. They also appreciate heat and warm socks; I think we have been successful in teaching an important lesson. I feel so happy that they get it!

☯

**Timothy Lewis**, Hangzhou
March 2008

Construction continues on our apartment complex. They are improving the first floor, so we have still been having water interruptions and lots of construction noise. The weather is getting warmer, however, which makes it easier to get outside and away from the apartment.

The boys have been home with us. They've been doing a really great job on their homeschooling, but it does make the apartment smaller having them home all day. However, we can move along at quite a fast pace, much faster than they move in regular public school so it has been fun and interesting for all of us.

☯

**Sue Lewis**, Hangzhou
May 2008

We are mailing boxes home, and I am taking the kids to say good-bye to their classmates because we never did that; we just didn't show up any more. I read a great book called *Third Culture Kids*[2] that talked about the process of moving, especially between countries. It said to build a RAFT: Reconciliation, Affirmation, Farewells, and Transition home. I would recommend it to families taking their kids overseas.


May 2008

We are coming to the end of a great year. Peter and Jack ended up homeschooling. It has turned out okay because Tim and I have had a chance to spend more time with the boys. Sophie loves her preschool (almost as much as we do) and has been able to pick up the language quickly. Our "jobs" have been the best we have had in years!

**Shana Tarter** and **Steven J. Platz**, Lijiang
August 2007

We visited Li's kindergarten. It seemed quite nice, and they will arrange for a driver for her each way. Kindergarten goes from seven thirty in the morning until seven o'clock at night and includes three meals a day, numerous hygiene breaks, and two and a half hours of napping. We'll have to see how that goes!


September 2007

Li's description of kindergarten included the following highlights: Li says, "I'm good. Today at kindergarten I had a good day at school. My favorite part of the day is eating. I met Amy, Lucy, Linda (English names)." She said that she spent naptime in a tent with a girl named Linda, and they talked the whole time. The teacher kept telling them to go to sleep, but they kept talking. We asked what they talked about, and Li said, "I don't know. She speaks Chinese." That somehow explains it.

I thought I knew how to ride a bike. But no one ever taught me the art of weaving in and out of buses and taxis. Some streets have what passes for a bike/cart/motorcycle lane, others, well, not so much. The taxis and buses are kind enough to honk at you shortly before they run you over. As Steve describes it, you simply ride into an intersection and then maintain your speed. If you change speed to avoid obstacles (like pedestrians), it throws everyone else off. The most challenging obstacles are the British-style roundabouts:

two lanes of traffic constantly entering and exiting the circle mixed with people and bikes. Li thinks it is all great fun and sits on the back of Steve's bike in her child seat eating sunflower seeds and shouting, "Faster, sled dog!" Shana appears to enjoy the chaos of the roundabouts in that periodically she will go around one and a half times. Li is ever watchful saying, "Where is Mommy going?" I think biking is similar to winter driving. There is a time to be plodding and a time to go for it, still with a sense of overwhelming caution. It is also amazing to see the variety of bikes, loads, and people pedaling around. I am not surprised to see a biker on a cell phone holding an umbrella while navigating the streets. I wonder what the locals would think about a stationary exercise bike.

October 2007

We continue to be amazed at how poorly the local towels and sponges absorb water. I used to think it would be impossible to actually make a 100% cotton towel not absorb water. The sponges work if there is enough surface area to spread out the spilled water until it no longer exists, but Chinese sponges do not actually hold onto water. Our new analogy: Li is learning Chinese. Her parents are also learning, and their brains are like Chinese sponges.

November 2007

**Haikus Bridge the Language Barrier**

I have had great success getting my students to be creative with haikus. Thinking if my students can do it, my daughter should be able to. Here are her results:

**Children**
Love mommy daddy
Swing and jump on the playground
Nap with Little Cow

**Silk**
Running in silk clothes
Feel shiny, cool, beautiful
Thank you to the worms

January 2008

## A Visit to Li's Orphanage

We arrived in Guilin today. The cold and rain is a bit brutal after a week at the beach in Sanya! Apparently we brought the rain. We had a single goal in Guilin: to visit Li's orphanage and to view her adoption file.

Our adoption agency representative from five years ago was able to set up a visit to the orphanage and arrange a translator which all worked very smoothly. We went from the hotel to the orphanage with our translator and met with two women who do all the babies' files. The older one "remembered" Li, or was at least there five years ago. She remembered my mother visiting two years ago, and I had a picture of them together. We met the man who named Li and learned that he meant for her middle name to mean "strong jade" (we were told precious jade originally)—that was great because most people can't translate the Chinese character for her middle name Yao. We saw the playroom built by a charitable group called Half the Sky, one of the young children's playrooms, and one baby room—all from the outside. We looked at Li's file that had very little in it and no information we didn't know. We did take a picture of the only picture in her file, one we had never seen. The staff seemed content to see us but not overly excited. It seemed routine for them. Our translator does adoption work in Guangzhou and was home in Guilin on vacation. He was young and nice. The whole tone was very easygoing. We joked with the man who named Li (who must be thirty at tops); he drives the babies and runs errands. No one had any real emotional response. We drove by her "finding place," but in the past five years it has been converted from a hospital to an apartment building so we could only take pictures from the outside. We asked about her foster mother (who she was only with for a month and we never knew her name). We asked if she was still caring for babies. They said that they weren't allowed to give us a name, and they had forgotten who it was, and many of the foster families from five years ago no longer took kids.

I am not sure what we expected, but I think it was what happened. We learned a few tidbits, but nothing more. Li didn't feel any connection, and we weren't allowed to go into any of the rooms with kids. We were definitely shown the model rooms. I think also being in China for four months has made so many things feel routine that there were no big surprises to be had. Perhaps if we had been with a group gearing up for this visit, we would have been allowed to spend more time or actually go into rooms with babies, but they were certainly not offering us that opportunity.

We are glad we had the chance to visit and take some pictures. Perhaps we can return when Li is older, and she may have a stronger response to the place she spent the first ten months of her life.

June 2008

### The Olympic Torch Made It and So Did We

We felt a little sorry for ourselves having to get up at six thirty in the morning and catch a bus for our "torch duty," but then again, the students and non-foreign teachers from the College were on duty at five thirty! The days and weeks leading up to the Olympic Torch's arrival have been shrouded in mystery and speculation. Our class schedules have changed on an hour's notice, as of yesterday the College was still negotiating its role in the affair with the local government and, of course, the torch route was secret. At first, it appeared that we, the foreigners, were meant to be the showpiece for the local government for our loyalty to China and our support of the torch. We all politely refused that honor, but nevertheless found ourselves on a bus full of foreign teachers and students from the two colleges in Lijiang and the head of the Lijiang Foreign Affairs Department (who knew we had one?). Instead of heading into town as we had expected, we headed north into Jade Dragon Snow Mountain Park. We found ourselves lining a corridor full of traditionally dressed minority people (at least a thousand) and students in matching t-shirts. Flags were ubiquitous. After our arrival, we learned there would be a three and a half hour wait. We had been told not to bring any bags or food for fear of "issues" so you can imagine how painful the wait was with a tired, hungry, under-clothed six-year-old. Since we had expected to be in town, we wore t-shirts and raincoats, fine for town, not good for the park which is over ten thousand feet in elevation.

Eventually, of course, the excitement began. The buses bearing torch bearers dropped them off at their designated stations, and we had a front row seat for the handoff of Torch Bearer #173 and #174. Number 173 was a big white guy, story unknown! After the brief event complete with drumming from the Tibetans and chanting from the Chinese, we waited for another hour and a half until the torch bearers were reloaded in their buses and taken back down the hill. We made it home by half past noon, in time for a nap.

In some ways, the actual event was anticlimactic, but in other ways it was astounding. The minority costumes were beautiful, the mountain a stunning backdrop, the actual torch handoff occurred less than ten feet from us, and it is likely we will make the local newspaper given the number of times we were photographed and interviewed.

Beijing, here we come! We Came, We Saw, We Survived!

July 2008

**The End! At Least Temporarily**

Our last two weeks in China were a whirlwind of packing, examinations, dinners, and many farewells. For as much effort as we put into our finals, it is disappointing to know that our grades probably won't actually count. In other words, the students that we fail will simply be promoted into the next class regardless. Then next year's unsuspecting foreign teachers will inherit the same problems that we did. We had two official farewell dinners. Both times we were segregated into a separate table for the foreign teachers and refused the opportunity to mingle. Such heavy-handedness was imposed by the Dean of the English Department. He did ask us to stay next year while we were taking a departmental photo three days before leaving China!

We were able to spend an afternoon with our friend and her family. Her six-year-old daughter and Li entertained us with dance performances and songs for the afternoon. We had some great meals with friends and students and generally felt sad to be leaving. The good news is that by the time we get back here again, most of our students will have graduated, and we can visit them all over China.

One of the most memorable events of our departure was the good-bye party at Li's school. We told her teacher we wanted to come by to take some pictures and bring a few small gifts. Upon our arrival, we discovered three chairs waiting for us at one end of the room and the kids ready to sing and dance for us. We put tattoos on all the kids and gave out treats. Li gave away many treasures, but ended up with about the same amount in return. There was a giant cake and lots of excited screaming, and of course, some tears.

*Despite an earthquake, scabies, and mildewed mattresses, all of these families found their year in China to be an enriching experience for both parents and children.*

# 7

# Going Home
## *Man zou, Zhongguo!*
## *(*Take It Easy, China!*)*

Things are winding down here or are they winding up? After a year of teaching idioms to the Chinese I'm not sure anymore. I've somewhat lost the ability to say what I mean. Or is it mean what I say?

—John McGee

*At this juncture, China has become "home" for most of these travelers, and China will have a home in their hearts and minds for decades to come. After a year abroad, their understanding of home shifts and enlarges. Many teachers decide to stay more than one year. The temptation to stay afflicts even those who return to the United States as planned.*

☯

### Jennie Richey, Nanjing
March 2002

We are now well into our eighth month of the China experience, which leaves only a short four months before our scheduled departure back to our homeland. Although we've been toying with the idea of staying on another year, we're still not sure. To leave in only four months is going to entail us uprooting ourselves from a life we've grown to love, but to stay another year would mean another year away from the comforts of Seattle, driving, homemade baked goods, Mexican food, dryers, tap water, salad, and most importantly, our families and friends.

☯

### Jim Boyd, Nanjing
May 2004

I wanted to send you a quick note to let you know that our experience has been *fantastic* in all ways. China is truly a beautiful country with wonderful people, food, culture, and scenery. We have been able to travel to almost all parts of the country and have seen over thirty-five or forty different cities, villages, and towns. We have over five thousand digital photos to share our experience. We have also been interviewed on TV here in Nanjing. Because of our age and our adopting Haley, we have had a lot of interest in our family. We are like movie stars.

We have gone very deep below the surface and feel that we have seen the real China. We have seen all of the major tourist sites in the country, as well as had dinner in students' homes in their towns. We have also had many of our students come to our apartment and cook dinner for us. What an experience we have had!

My teaching has been the most rewarding thing I have done in my whole career. I love it very much. We would like to stay many more years, but we have to get Haley into school at home. The international schools here are too expensive. We are coming home.

**Mary Barton**, Nanjing
June 2004

While I am writing this final update I am thinking about the things I won't miss and those that I will miss. I want to keep my thoughts positive as I leave this great country so I will just mention a few things I will miss: Road One with its hubbub of activity 24/7, buying fresh fruits and vegetables half a block away, laughing with my students and coaching them in baseball, the simple life, DVD shopping, teaching at the university, weekly facials, my roommates, other foreign teachers, this campus, teaching line dancing, freedom from palm pilots, cell phones, pagers, yadda, yadda; all-nighters with *West Wing* and *Alias*, and most of all, the deep friendships I have made with my students. They have unbelievably touched my heart. I can't believe how lucky I have been.

**Rodney Chin**, Chengdu
August 2001

Alice, this China trip was certainly the experience of a lifetime! It really helped put things more into perspective. Truly, the best education one can ever attain is by visiting different countries and living there.

The Chinese really do go all out for their foreign teachers. It's very tempting to stay an extra year, but I know that I have too many responsibilities back home for another year of indulgence! The first month was difficult for me, but after that everything fell into place. My classes were so good that it was like driving a car with cruise control, and I was merely steering them, getting them through the long and winding road of English! In my opinion, a good class has fun together both in and out of the classroom.

Some people can easily adjust to this new environment and become effective teachers; for others, the transition is nerve-racking. They may lose the confidence of the class, and ultimately, themselves as well.

Thanks for everything you've done, directly and indirectly; this year has been so influential to my life that I feel like a different person. I hope that in the future, others can experience this feeling as well.

**Michael Hsu**, Tianjin
November 2003

You were right. I remember you saying that China has certain addictive qualities, and you are absolutely right. I am hooked—hooked to the point where I am thinking about next fall, the next step in my life, and I am only thinking about and fixated on one thing: China.

My thoughts are turning to graduate school, and I have decided (a no-brainer, really) to apply to Asian Studies programs.


May 2004

**Misty Nostalgia**

As the end of my time here draws ever nearer, I stand amazed at the things I have learned, places I have seen, people I have met, and the experiences I have amassed during this life-changing year. (Wow, this sounds a lot like the retrospective that Miss America gives at the end of her yearlong reign, you know, the voice-over that accompanies images of her making the one last regal, slinky stalk across the stage.)

But, truly, I am sometimes literally breathless when I consider the scope of my adventures in China that have covered the full breadth of the country and the full range of emotions.

I enjoyed my return to Shanghai. I met up with one of the students from our program last summer, and was overcome with misty nostalgia as I passed by the parking lot near the Yu Yuan Gardens, where we were spilled—drenched in sweat and delirious with shock—into our first full day in China. That moment is, at the same time, close in my memory, and yet so unreachably in the past.


❧


**Barbara Kramarz**, Shanghai
April 2006

I've decided to move on from Shanghai in June. I still remain totally fascinated with this incredibly dynamic city, but some inner voice says it's time. Wish I knew what and where, but that essential information will just have to unfold. I can't say that China was anywhere on my horizon two years ago, and look what happened. I'll always be grateful to you for threading my way through the needle!


❧


**Eva Tam**, Fuzhou
June 2007

The semester will be over in a few weeks, and then I'll fly back to the United States. For me, it's amazing to think that I left the United States in July 2006, and now I will be returning in July 2007. It wasn't easy being away from home for a year, but the experience has made me a stronger person. The experience has made me realize how much I do miss my family, friends, and home, and how different China is. I thought I had a good idea of what China is like, but that was because I hadn't experienced living in a *real* Chinese city. Yes, Shanghai is in China, but it is atypical of a Chinese city. Fuzhou, however, has a blend of both Western and Chinese elements. Here, I am able to find cheese, tortilla chips, salsa, Tabasco, even Pringles, but I can also find babies with split-pants and people spitting on the bus too. I hear stories from the students about wearing black, blue, and green colored hair clips and how each color represents the death of a different relative. I learned that some students have brothers or sisters, actual brothers or sisters. In Shanghai, a brother or sister usually meant cousin, but in Fuzhou, a lot of the time it means brother or sister.

One thing I will miss about China is the friendly faces. Every time I walk to and from the university, I see a friendly face and receive a *"Ni hao."* Sometimes I am greeted by the old woman and man who guard the gate, the driver, and the students. There are many things that I will miss, but I will be happy to see my friends and family again soon.

I'll end this letter with farewell Fuzhou, I shall always remember you, and hello America, I'm coming back home!

*And some teachers depart temporarily with plans to return.*

**Susan Burnett**, Shanghai
June 2008

I leave one week from today for the United States. It's going to be interesting to be in the States after being on foreign soil for so long, and I'm looking forward to my perspective of China once I'm away, just as I was looking forward to the perspective of the States from China when I came here. I was in touch with several of my Chinese students yesterday, and realized that I'll be glad to be back in China in August, as I truly have made some good friends here.

**Theresa**, Tianjin
March 2008

Although getting adjusted was difficult at first, I am so glad I have chosen to stick it out. I am actually enjoying it here in China rather than just waiting for it to be over! Taking Chinese classes has made all the difference in the world, and I highly recommend that to teachers joining the program next year. I am actually planning on staying in China a little bit longer; however, I'd like to move to Beijing so I'll start scouting out jobs there shortly.

**Daniel**, Beijing
December 2008

I won't be teaching next semester. Actually tomorrow will be my first day of official China teaching retirement. I just finished my last three classes today. It was a very touching experience as my students almost brought me to tears with letters and cards and spoken words. As I said good-bye to them I could see some tears well up in some of their eyes which made it all the more difficult. You may earn more money in the corporate world or respect compared to teaching in China, but the "personal" aspect of the teaching job is fulfilling and unforgettable. Anyway, you know all of this.

I plan to return home to Chicago in the next couple of weeks. After visiting family for a few weeks and a quick trip to Boulder, I plan to return to China to study Chinese for a semester or so and just be a student—no job. I'm not exactly sure yet, maybe somewhere in *dongbei* [*northeast China*].

*Of course, some teachers breathe a sigh of relief when it is time to leave, and still experience mixed emotions.*

**Karen Raines**, Shanghai
May 2008

I'm packing up my bags, and I'm ready to get out of here! Today, I met a colleague at the local Starbucks (where everybody knows our names). She told me I was going to miss the students, the people, and the energy of China. I responded that I could not wait to miss everything! She is right; however, here are moments when I fall in love with China. For instance, when I went to the post office yesterday I had an only-in-China experience. I was shipping some of the shoes I acquired over the year, and the female worker going through my belongings (to make sure I was not sending anything illegal) pointed at my shoes and said, *"Hen hao"* [*very nice.*] She then proceeded to try on my shoes! I smiled widely and then laughed out loud when she actually started modeling the shoes for me. Only in China! I will cherish my time here, but I'm ready to be elsewhere—at least for a while.

*Ironically, Karen returned in the fall.*

**October 2008**

Can you believe that after all of the sadness, after all of the questions about my future, after all of the meatless nights, I have come back to China for another year?! I think I am probably more shocked than anyone else that I returned. When I got back to the States I felt like my journey in China wasn't quite complete. I decided that one really needs to be here two years to fully appreciate the country and the experience. The first year can be used for understanding the system, working through culture shock, and garnering teaching experience; the second year can be used to dig below some of the well-polished layers that make up Chinese society, culture, and thought.

I have my own apartment now, and I cannot believe that I spent a year in a hotel room. While looking for an apartment, I thought of the Virginia Woolf quote: "A woman must have money and a room of her own." I don't have the money, but it definitely feels good to actually have a little corner to call my own in this vast city. I would also argue that in addition to money and a room, a woman—or any person—also needs a view. It doesn't have to be beautiful but it has to be a view that inspires, emotes, and imbues. I look out at my gorgeous view of downtown every night, and I'm actually thankful that I can call Shanghai my city and my home. Unlike last year, I feel that my life here is a privilege rather than a burden.

*Once China feels like home, the question becomes, what will it be like to return to the United States? Experiences of reverse culture shock are to be expected.*

**Jack Early,** Qingdao
January 1998

**Approaching Reentry**

Do our families and friends still like us? They may get very bored if we start talking about China. We'll be like the fictional Farkle family that couldn't stop talking about their summer vacation.

We have changed. You cannot live outside the United States for a period of time and then look in and not see it differently. We often shake our heads reading *USA Today* at the inane stuff that goes on in America. Do our Congressmen really say some of the dumb stuff I read? Or is it just a hoax? Are we Americans always as pretentious as we sound? Unfortunately, what most often gets shipped out of America is the top level of trash in the form of our pop culture.

As I write this, I feel like I'm hearing the pilot say over the intercom, "Ladies and Gentleman, we've started our descent home. We'll be touching down in approximately five and a half months. We're sorry for the slight disturbances incurred along the way, but we hope you've enjoyed the China years. Please begin making your final adjustments."

**Dana Hagengruber**, Tianjin
June 2007

Alice, thank you so much for the advice! I just hadn't been thinking about "reverse culture shock" at all—even though I knew there would be some. I'm actually starting to feel that already. I've surprised myself to find that my mind is starting to "pull back" from China. I just hadn't been thinking about the fact that, since no one else came with me to China, no one else would have that perspective or want me to talk about it all the time. That certainly will take some getting used to.

Of course, I would do it again in a heartbeat.

*A final good-bye.*

**Heather Bugni**, Lijiang
July 2008

### *Man Zou*, **Lijiang** [*Take it easy, Lijiang*]

Our apartment is empty; our backpacks are packed; our finals are graded. We are saying our good-byes to Lijiang. It has absolutely fascinated us and captured our hearts. We feel such a connection with this beautiful little mountain valley. It's hard to leave. It's sad to think we won't be riding the Number 11 bus around town. We won't have to go to dreaded English Corner on Wednesday evenings. No more dilapidated classrooms with random electrical fires. No more dinners with friends over chicken feet hot pot. No more Naxi women chuckling. No more students asking me if someday they can come to my wedding. No more leaky bathtub and broken toilet seat. No more biking to class with a view of Yulong Mountain. No more Naxi music blaring downtown. No more weekend bus rides on the dramatic Yunnan mountain roads. Patrick and I feel so blessed to have lived here for the past year, and it feels devastating to say good-bye to our friends, students, and life here. *Man zou*, Lijiang, take it easy.

**Heather Bugni** and **Patrick Tartar**, Lijiang (traveling in Laos)
September 2008

### Watching the Beijing Games

All year long our students have excitedly asked us, "Will you go to Beijing to see the Olympics?" And all year long we've replied, "No, it's too expensive. But we're looking forward to watching it on TV!" Our students loved this response and would eagerly add that this was how they too would watch the games.

Watching the Olympic Games over the past few weeks has felt like a culmination of our year in China. Every Chinese person I have interacted with—my students, friends, local restaurant owners, our Naxi friend, or a random person I was seated next to on the bus, everyone—has been eagerly anticipating the Olympics with the hope that this will show the world how modern and strong China really is.

When we settled into our dingy Laotian hotel room and turned on the Opening Ceremonies being broadcast on a Thai network, I was surprisingly overcome with emotion. As I continued to watch the Games and saw China continuing to rack up gold medals, I felt a strange satisfaction and found myself rooting for China. Never before had I realized that it was possible for the Olympics to be so important to a national identity. For the first time, I felt myself overcome with the odd feeling of Chinese nationalistic pride. Don't get me wrong, I have severe concerns about the Chinese government, but for the Chinese people to feel proud of themselves for a Games well done brings me immense joy.

With the Olympics now successfully complete, it feels like the perfect closure to our year in China. *Jia You Zhongguo!* [*Loosely translated, "Go for it, China!"*]

# 8

# Epilogue
## *Looking Back*

Is it over or is it just beginning?

—Carl Siegel

❧

**Jack Early**, Qingdao
January 2001

When I think of China, I see many hardships still and find many of her decisions awkward, but in the end I can do nothing for the path of China. For me, it's very personal. I think of the faces I know, and the faces I miss. In no small way, we affected each other. Maybe that's where it all starts.

❧

**Michael Hsu**, Tianjin
July 2004

Of course, my thoughts often drift back to China, and I am already plotting in my head and dreaming in my sleep of a return voyage. My father came to visit me in May; he had not been back to the Mainland since he left at the age of five. He has been telling my mother and sister of the zaniness, craziness, and excitement of adventures in China. It won't be long before we all take a trip across the pond, I think! Interestingly, due to coincidence or fate, all of my father's siblings (my two uncles and an aunt) have been to China this year at different times for different reasons. It is a first in Hsu family history! After so many years away, it is exciting to see the clan dipping its toe back into the water, or at least, back into the doorjamb (if I may mix metaphors)!

❧

**Carl Siegel**, Shanghai
June 2005

Why I owe you for the last ten months, three moments in brief:

First, I now teach summer school at a unique summer program for local middle school students in San Francisco. It's what I've been doing for going on four summers. We happen to be at a local public high school, and the regular school year teacher is Ms. Li who teaches Chinese. So while I teach, I can gaze at the three walls and see nothing but basic Chinese characters that I can now read! It's a thrill, and it also seems like some sort of sign that I happen to be teaching in America in a Chinese classroom.

Second, since I'm in San Francisco and in a certain neighborhood, most of my students are Chinese. Now, of course, most only speak English and Cantonese, but a handful speak Mandarin. It's really fun to swap stories and compare Chinese to Chinese-Americans.

*Anna Maher visits Tai Shan and makes a friend. Photo by Robert Maher.*

And third, I'm now going to send out a letter to the sweetest Chinese girl who I may be dating when I return to Shanghai in August. Who knows?

January 2008

Just to let you know I plan on returning to Shanghai in February. Can't stay away. I'm still working sports events, but definitely keep in touch with all my old friends at the university. In case you didn't know, I also took five weeks to lead sixteen American high school students through three community service projects in China back in July. Now I'm their program developer for next year's program. So yes, I'm "continuing to make a difference in the world." Crazy!

**Bryna**, Fuzhou
February 2007

I've been at the University of Oregon since September. I was accepted to their PhD program with a full ride, and I'm quite happy to be here! I've been teaching both Chinese language and Chinese culture and literature, and while it's very different teaching American students as compared to Chinese students (as well as a second language vs. my native language) the experience I got working in Putian has been invaluable. I still write to my kids every so often, and they write to me. I'm hoping to go back to China to teach again once I finish my PhD (depending on the job situation here), and I will certainly let you know when I'm ready for that.

**Kevin A. Gee**, Guangzhou
July 2007

This is Kevin Gee, remember me? I'm way back from 1999 when you helped me get placed at Zhongshan University. Thought I'd write and touch base. It's been a busy several years. I stayed an additional year in Guangzhou after 1999–2000, returned to the States in 2001, and got my master's in International Affairs (China focus, of course) at the University of California, San Diego in 2004. I'm now at Harvard pursuing my doctorate and hope to be doing my dissertation research in China. I'm focusing on education policy and the economics of education. I'm basically interested in evaluating the effectiveness of education policies across the developing world. I've been back to China almost every year visiting good friends from my time at Zhongshan University, as well as family in the Guangzhou area.

**S. Lauren Carpenter**, Tianjin
January 2009

It's been quite a while, and I'm not sure if you remember me, but I'm Lauren Carpenter, one of the CCC group sent to Nankai University back during the 2004–2005 year. A lot has happened to me since then. I came back to the States two weeks ago, after spending the past four and a half years in China. Unfortunately, I left a husband behind! He is going to join me in a few months after the immigration process is finished. Meeting him was largely due to a series of events that were triggered by my trip to China with CCC in 2004, and for that I'll never regret my decision to join the program!

In the intervening years, I've been a teacher, student (I graduated with an MBA from Oklahoma City University's Great Wall Program this past December), put together a Chinese/Western wedding, hosted family members visiting China, and have had some really amazing travel experiences. China is truly a second home to me, despite its many infamous frustrations. I have returned to the States to finally "settle down," start my career, and prepare for my husband to join me here and go through some major culture shock.

**Tim Gerber**, Shanghai
May 2009

My whole goal is getting enough Chinese to *teach*! So, I will try to convince them [*the funding agency*] that it is worth it for them to send me for two years so I could fulfill this goal and promote lifelong engagement between China and other countries including America. I am, like you, very passionate about the need for this, and I would love to be in a position as a Chinese teacher to perpetuate this engagement!

Since I came back, I have stayed very engaged with China, taking on conversation partners from China at the University of South Carolina so China is still very much in my heart and my head. I think this is the time for me where I can ramp it up and take it to the next level. The Shanghai and China experiences as you know were incredible. Now, this might be my time to take it the whole nine yards.

**Collin Starkweather**
June 2010

I'm still in Chicago, continuing my work as an economist. Business was particularly good last year despite the downturn. And though I hope to return to China at some point for more than a brief visit, my feet are firmly planted in the domestic financial sector for the time being.

**Tom Brennan**, Tianjin
2001

Hope all is going well. I'm still working at Thunderbird School of Global Management in Phoenix, and I'm loving it! I got sent to China and the Middle East last year and Europe this year. As far as the future, we'll see. I'd still like for it to involve China in some way, shape, or form. Take care and good luck with the program.

**Kimberley Te Winkle**, Tianjin
December 2010

I've just submitted my PhD thesis at University College London, Institute of Archaeology, where I researched how rural communities in China value their architectural heritage and work to preserve this and other cultural features, specifically in Kangding and Danba Counties in Sichuan; Yongding County in Fujian, and Kaiping in Guangdong. A process of study very much influenced by my time teaching.

**Alex Weymann**, Shanghai
December 2010

Hi Alice,

I am currently a pediatrician in residency at the Children's Hospital of Philadelphia! Can you believe it? After my car accident in 2000 and finishing out the year, I went back to New York City and got a second surgery, as well as lots of physical therapy. Sadly, my leg was not getting better, and I was told by my surgeon that I would never walk more than one city block without pain! I did a master's program at Harvard in Mind, Brain, and Education, and while there, won a grant from the Chinese Scholarship Council to go back to Shanghai and study Chinese full time at Fudan University! I took the opportunity and went back for another year! I loved studying Chinese. After that trip, I decided to go back to medical school, and I enrolled in a post-baccalaureate program at Bryn Mawr, PA, because I did not have all of my science classes. Then, I went to medical school in Rochester, NY, and now I'm almost done with residency!

Can you believe our paths? I still am totally obsessed with China. I'll tell you a funny thing. When I got the idea to go to China via the Colorado China Council, it was much the idea of my friend from college. She bailed on the trip at the last second because she got a very good job in Washington. So, I went alone. I remember talking to you about the city I would go to. There were two options: Tianjin and Shanghai. And I asked you very naively, "What's the difference between these two cities?" You probably thought at that moment that China would eat me up. I didn't even know that Shanghai was one of the largest cities in China! Luckily, you helped me choose Shanghai, and I have had a place in my heart for it ever since.

Thank you for your passion for China—it truly was infectious!

*And the final word from one who didn't "get away." Peggy Rosen has been in China since 2003.*

**Peggy Rosen**, Shanghai
January 2011

Often people who are working and living in China are asked, "What made you decide to come to China?" My usual joking answer to this question has been, "I ran away from home." Or, "My life was boring, and I was looking for excitement." I believe the real answer was and has been a little bit of both. I certainly wasn't running away from anything, but running to some-thing, and I found it. My life has certainly not been boring for the past few years, and when I didn't find excitement, it usually found me. I have met scores of people, and made lasting and meaningful friendships with both expats and Chinese. This is something a person in their sixties does not usu-ally have the opportunity to do. Perhaps I could be the poster girl for AARP!

I have taught hundreds of students, all of whom in return taught me something about their culture, about myself, about patience, about compas-sion, about perseverance, about humor, and about love, and on and on. I have not only had the opportunity to teach in China, but have had other spectacular and unexpected opportunities presented to me—some big, some small, but all very meaningful.

I honed my skills as a creative teacher in China. I became a published writer in China. I appeared on Chinese TV. I met and conversed with world-renowned authors, was introduced to a prince and a governor, and I wit-nessed world-class competitions of some of the best athletes of our generation. None of these opportunities would have happened to me back in the United States. These are the "big" memories. However, the memories that will last the rest of my life were those which were heartwarming coming from the everyday Chinese person. Some of these things have been "random acts of kindness," and others the true desire to welcome and befriend a foreigner. Nothing meant more to me than being invited to share a dinner for Chinese New Year with a student and her parents in their humble apartment. A former student and his family have welcomed me into their inner circle of relatives and consider me part of their family. There were countless times that people just wanted to help—such as the little lady who wanted to make sure I got on the right bus at the right time in the right seat at a long-distance bus station.

There have been many funny instances with language and communica-tion, or perhaps miscommunication. My Chinese is still not very good, but I get by. I may have said this before in an email to you, but when coming to teach in China, it is important to pack a smile and your sense of humor.

Over the years that I have been here, China has changed, is changing, and will continue to change every day. The opportunities continue to be here for the taking, but most importantly, for the offering. Teaching in China is life altering, if you want it to be.

*For a few like Peggy Rosen, China is a place to put down new roots. For many former CCC teachers like Carl Siegel, Kevin A. Gee, and Alex Weymann, China is a place to return to for work, study, and pleasure. Jim Boyd and his family lived in Nanjing from 2003–2004 with their daughter. After returning to the United States, Jim Boyd and Susan Keough adopted a second daughter. In 2010, the family taught in the Colorado China Council's three-week summer program in Nanjing. In August 2011, they embarked on another full year of living in China—China, ever-changin* **,** *ever-alluring.*

# Notes

## PREFACE

1. The word "teacher" is used loosely throughout both books. While all participants had to have a minimum of a BA degree to participate in the program and many people had MAs and PhDs, few were actual professional teachers in the traditional sense until they left China.

## CHAPTER 1: CHINA ARRIVAL

1. The *Little Red Book* is a compilation of quotations by Mao Zedong (1893—1976), leader of the Chinese Communist Party at the time of its victory in the Chinese Civil War, first Chairman of the People's Republic of China (1954–1959), and de facto leader of the PRC until his death.

2. Hot pot is a bowl of boiling broth/oil set right at your table to which you add thinly sliced meats, seafood, and vegetables and cook fondue style.

3. *Kuai* is a colloquial term for the Chinese *yuan*, which is the primary monetary unit. Chinese currency is called *renminbi* (RMB) or "the people's money." In 2000, the exchange rate was 8.28 yuan to one US dollar. In 2011, the rate is 6.53 yuan to one US dollar.

4. Sun Yat-sen (1866–1925), called "Father of Modern China." After the overthrow of the Qing Dynasty in 1912, he became the provisional president of the Republic of China.

5. The Long March (1934–1935) was a legendary journey of about six thousand miles undertaken when the Red Armies of the Communist Party retreated from south to north China while being pursued by the Chinese National Party army (Kuomintang).

## CHAPTER 2: TEACHING

1. English Corner is an informal gathering of individuals who want to practice speaking English, ideally with a native speaker.

2. *Ipse dixit* is Latin for an unproven assertion.

## CHAPTER 3: CROSS-CULTURAL EXPERIENCES

1. Nationalists or Nationalist Party, also known as the Kuomintang or KMT, ruled much of China from 1928 until 1949 when it was defeated by the Communist Party of China (CPC). It was then forced to retreat to Taiwan in 1949 during the Chinese Civil War.

2. *China Today* reports CPC membership of nearly seventy-eight million at the end of 2009.

3. *The Romance of the Three Kingdoms* is a historical novel about the rival lords who lived during the end of the Han dynasty around 200 B.C.

## CHAPTER 5: TRAVEL

1. *Hutongs* are the narrow lanes that are unique to Beijing neighborhoods composed of traditional Chinese homes with courtyards.

## CHAPTER 6: FAMILIES COPING

1. Many universities/colleges were beginning to allow their foreign faculty to live off campus in subsidized rented housing.

2. David C. Pollock and Ruth E. Van Reken, *Third Culture Kids: The Experience of Growing Up Among Worlds* (Boston: Nicolas Brealey Publishing, 2001, 2009).

# Sources

## CHAPTER 1: CHINA ARRIVAL

### Population Statistics

GeoHive.com; source cited is National Bureau of Statistics of China. 2008 Population Estimates. http://www.geohive.com/cntry/china.aspx.

### Currency Exchange

Board of Governors of the Federal Reserve System. Statistics and Historical Data. Historical Rates for China. January 3, 2000 to April 22, 2011. http://www.federalreserve.gov/releases/H10/hist/dat00_ch.htm.

## CHAPTER 2: TEACHING

Primary, junior, and senior school enrollment. Ministry of Education of the People's Republic of China. Education Statistics 2009 (published December 2010). http://www.moe.edu.cn/publicfiles/business/htmlfiles/moe/s4972/index.html.

## CHAPTER 3: CROSS-CULTURAL EXPERIENCES

### Symptoms of Culture Shock

Phyllis L. Thompson, ed. *Dear Alice: Letters Home from American Teachers Learning to Live in China* (Berkeley: Institute of East Asian Studies University of California, 1998), 222.

### Communist Party Membership in China

ChinaToday.com. China Information and Sources. The Communist Party of China. http://www.chinatoday.com/org/cpc/.

# Blogs

This book is indebted to the emails of the contributing writers and the following blogs:

Heather Bugni and Patrick Tartar. *Where in the World Are Heather and Patrick?* (blog) August 2007—September 2008, http://www.lawgate.net/heather2007/default.asp.

Ken Driese. *Ken, Ellen and Bei in China* (blog) July 2005—January 2007, http://kdriese.blogspot.com/.

Tim Lewis. *The Lewis Family Goes to China* (blog) January 2007—July 2008, http://lewisesinchina.blogspot.com/.

*Steve, Shana and Li in China* (blog) May 2007—August 2008, http://sltsjpchina.blogspot.com/.

For additional blogs by teachers in China and other suggested reading material, see the Colorado China Council website at www.asiacouncil.org.

# Index

*Note:* Page numbers followed by an italic *p* refer to photos.

# About the Editors

**Alice Renouf** has been executive director of the Colorado China Council (CCC) since the late 1970s. Under her aegis, with advisory board support, CCC has undertaken academic symposia, multimedia events, musical performances, major national art and archeological exhibits, and conferences on business and health care, and has organized and hosted high-level scientific, business, and academic delegations. In the 1980s CCC worked extensively with the state, businesses, and universities interested in establishing links with China as well as helping to establish the Colorado-Hunan and Denver-Kunming relationships.

Since 1991, Alice has personally placed and helped train well over seven hundred people to teach in China. As a direct result of the China Teachers Program, she conceptualized and initiated the book *Dear Alice: Letters Home from American Teachers Learning to Live in China* (1998), based on letters received from thirty-six teachers in China.

She did her undergraduate and graduate work in Asian studies and Chinese history. In 1970 she was a graduate student in Taiwan and has since made over thirty trips to China to develop cultural and academic bridges. For many years Alice worked at the University of Colorado in its Office of International Education and Asian Studies Department.

**Mary Beth Ryan-Maher** has written about China, poetry, and medicine. Her work has appeared in *American Book Review*, *Anesthesiology Now*, and *The Manhattan Times*. She holds degrees in literature from the City University of New York and in English and Spanish from Marquette University. She has taught at every age level from teenagers to university students to adult learners. After teaching in Kunming, she co-led the Colorado China

Council's Summer Institute for new teachers for four summers in Shanghai. She edits the newsletter of the Friends Committee of Fort Tryon Park Trust and is a full-time grant writer. She lives in New York City with her husband and two daughters. They cook Chinese food at least twice a week.

# About the Calligrapher

As a devoted artist, **Harrison Xinshi Tu** has created numerous works of calligraphy, many of which have been selected for exhibitions in the United States, Japan, Korea, and Singapore. Two of his calligraphy artworks are in the permanent collection at the Denver Art Museum. Mr. Tu has consistently received high recognition, including Outstanding Calligrapher Award, Beijing (2008); Naropa University Art Gallery exhibition, Boulder, Colorado (2003); Shanghai Library personal exhibition (2000); China National Art Gallery, Beijing, personal exhibition (1998); American Biographical Institute, International Cultural Achievement Award (1997); and the World Chinese Calligraphy and Painting Contest, Gold Medal (1996).

While living in the United States, Mr. Tu has become a devoted proponent of exchange and mutual understanding between the East and West. Since 1994, he has served as editor-in-chief of the *Chinese American Post*. He is also visiting professor at Naropa University, Boulder, and Colorado College, Colorado Springs, where he teaches Chinese calligraphy and culture. His publications include *The Wisdom and Art of Chinese Calligraphy* (1998) and *A Calligrapher's Yi Jing* (2004).